Study Guide for Sigelman's
Life-Span Human Development

Third Edition

Elizabeth Rider
Elizabethtown College

Brooks/Cole Publishing Company

I(T)P® An International Thomson Publishing Company

Pacific Grove • Albany • Belmont • Bonn • Boston • Cincinnati • Detroit
Johannesburg • London • Madrid • Melbourne • Mexico City • New York
Paris • Singapore • Tokyo • Toronto • Washington

Senior Assistant Editor: *Faith B. Stoddard*
Editorial Assistant: *Stephanie M. Andersen*
Production Coordinator: *Dorothy Bell*
Cover Design: *Roy R. Neuhaus*
Printing and Binding: *Patterson Printing*

For more information, contact:

BROOKS/COLE PUBLISHING COMPANY
511 Forest Lodge Road
Pacific Grove, CA 93950
USA

International Thomson Publishing Europe
Berkshire House 168-173
High Holborn
London WC1V 7AA
England

Thomas Nelson Australia
102 Dodds Street
South Melbourne, 3205
Victoria, Australia

Nelson Canada
1120 Birchmount Road
Scarborough, Ontario
Canada M1K 5G4

International Thomson Editores
Seneca 53
Col. Polanco
11560 México, D. F., México

International Thomson Publishing GmbH
Königswinterer Strasse 418
53227 Bonn
Germany

International Thomson Publishing Asia
60 Albert Street
#15-01 Albert Complex
Singapore 189969

International Thomson Publishing Japan
Hirakawacho Kyowa Building, 3F
2-2-1 Hirakawacho
Chiyoda-ku, Tokyo 102
Japan

Printed in the United States of America

10   9   8   7   6   5   4

ISBN 0-534-35962-0

CONTENTS

This Study Guide was written to help you better understand and remember the material presented in Life-Span Human Development, 3rd edition by Carol Sigelman. Most students associate "a better understanding" of material with increased study time. However, the <u>way</u> you study is as important as how much time you spend studying. In thinking about studying and whether you "know" the material, it's helpful to consider Bloom's taxonomy, which is a hierarchical yet overlapping set of learning objectives. Take a look at the following description of this hierarchy, including examples of questions that might be asked at each level.

1.   <u>Knowledge</u>--Being able to recite the definition from the book or instructor.
      EX: Define "accommodation"

2.   <u>Comprehension</u>--Putting a definition in your own words.
      EX: Explain the concept of accommodation in your own words.

3.   <u>Application</u>--Being able to *use* principles.
      EX: Indicate how accommodation relates to the process of equilibration. Or use your understanding of learning principles to help a parent modify a child's inappropriate behavior.

4.   <u>Analysis</u>--Breaking a principle down into component parts and understanding how the parts relate.
      EX: Compare and contrast accommodation to assimilation. Or discuss how Piaget's concept of nurture is different from Freud's concept of nurture.

5.   <u>Synthesis</u>--Putting old knowledge together in new ways.
      EX: In what way(s) would Piaget's description of the stage of preoperations need to be modified in order to better "fit" recent research in this area?

6.   <u>Evaluation</u>--Making judgments about material *based on knowledge*.
      EX: Evaluate the usefulness of Piaget's concept of equilibration.
      Provide justification for your response.

When you are in the process of learning material, ask yourself questions such as: To what extent do I know this material? Could I give a definition? Could I explain it to someone else? Could I solve a real-life problem by applying this information? Would I even recognize a real-life problem to which this information is relevant? Can I compare this information to something I learned from the last chapter? Can I critically evaluate this material using one or more criteria? The more of these questions you can answer, the better you understand the material.

Knowing material to the extent represented by the lower ends of the hierarchy may allow you to pass a course, but you may not do well in the course even though you may have spent many hours memorizing factual information. Find out what the expectations for the course are from your instructor. Use the Study Guide to help achieve a better understanding of the material in the text.

Organization of the Study Guide

Each chapter of Study Guide contains the following sections:

Chapter Overview provides a general picture of what is in each chapter. This is meant to orient you to the chapter in the text and certainly does not replace reading the chapter.

Learning Objectives are questions that you should be able to answer after you have read and studied a chapter. Read these first before you begin a chapter so that you have an idea of what to focus on as you read.

Summary and Guided Review guides you through the main points in each chapter. As you read through the summary, fill-in the blanks with the terms that appropriately complete a sentence. There are questions in parentheses scattered throughout the summary; these are meant to encourage you to think actively as you are reading and connect this summary to the more detailed information provided in the text. The questions are in bold type so that they stand out from the surrounding text. This will allow you to focus on the questions even if you do not fill-in the blanks of the guided review. Finally, each Summary and Guided Review uses the same headings and subheadings from the text to help keep you oriented to the text chapter and allow you to work on specific sections.

Review of Key Terms is an exercise designed to facilitate study of important terms, which are in bold type in the textbook. For each one, you need to complete the sentence with the appropriate term.

Multiple Choice Self Test consists of 15 multiple choice questions that you can use to check your understanding of key concepts in a chapter. These are comparable to the multiple choice questions that are available to your instructor in the corresponding Test Bank and should serve as a good review in classes that use multiple choice tests.

Application Questions require you to think about the material on a fairly sophisticated level. You need to be able to discuss material in your own words, apply it to a problem of current interest, or synthesize and integrate several concepts to arrive at a new understanding of some problem. For the first question, a sample answer is provided so that you have a model of a good answer. Keep in mind that there may be other ways to correctly answer the question. For the other application questions, a hint is given about where you might relevant information in the text. These questions are comparable to the essay questions available to your instructor in the corresponding Test Bank and should serve as good practice in classes that use essay tests.

People and their Ideas is a short matching exercise included in some chapters to help you connect important people with their ideas. For the most part, this exercise includes the researchers and theorists who stand out as particularly influential in developmental psychology.

Additional Review of a particular issue is included in some chapters where appropriate. In many cases, this review focuses on a concept that was an important focus of a chapter and was summarized in a table or chart.

Answers are provided for the Summary and Guided Review, Key Terms, the Multiple Choice Self Test, People and their Ideas, and one Application question. Whenever you miss a question or term, go back to the textbook and reread that section so that you understand why an answer is correct or incorrect.

This is the third time I have written this Study Guide, and I wish to thank all the students who have used the previous editions and provided feedback. For this edition, I am most grateful to Vicki Watson, an Elizabethtown College student, class of '99, who assiduously checked each chapter for me.

Elizabeth Rider

CHAPTER ONE

UNDERSTANDING LIFE-SPAN HUMAN DEVELOPMENT

OVERVIEW

This chapter introduces the field of life span human development. The chapter begins by defining life span development and noting historical changes and cultural differences in conceptions of the life span. A large portion of the chapter is devoted to discussion of how developmentalists study life span changes. The goals of study include description, explanation, and optimization. Developmental study has progressed from the study of specific age groups to the study of the entire life span. There are seven assumptions of a life span perspective; these are described in this chapter and then echoed throughout the book.

Developmental research is guided by the scientific method and its emphasis on systematic observations. Researchers collect their data through self-report measures or behavioral observations. An important part of this chapter is the description of three developmental designs and their strengths and weaknesses. These designs--cross-sectional, longitudinal, and sequential--are valuable tools for describing development. In order to *explain* development, researchers use experiments to establish cause and effect connections between variables, or they use correlational studies to show relationships or suggest connections among variables. Experiments and correlational studies have both advantages and disadvantages for developmental questions. This chapter concludes by considering several problems that arise in studying development, namely the selection of participants and protecting participants' rights.

LEARNING OBJECTIVES

After reading and studying the material in this chapter, you should be able to answer the following questions.

1.   What is development? What processes underlie developmental changes across the life span?

2.   How has our understanding of different periods of the life-span changed historically? What cultural and subcultural differences exist in perspectives of the life span?

3.   What are the three goals of life-span developmental psychology?

4.   What are the seven assumptions of the life-span perspective on human development?

5. How is the scientific method used to study development?

6. What are the pros and cons of the two common methods of data collection used by developmental researchers?

7. What are the advantages and disadvantages of the cross-sectional and longitudinal designs?

8. How does the sequential design resolve the weaknesses of the cross-sectional and longitudinal designs?

9. What are the important features of the experimental method? What sorts of information can be gathered from an experimental study?

10. What are the important features of the correlational method? What sorts of information can be gathered from this type of study?

11. What problems or issues arise in studying development?

CHAPTER SUMMARY AND GUIDED REVIEW

The following summary provides an overview of the main points contained in this chapter of the text. Fill-in the blanks with terms that appropriately complete the sentence. Scattered throughout the summary are questions in parentheses. These are meant to encourage you to think actively as you are reading and connect this summary to the more detailed information provided in the text. You can answer these questions as you are filling in the blanks or you can complete all the blanks, then go back and reread the entire summary, addressing the questions in order to provide more depth of understanding.

WHAT IS DEVELOPMENT?
        Development consists of systematic changes and continuities that occur in an individual between conception and death. Developmentalists are concerned with three general areas of change, including (1) _____, (2) _____, and (3) _____ changes. Biologists typically define (4) _____ as physical changes occurring from conception to maturity and refer to the deterioration of an individual as (5) _____. Developmentalists, however, argue that both positive and negative changes occur throughout the (6) _____, and that (7) _____ refers to both positive and negative changes in the mature individual.

Developmental Processes

Developmental change results from both (8) _____, which refers to the genetically programmed biological unfolding of traits and behaviors, and (9) _____, which refers to changes resulting from experience.

HOW DO PEOPLE VIEW THE LIFE SPAN?

The life-span is typically divided into several phases. For example, Neugarten distinguished (10) _____ adults who are usually between the ages of 55 and 75 and healthy from (11) _____ adults who are age 75 or older and frail. A third group, the (12) _____, are over the age of 85 and frail. The age group, or (13) _____, to which a person belongs will in part determine the roles, privileges and responsibilities that person will be granted. Societal expectations or (14) _____ define how people should behave at different ages. (*Why are these important?*)

Historical Changes in Life-Span Phases

Historically, our conceptions of life-span development have changed significantly. Children in premodern times were viewed as miniature adults, treated harshly, and held to adult standards at a young age. Toward the end of the 19th century, (15) _____ emerged as a period of life distinct from adulthood. (*What events led to the development of this distinct period?*) Conceptions of adulthood have also changed, in part because of increased (16) _____; a longer empty nest period has focused attention on middle age. The number of adults in our society will also increase as the (17) _____, those born after World War II through 1964, ages. (*What are the societal implications of this increase in number of middle aged adults and eventually in the number of older adults?*)

Cultural Differences

The life span is viewed differently by different cultures. In Western societies, the life span is considered to be a straight line from birth to death. Other cultures, though, include an after-life or view the life span as circular rather than linear. Many cultures define old age in terms of how well a person (18) _____, not by their chronological age.

Subcultural Differences

Even within a society, subcultures vary in their conception of the life span. For example, in some U.S. subcultures, the age norms for becoming mothers and grandmothers are younger than in other subcultures.

WHAT IS THE SCIENCE OF LIFE-SPAN DEVELOPMENT?

Developmental psychology is the branch of psychology that studies the changes that occur between conception and death.

Goals of Study

One of the goals of life-span developmental psychology is the (19) _____ of normal development and individual differences. In addition to this, developmentalists try to (20) _____ and (21) _____ development. (*Can you give an example of each goal?*)

Origins

The study of development began with observations that were recorded in (22) _____. The person usually credited as the "founder" of developmental psychology is (23) _____. He pioneered the use of (24) _____ to more objectively collect information from larger numbers of children.. Hall viewed the entire life span as important for study, but is probably most associated with the study of adolescence and his view that this period of the life span is characterized by (25)_____.

Today's Perspective

For a number of years, researchers tended to focus on a specific age group, such as the study of infants or (26)_____, the study of old age. Today, the study of development assumes a life-span perspective with seven assumptions:

1.	Development is a (27) _____ process.
2.	Development is (28)_____, rather than following a single universal path.
3.	Development includes both gains and losses at every age.
4.	There is (29) _____ in human development, which means we can change in response to our experiences.
5.	Development is shaped by the (30) _____ context in which it occurs.
6.	Development is influenced by multiple factors.
7.	Complete understanding of development requires input from multiple disciplines.

(*Can you give an example of each of these themes that illustrates the importance of the theme to the study of life-span development?*)

HOW IS DEVELOPMENTAL RESEARCH CONDUCTED?
The Scientific Method

Understanding development is best accomplished through the scientific method, which stresses that conclusions should be based on systematic, unbiased observations (data). To describe or explain a set of observations or facts, scientists develop (31) _____. To test the validity of a theory, specific predictions or (32) _____, can be generated and should hold true if the theory is in fact valid.

Data Collection

There are two general ways to measure behavior. People can be asked to provide information about themselves using several types of (33) _____ measures such as interviews or questionnaires. (*What are several weaknesses of collecting data this way?*) Alternatively, researchers might use a kind of behavioral observation called (34) _____ observation to directly measure people's behavior in their everyday surroundings. (*What are advantages and disadvantages of this measurement technique?*) Sometimes, researchers control some of the conditions under which they collect observations by using (35) _____ observation.

Developmental Research Designs

There are three research designs frequently used to describe developmental change across the life span. In a (36) _____ design, the performances of people of different age groups are compared, which yields information about age (37) _____. In a (38) _____ design, the performance of the same group of people is measured repeatedly over time, yielding information about age (39) _____. The findings of developmental studies can be influenced by three factors. (40) _____ reflect the effects of getting older. Effects of (41) _____ reflect the influences of being born in a particular historical context, and effects of (42) _____ reflect the influences of particular events that occur at the time data are collected. In a cross-sectional study, findings may reflect (43) _____ effects in addition to age effects because people of different ages are studied. Because people in a longitudinal design are repeatedly tested at different times, findings from this design may reflect changes due to (44) _____ effects in addition to age effects. The (45) _____ design combines the cross-sectional and longitudinal designs in a single study in order to disentangle effects due to age, cohort, and time of measurement. (***Can you describe situations where it would be appropriate to use each of these designs? What could you conclude about age effects from studies using each of these research designs?***)

Explaining Development

In an effort to explain behavior or identify causes of developmental change, researchers often use an (46) _____ . The researcher manipulates or changes some aspect of the environment, called the (47) _____ variable, and measures the effect that this has on the (48) _____ variable. In addition to manipulation of the variable of interest, participants in a true experiment must have an equal opportunity to end up in any of the groups, which is achieved through (49) _____ . Finally, in a true experiment, all factors other than the independent variable must be held constant, a procedure called (50) _____. (***What are two major limitations of the experimental method?***) In some cases, when participants cannot be randomly assigned to groups, researchers might conduct a (51) _____.

Some developmental questions cannot be answered by experimentally manipulating the environment. In these cases, researchers may use the (52) _____ method, which involves determining whether two or more variables are related. (***Can you provide an example of a question studied with this method?***) The strength of the relationship between two variables is generally assessed with a (53)_____, which can range in value from -1.00 to +1.00. (***Can you describe a relationship that would have a large negative correlation and one that would have a large positive correlation?***) A major limitation of the correlational method is that it does not establish a (54) _____ relationship between the variables. (***Can you explain why the correlational method is not able to do this?***)

WHAT PROBLEMS ARISE IN STUDYING DEVELOPMENT?

There are a number of other issues for researchers to consider.

Choosing Samples

Researchers cannot typically study all members of a population in which they are interested, so they select a (55) _____ from this population. Ideally, a (56) _____ sample is selected so that all members of the population have an equal chance of being selected. This allows the researcher to generalize to other members of the population. Researchers studying age changes or age differences may have difficulty ensuring that their groups are comparable on all characteristics except age. (***How might researchers ensure that groups are similar?***)

Protecting the Rights of Research Participants

Researchers need to protect their subjects from physical or psychological harm by following certain standards of (57) _____. This involves informing participants of what the research will involve so that they can provide (58) _____. It also means that the researcher will (59) _____ participants after the study to inform them of its true purpose. Finally, participants must be protected from harm and guaranteed that their responses will be (60) _____.

REVIEW OF KEY TERMS

Below is a list of terms and concepts from this chapter. Use these to complete the following sentence definitions. You might also want to try writing definitions in your own words and then checking your definitions with those in the text.

age effects	life-span perspective
age grades	longitudinal design
age norms	maturation
aging	naturalistic observation
baby biographies	old-old
baby boom generation	oldest old
centenarian	plasticity
cohort effects	population
correlational method	quasi-experiment
correlation coefficient	random assignment
cross-sectional design	random sample
dependent variable	research ethics
development	sample
environment	scientific method
experiment	sequential design
experimental control	social clock
gerontology	storm and stress
growth	structured observation
hypothesis	theory
independent variable	time of measurement effects
learning	young-old

1.   _____ refers to the relatively permanent changes in behavior that result from experiences or practice.

2.   _____ is a technique for systematically and objectively using observations to determine the merits of one's thinking.

3.   A(n) _____ is a research technique in which some aspect of the subject's environment is manipulated or altered see if there is any change in the subject's behavior.

4.   People who are at least 100 years old are called _____.

5.   A(n) _____ is a testable prediction resulting from a theoretical position.

6.   Standards of conduct that investigators must ethically follow in order to protect subjects from harm are _____.

7.   The _____ is a research design that involves determining whether two or more variables are related.

8.   _____ is a method in which hypotheses are tested by observing behaviors under naturally occurring conditions.

9.   Systematic changes in a person occurring between conception and death are collectively referred to as _____.

10.   Recorded observations of an infant's behaviors over a period of time constitute a _____.

11. A _____ is used to measure age-related change by studying participants from different age groups repeatedly over time.

12. A person's _____ consists of all the external physical and social conditions that can influence the person.

13. _____ result from being part of a group of people born about the same time and exposed to similar cultural and historical events.

14. _____ is a technique that ensures that all research participants have an equal chance of being included in all experimental conditions.

15. A _____ is a statistical value that represents the extent to which two variables are systematically related.

16. The physical changes that occur from conception to maturity are called _____.

17. _____ are distinctive periods of the life span, usually delineated by ages.

18. _____ refer to the historical events that occur when data are collected, which may influence findings.

19. In a _____, age-related differences are measured by simultaneously studying subjects from different age groups.

20. The _____ is an approach to the study of development that focuses on changes occurring from conception to death of a person.

21. Adults who are over the age of 85 and usually frail are referred to as the _____.

22. _____ are expectations about how people should act at different ages.

23. Changes that occur in a mature person are considered the _____ process.

24. _____ refers to a genetically programmed biological plan of development, relatively independent of effects of the environment.

25. The _____ refers to the large generation of people born from the end of WWII to about 1964.

26. Adolescence has sometimes been characterized as a period of _____ by those who believe it is a turbulent period of change.

27. In an experiment, the _____ is the aspect of the environment that the investigator deliberately manipulates in order to discover what effect this has on behavior.

28. Psychologists develop _____, which are sets of rules or principles that describe and explain some behavior.

29. A subset of subjects from a larger population of interest is a _____.

30. A _____ is similar to an experiment, but participants are not randomly assigned to groups.

31. A technique that ensures that all factors besides the independent variable are controlled or held constant is _____.

32. _____ is the study of aging and old age.

33. The _____ refers to the sense that life events should occur at a particular time, according to a schedule dictated by age norms.

34. In a _____, age-related changes are measured by repeatedly studying the same individuals over time.

35. In an experiment, the _____ is the aspect of a participant's behavior that is observed or measured in order to determine whether the independent variable had an effect.

36. A _____ is when participants are drawn from the larger population of interest such that all members of the population have an equal chance of being selected for the sample.

37. The _____ are adults over the age of 75 who often have declines in abilities and need assistance from others.

38. Researchers sometimes use the technique of _____ to create conditions that will elicit the behavior of interest.

39. _____ refers to the ability to change in response to positive or negative experiences.

40. Researchers would like to be able to generalize their research findings to a _____ after studying a subset of this group.

41. _____ are adults between the ages of 55 and 75 who are basically healthy and active.

42. In research, the consequences of getting older are called _____.

MULTIPLE CHOICE SELF TEST

For each multiple choice question, read all alternatives and then select the best answer.

1. Development results from biologically programmed changes called _____ and from specific environmental experiences called _____.
   a. aging; learning
   b. learning; growth
   c. maturation; learning
   d. age changes; age differences

2. Neugarten uses the term "old-old" to refer to individuals who are
    a. past retirement age
    b. between 55 and 75 and still active
    c. over the age of 85 and frail
    d. between 75 and 85 with some impairments in functioning

3. A 65-year-old woman who feels as though it is time for her to become a grandmother is feeling the influence of
    a. age grade
    b. social clock
    c. age norms
    d. physiological needs

4. What are the most striking historical <u>changes</u> in how the life span is perceived?
    a. Infancy and childhood are regarded as important periods of time.
    b. Adulthood is viewed as more important than childhood.
    c. Periods of adolescence and middle adulthood have emerged.
    d. Increasing birth rates have focused greater attention on infancy.

5. An increase in life expectancy during the past century has resulted in
    a. an increased awareness of, and interest in, middle adulthood
    b. more attention to adolescence as a distinct period of the life span
    c. changes in the way we treat our children
    d. more research on infant capabilities

6. The goals of developmental psychology are BEST described by which of the following?
    a. Developmental psychologists seek to modify behavior wherever possible.
    b. Developmental psychologists seek to identify behaviors that should be changed.
    c. Developmental psychologists seek to construct a single unifying theory to explain development.
    d. Developmental psychologists seek to describe and explain behavior, and where possible, optimize behavior.

7. One of the assumptions of the life-span perspective is that development is multidirectional. This means that
    a. development is caused by any number of factors and determining which cause is most influential can't be done
    b. developmental changes are universal across most people
    c. developmental outcomes can never be predicted
    d. development at all ages consists of some gains and some losses as well as some abilities that remain the same

8. Another assumption of the life-span perspective is that there is plasticity in development. This means that
    a. most of our acquisition of new skills will occur during infancy when our brains are not fully developed
    b. developmental changes can occur in response to our experiences across the life span
    c. development is never really complete
    d. all skills can be developed at any time of the life span

9. Which of the following is an example of using naturalistic observation to collect data?
   a. watching how children behave on their playground
   b. asking participants to orally answer questions rather than fill out questionnaires
   c. asking parents to keep track of their children's TV viewing habits
   d. seeing how children behave when they are asked to play a game with unfamiliar children

10. Cross-sectional designs provide information about age _____; longitudinal designs provide information about age _____.
    a. differences; changes
    b. changes; differences
    c. differences; differences
    d. changes; changes

11. Cross-sectional designs confound age effects with _____; longitudinal designs confound age effects with _____.
    a. cohort effects; cohort effects
    b. time of measurement effects; cohort effects
    c. cohort effects; type of measurement effects
    d. cohort effects; time of measurement effects

12. If you wanted to assess individual changes over time in prosocial behavior, you would need to use
    a. a longitudinal design
    b. a cross-sectional design
    c. a correlational design
    d. an experimental design

13. Suppose you have one group of children role play (children assume the role of someone else) while another group of children does not role play. You then observe the level of empathy in children from both groups as they interact with other children. The independent variable would be
    a. whether children role played or not
    b. children's level of empathy
    c. the relationship between role playing and level of empathy
    d. children's ability to role play

14. A positive correlation between viewing televised violence and aggressive behavior would indicate that
    a. children who watch less televised violence tend to be more aggressive
    b. children who watch more televised violence tend to be more aggressive
    c. increases in aggression are caused by watching more televised violence
    d. watching televised violence is not related to level of aggressive behavior

15. Ensuring that all subjects have an equal chance of participating in any of the experimental treatments is accomplished
    a. through experimental control
    b. by selecting a random sample from the population
    c. through random assignment
    d. by administering a questionnaire

REVIEW DEVELOPMENTAL RESEARCH DESIGNS

For each of the major developmental designs, indicate the procedure used to conduct the study, the type of information that can be gained, and the major advantages and disadvantages. Use Table 1.2 in the text to check your answers.

	Cross-Sectional	Longitudinal	Sequential
Procedure			
Information			
Advantages			
Disadvantages			

APPLICATION QUESTIONS

By answering the following questions, you will strengthen your understanding of the material in this chapter. These questions require higher level thinking skills such as integration and application of concepts. To get you started, there is a sample answer or outline provided for the first question. This illustrates one possibility, but there are other answers you could provide that might be just as good. For the other questions, you can check yourself by referring to the text (a hint is provided), or by asking a peer or your instructor to review your answer.

1. Many people in our society are interested in the possibility of "speeding up" some aspect of development, such as the ages when children can print or read. Similarly, parents are often concerned about providing appropriate learning experiences for their children to enhance their abilities. Design a study to test the possibility that some specific aspect of development can be accelerated. Indicate the type of design and the variables used to test this hypothesis. [Sample answer provided]

2.   Another current concern is the effect of divorce on children of all ages. Design a study to assess whether divorce has a negative impact on children at different ages. Specify the type of design needed for this question and how you would measure the impact of divorce.
[Hint: Review the sections in the chapter on conducting developmental research, particularly Developmental research designs" and "Explaining development."]

3.   Suppose you would like to study how nutrition, both before birth and after birth, affects the three major areas of development: physical, cognitive, and psychosocial. How would you ethically conduct this study? Discuss factors that would need to be considered when designing an ethical study and specify how you would define and measure your variables.
[Hint: Review the section on "What problems arise in studying development?" and the discussion of the limitations of correlational experimental methods in the subsection on "Explaining development."]

4.   The age range for when it is considered appropriate to engage in various activities (e.g. sexual intercourse, marriage, settling down in career, having children, etc.) has changed over the years. How and why?
[Hint: Review the section on "How do people view the life span?" and consider the implications of historical events and cultural differences on our perception of the life span.]

ANSWERS

Chapter Summary and Guided Review (Fill-in the blank)

1.	physical	25.	storm and stress
2.	cognitive	26.	gerontology
3.	psychosocial	27.	lifelong
4.	growth	28.	multidirectional
5.	aging	29.	plasticity
6.	life span	30.	historical/cultural
7.	aging	31.	theories
8.	maturation	32.	hypotheses
9.	learning	33.	self-report
10.	young-old	34.	naturalistic
11.	old-old	35.	structured
12.	oldest old	36.	cross-sectional
13.	age grade	37.	differences
14.	age norms	38.	longitudinal
15.	adolescence	39.	changes
16.	life expectancy	40.	age effects
17.	baby boom generation	41.	cohort
18.	functions	42.	time of measurement
19.	description	43.	cohort
20.	explain	44.	time of measurement
21.	optimize	45.	sequential
22.	baby biographies	46.	experiment
23.	G. Stanley Hall	47.	independent
24.	questionnaires	48.	dependent

49. random assignment
50. experimental control
51. quasi-experiment
52. correlational
53. correlational coefficient
54. causal

55. sample
56. random
57. research ethics
58. informed consent
59. debrief
60. confidential

Review of Key Terms

1. learning
2. scientific method
3. experiment
4. centenarian
5. hypothesis
6. research ethics
7. correlational method
8. naturalistic observation
9. development
10. baby biography
11. sequential design
12. environment
13. cohort effects
14. random assignment
15. correlation coefficient
16. growth
17. age grades
18. time of measurement effects
19. cross-sectional design
20. life-span perspective
21. oldest old

22. age norms
23. aging
24. maturation
25. baby boom generation
26. storm and stress
27. independent variable
28. theories
29. sample
30. quasi-experiment
31. experimental control
32. gerontology
33. social clock
34. longitudinal design
35. dependent variable
36. random sample
37. old-old
38. structured observation
39. plasticity
40. population
41. young-old
42. age effects

Multiple Choice Self Test

1.	C	6.	D	11.	D
2.	D	7.	D	12.	A
3.	B	8.	B	13.	A
4.	C	9.	A	14.	B
5.	A	10.	A	15.	C

Application Questions

1.   *You would need to use a longitudinal or sequential design to determine whether development could be accelerated. Acceleration is really looking at whether or not some experience produces change over time. A cross-sectional design wouldn't work because this would provide information about age differences but not about whether individuals change over time as a result of their experiences. Further, if you wanted to show that acceleration was* <u>caused</u> *by a particular program, you would need to use an experiment.*

Suppose you're interested in speeding up the age at which children read. After selecting a group of representative participants, these participants would be randomly assigned to either a treatment condition or the control group. In the treatment condition, children would spend one hour every day in a special program designed to foster reading, while children in the control condition would not get any special treatment. Children would begin the program when they were 18 months old and continue for at least 8 years. Both groups of children would be tested on their reading progress every 6 months until they were 9 or 10 years old. If children in the treatment group read at an earlier age and/or progressed faster once they started reading, then we could conclude that this particular aspect of development could be accelerated by this particular type of treatment.

You could also use a correlational study to study this question if you couldn't randomly assign children to different groups. To do this, you might measure the performance of children who were already in a special reading program and compare them to children in a regular reading program to see if one group tends to have higher reading scores than the other. The problem with this is that children in the two groups might have been different to begin with, which may account for why some of them were in the special reading group and others were not. Also, you wouldn't have control over what was in the program or how long it lasted.

CHAPTER TWO

THEORIES OF HUMAN DEVELOPMENT

OVERVIEW

This is an important foundational chapter for the rest of the text. The major developmental theories, which come up in most of the subsequent chapters, are introduced and evaluated here. Before getting into specific theories, the qualities of a good theory are discussed, as are the basic developmental issues that the theorists are trying to understand. These issues are: assumptions about human nature, nature and nurture, activity and passivity, continuity and discontinuity, and universality and context-specificity.

Five major theories are discussed: Freud's psychoanalytic theory with its psychosexual stages and three personality structures, Erikson's neo-Freudian psychoanalytic theory with its eight psychosocial stages, Skinner's and Bandura's learning theories, Piaget's cognitive-developmental theory, and Bronfenbrenner's ecological theory, which is an example of a contextual theory. You should be able to describe the distinct features of each theory, compare and contrast issues among the theories, and evaluate the contributions of each theory. A good understanding of these theories will be useful to you as you read other chapters in the text. The chapter ends by considering three general world views--organismic, mechanistic, and contextual--and relating these to the developmental theories.

LEARNING OBJECTIVES

After reading and studying the material in this chapter, you should be able to answer the following questions.

1.   What are the characteristics of a good theory?

2.   What are the five basic issues in human development? Where does each theorist stand on each of these issues?

3.   What are the distinct features of Freud's psychoanalytic theory? What are the strengths and weaknesses of the theory?

4   How does Erikson's theory compare to Freud's theory? What crisis characterizes each of Erickson's psychosocial stages?

5. What are the distinct features of Skinner's operant conditioning theory and Bandura's social-learning theory? What are the strengths and weaknesses of the learning theories?

6. What is Piaget's basic perspective on cognitive development? What are the strengths and weaknesses of Piaget's theory?

7. What are the main features of the contextual theory of development? What is Bronfenbrenner's ecological approach? What are the strengths and weaknesses of the contextual perspective?

8. What are the three major world views? Which theories are consistent with each view?

CHAPTER SUMMARY AND GUIDED REVIEW

The following summary provides an overview of the main points contained in this chapter of the text. Fill-in the blanks with terms that appropriately complete the sentence. Scattered throughout the summary are questions in parentheses. These are meant to encourage you to think actively as you are reading and connect this summary to the more detailed information provided in the text. You can answer these questions as you are filling in the blanks or you can fill-in all the blanks, then go back and reread the entire summary, addressing the questions in order to provide more depth of understanding.

THE NATURE OF THEORIES

Theories of human development try to organize and explain the facts and observations about a particular phenomenon. Some theories do a better job of this than others. Good theories can explain a wide range of observations but are also (1) _____ in that the principles needed for explanation are simple and concise. In addition, good theories can generate hypotheses that can be tested, either confirming or disconfirming the theory. This means the theory is (2) _____. Good theories also should be supported by the research conducted on them.

BASIC ISSUES IN HUMAN DEVELOPMENT

There are five basic issues concerning what humans are like and how development occurs. (*Where do you stand on these issues and how do your views compare to the views of the major developmental theorists? See Boxes 2.1 and 2.7 in the text.*)

Assumptions about Human Nature

One basic issue concerns our assumptions about human nature. In particular, are people inherently good or bad, or are they a (3) _____, meaning they are neither inherently good or bad but develop according to their experiences.

Nature and Nurture

Another basic issue concerns whether development results primarily from biological forces, called (4) _____, or environmental experiences, called (5) _____.

Activity and Passivity

A third issue concerns whether people actively produce developmental change or are more passively shaped by biological and environmental forces outside of their control.

Continuity and Discontinuity

A fourth issue is whether development is continuous or discontinuous. Continuity implies gradual and (6) _____ change, while discontinuity implies abrupt and (7) _____ change. Developmental stages are often proposed by theorists who believe development is (8) _____.

Universality and Context-Specificity

A final developmental issue is whether we all follow the same universal path of development or whether we each follow different, context specific paths of development.

FREUD: PSYCHOANALYTIC THEORY

Instincts and Unconscious Motives

Freud's psychoanalytic theory proposes that humans have basic biological urges that must be satisfied. Two powerful biological forces that motivate behavior are the life and death instincts. We are often unaware that these instincts motivate behavior because they are (9)_____.

Id, Ego, and Superego

Freud believed that there were three personality components. At birth, the personality consists of only the (10) _____, which seeks to satisfy a person's instincts. During infancy, the (11) _____ begins to develop and tries to realistically satisfy the demands of the id. The third component of the personality is the (12) _____, which begins to develop during early childhood and functions as a person's internalized moral standards. Problems may develop if the available (13)_____ is not evenly distributed among the three personality structures.

Psychosexual Development

Freud believed that the most important life instinct was the sex instinct; the psychic energy of the sex instinct is called the (14) _____ . Although we are presumably born with this instinct, the psychic energy associated with it changes focus over development. This is reflected by progression through Freud's stages of (15) _____ development. During the first stage, the libido seeks pleasure through (16) _____ activities. This focus shifts to (17) _____ activities during the second psychosexual stage of development. During the (18) _____ stage of development, boys and girls become interested in their genitals and are influenced by the presence or absence of a penis. Freud proposed that boys experience the (19) _____ during this stage, characterized by desire for their mother and jealousy and fear of castration from their father. Resolution of these feelings involves repression of boys' desire for their mother and (20) _____ with their father. Girls experience the (21) _____ during this stage, which is characterized by desire for their father and resentment towards their mother. These feelings may simply fade away. (***What explanation is given for the difference in how boys and girls resolve the complexes of this stage?***) During the (22) _____ period, the psychic energy of the sex instinct becomes focused on socially appropriate activities such as schoolwork. The (23) _____ stage is the final psychosexual stage and occurs with the onset of puberty. It is characterized by mature love with the goal of biological reproduction.

Freud emphasized the influence of inborn biological drives but also recognized that early experiences could have a long-term effect on personality development. During any psychosexual stage, conflict among the personality components may create anxiety that is alleviated by use of (24) _____. One example is (25) _____, which occurs when the psychic energy remains tied to an early stage of development. Another example is (26) _____, which involves returning to an earlier, less traumatic stage of development.

Strengths and Weaknesses

One of the criticisms of Freud's theory is that many of the concepts cannot be tested, which means the theory is not (27) _____. Freud also offered biased interpretations of many phenomenon. Freud's theory is valuable because it focused attention on unconscious motivation, early family experiences, and emotions.

ERIKSON: NEO-FREUDIAN PSYCHOANALYTIC THEORY

Erik Erikson was another psychoanalytic theorist, a neo-Freudian, who was distinct from Freud in several ways. Erikson focused less on sexual instincts than Freud and more on societal forces. He also had a more positive view of human nature and believed that development continued through adulthood. Erikson also emphasized the rational ego more than the irrational id.

Psychosocial Development

Erikson proposed that maturation and society together create eight life (28) _____, which correspond to eight psychosocial stages of development. Each crisis can be resolved positively or negatively and unresolved crises can have an effect on later development. In the first psychosocial stage, infants must learn to develop a sense of (29) _____. Toddlers struggle to develop (30) _____ rather than shame and doubt. Preschool-age children must learn to (31) _____ activities and set goals without coming into conflict with others. In the fourth stage, elementary school children develop a sense of (32) _____ by mastering the cognitive and social skills important in school. Adolescents struggle to develop a sense of (33) _____ as they try to define who they are. Adolescents who have difficulty figuring out who they are experience (34) _____. Young adulthood is the time for establishing (35) _____ in a committed relationship. Middle aged adults are concerned with whether or not they have produced something meaningful that will live on after them, which is an issue of (36) _____. In the last psychosocial stage, older adults try to find meaning in their lives and develop a sense of (37) _____ rather than despair.

Strengths and Weaknesses

Like Freud, Erikson's theory has been criticized because it is difficult to test. Erikson also does not adequately explain development. The theory has been praised for focusing attention on adolescent and adult development.

LEARNING THEORY

John Watson believed it was not possible to study unconscious motivations or mental processes and developed a "school" of psychology called (38) _____. Watson believed that only overt behaviors were appropriate for study and that learned associations between a person's actions and external stimuli were the bases of human development.

Skinner: Operant-Conditioning

Many of Watson's ideas have been advanced by B.F. Skinner, who demonstrated that existing behaviors become more or less probable depending on the consequences of the behaviors. This form of learning is called operant conditioning. A (39) _____ is anything that increases the likelihood of future responding and a (40) _____ is anything that decreases the likelihood of future responding.

Bandura: Social Learning

Another learning theorist, one who emphasized the importance of cognition, was Albert Bandura. His social learning theory makes the claim that humans are active processors of environmental information. Bandura believes that (41) _____ learning is the most important mechanism through which development occurs. Bandura also believes that development occurs through a constant give-and-take relationship between a person and the environment, called (42) _____.

Strengths and Weaknesses

A strength of learning theories is that precise hypotheses can be generated and tested. In addition, the principles apply to learning across the entire life span, and they are applicable to many developmental phenomenon. Learning theories have been criticized for not clearly showing that learning causes developmental changes and for oversimplifying developmental processes.

COGNITIVE-DEVELOPMENTAL THEORY
Piaget: Intellectual Development

Piaget focused on cognitive development and proposed that children actively (43) _____ their understanding of the world based on their experiences. Cognitive development results from the interaction of maturation and environment. As children mature, they develop more complex (44) _____, which are organized patterns of thought or action that are used to interpret experiences.

Cognitive Development

Piaget proposed four stages of cognitive development, which form an (45) _____, meaning that children progress through the stages in order with no skipping. Infants are in the (46) _____ stage because they learn about the world through their sensory experiences and their motoric responses to these experiences. Preschoolers are in the (47) _____ stage, which is characterized by use of (48) _____ and lack of logical thought. School-aged children are in the (49) _____ stage and can logically solve problems by applying a number of mental operations. They typically use a trial-and-error approach to solving problems. Adolescents are in the (50) _____ stage, which is characterized by systematic hypothesis testing and logical reasoning on abstract problems.

Strengths and Weaknesses

Piaget's theory has been very influential. Piaget's descriptions of cognitive development have largely been supported by research. However, he has been criticized for not adequately considering the influence of social factors on cognitive development. In addition, research suggests that cognitive development is not nearly as stage-like as Piaget proposed.

CONTEXTUAL THEORY

Contextual theories propose that development results from an ongoing relationship between a changing person and a changing environment.

Bronfenbrenner: Ecological Approach to Development

Urie Bronfenbrenner focused attention on the (51) _____ in which development takes place. He developed an ecological theory that truly integrates nature and nurture. According to this theory, there are various environmental systems that interact with a person. The system closest to the individual is the (52) _____ system. A person's immediate environments are interrelated through the (53) _____ so that events in one impact on behavior and events in another. Children can also be influenced by the (54) _____, which includes social settings that are not directly experienced but still influential. The broadest context in which development occurs is the (55) _____. (*Can you provide an example of each type of environmental system?*)

Strengths and Weaknesses

Contextual theories are valuable for pointing out the importance of the context of development. Most contextual theories are broad and not fully developed. Indeed, it may not be possible to develop a specific contextual theory because at the very heart of these theories is the notion that development depends on the unique and continuous interactions between a person and their world.

THEORIES AND WORLD VIEWS

The theories presented in this chapter can be classified according to their general world view.

The Organismic World View

Those theorists who compare humans to other living organisms adopt the organismic world view of development. According to this view, humans are organized wholes, active in their development, and internal forces are primarily responsible for development. (**Which theories fit this world view?**)

The Mechanistic World View

According to this world view, humans are like machines. They are a collection of parts, relatively passive in their development, with continuous changes, and many different developmental paths. (**Which theories fit this world view?**)

The Contextual World View

Those theorists who use historical events as a metaphor for human development ascribe to the contextual world view. According to this view, the person and their environment are both active in the person's development. (**Which theories fit this world view?**)

Changing World Views

The theories and world views of development change and increase in complexity as we learn more about human development. Most developmentalists do not adopt static positions on development, but assume a multifaceted view.

REVIEW OF KEY TERMS

Below is a list of terms and concepts from this chapter. Use these to complete the following sentence definitions. You might also want to try writing definitions in your own words and then checking your definitions with those in the text.

activity/passivity issue

autonomy versus shame and doubt

behaviorism

concrete operations stage

constructivism

contextual theories

contextual world view

continuity/discontinuity issue

defense mechanisms

developmental stage

eclectic
ecological approach
ego
Electra complex
exosystem
fixation
formal operations stage
generativity versus stagnation
id
identity versus role confusion
industry versus inferiority
initiative versus guilt
instinct
integrity versus despair
intimacy versus isolation
libido
macrosystem
mechanistic world view
mesosystem
microsystem

nature/nurture issue
observational learning
Oedipus complex
operant conditioning
organismic world view
preoperational stage
psychoanalytic theory
psychosexual stages
punisher
reciprocal determinism
regression
reinforcer
sensorimotor stage
social learning theory
superego
tabula rasa
trust versus mistrust
unconscious motivation
universality/particularity issue

1.   With the defense mechanism of _____, a person reverts to an earlier, less traumatic stage of development.

2.   The psychosocial conflict during elementary school in which children need to acquire important academic and social skills is called _____.

3.   According to the _____ school of psychology, researchers and theorists should focus on observations of overt behavior rather than unobservable mental processes.

4.   In Piaget's _____ stage of cognitive development, school-aged children can reason logically about concrete problems.

5.   According to _____, humans develop actively through a continuous reciprocal interaction between them and their environment, rather than being passively shaped by their environment.

6.   The basic principle of _____ is that behaviors become more or less probable depending on the consequences they produce.

7.   The _____ is a general philosophical assumption that views humans as similar to machines.

8.   The _____ concerns the question of whether development is primarily the result of biological or environmental forces.

9.   The _____ concerns whether humans are actively involved in their development or passively influenced by factors beyond their control.

10. According to Freud, the _____ is the most primitive component of personality, seeking immediate satisfaction of instincts.

11. A period of life characterized by a cohesive set of behaviors or abilities that are distinct from earlier or later periods is called a _____.

12. In the psychosocial stage of _____, a young child tries to accept more grown-up responsibilities that she/he may not be able to handle.

13. The _____ is Freud's term for a young boy's desire for his mother and the accompanying feelings of rivalry with father and guilt.

14. _____ are unconscious techniques used by the ego to protect itself from anxiety.

15. The _____ is largest cultural context in which development occurs.

16. _____ is the belief that children have no inborn tendencies, but their outcome depends entirely on the environment in which they are raised.

17. Piaget's first stage of cognitive development during which infants learn about the world through their sensory experiences and their actions is the _____ stage.

18. _____ is a form of learning that results from observing the behavior of other people.

19. Any consequence that decreases the probability that a response will occur in the future is a _____.

20. _____ hold that development arises from the ongoing interrelationships between a changing organism and a changing world .

21. The _____ is a general philosophical assumption that compares humans to other living organisms.

22. Piaget believed in _____, the belief that children actively build their own understanding of the world.

23. The question of whether development is smooth and gradual or somewhat abrupt is the focus of the _____.

24. _____ refers to the influence of information that is in memory but is not recalled at a conscious level.

25. Freud's term for the sex instinct's psychic energy is _____.

26. Adolescents are faced with developing a sense of who they are socially, sexually, and professionally during the _____ stage.

27. The defense mechanism of _____ is when development becomes arrested because part of the libido remains tied to an earlier stage of development.

28. The interrelationship among microsystems is referred to as the _____.

29. In Piaget's _____ stage of cognitive development, preschoolers are able to use symbols but lack logical reasoning.

30. Any consequence that increases the probability that a response will occur in the future is called a _____.

31. In the psychosocial conflict of _____, toddlers must learn some independence.

32. The personality component that seeks to realistically satisfy instincts is called the _____.

33. The psychosocial conflict of middle adulthood that involves being productive in one's work and with one's family is called _____.

34. In the psychosocial stage of _____, young adults strive to develop strong friendships and intimate relationships.

35. The _____ is a general model for human development based on historical changes.

36. In Piaget's _____ stage of cognitive development, adolescents can reason logically about abstract concepts and hypothetical ideas.

37. The personality component that contains values and morals learned from parents and society is called the _____.

38. The most immediate environments that a person experiences is the _____.

39. Freud used the term _____ to refer to a young girl's envy and desire for her father and the corresponding feelings of jealousy toward her mother.

40. A person with an _____ view believes that none of the major theories of human development can explain everything, but each has something to contribute to our understanding of human development.

41. The theory that humans are active, cognitive processors of information from the environment, rather than passive recipients of information from the environment is the _____ theory.

42. An _____ is an inborn biological force that motivates behavior.

43. The psychosocial conflict of _____ occurs late in life when individuals assess their life and evaluate whether it has been meaningful.

44. According to the _____ theory, humans are driven by unconscious motives and emotions and are shaped by early childhood experiences.

45. The _____ addresses whether developmental changes are common across people or are different for each person.

46. The _____ is a social setting that indirectly influences a child's development.

47. Children progress through the _____ as the libido shifts from one part of the body to another.

48. The _____ to development focuses on the influences of nature and nurture by examining a person's development within a series of environmental layers.

49. During the _____ psychosocial stage, infants strive to achieve a basic trust in others.

MULTIPLE CHOICE SELF TEST

For each multiple choice question, read all alternatives and then select the best answer.

1. A theorist who believes that humans progress through developmental stages is likely to believe in
   a. discontinuous changes
   b. continuous changes
   c. quantitative changes
   d. multiple paths of development

2. The universality/context-specificity issue concerns
   a. the degree to which developmental changes are quantitative or qualitative in nature
   b. the extent to which developmental changes are common to everyone or different from person to person
   c. whether development is multiply caused
   d. whether development follows universal paths determined by genetic factors or by environmental factors

3. According to Freud's theory, the _____ must find ways of realistically satisfying the demands of the _____.
   a. superego, ego
   b. defense mechanisms, id
   c. id, ego
   d. ego, id

4. Boys resolve their Oedipus complexes by
   a. fearing their father
   b. identifying with their father
   c. distancing themselves from their parents
   d. redirecting their psychic energy to another part of their body

5. Regression occurs when
   a. a person reverts to an earlier stage of development
   b. a person pushes anxiety-provoking thoughts out of conscious awareness
   c. development becomes arrested because part of the libido remains tied to an earlier stage of development
   d. psychic energy is directed toward socially acceptable activities

6. Which of the following BEST characterizes Erikson's position on the nature-nurture issue?
   a. He emphasized nurture more than nature.
   b. He emphasized nature more than nurture.
   c. He emphasized nature and nurture equally.
   d. He didn't really take a stand on this issue.

7. According to Erikson, the main task facing adolescents is
   a. developing a sense of identity
   b. achieving a sense of intimacy with another person
   c. mastering important academic tasks
   d. building a sense of self-confidence

8. A basic premise of John Watson's behaviorism is that development is
   a. a series of qualitative behavior changes
   b. a continuous process of change dependent on learning experiences
   c. a combination of inborn tendencies and environmental experiences
   d. best understood by studying mental activities

9. Which of the following explanations for developmental change would a social learning theorist be most likely to give?
   a. Children are unconsciously motivated by internal conflict.
   b. Children observe the world around them and actively process this information.
   c. Children are passively influenced by environmental rewards and punishments.
   d. Children actively construct an understanding of the world through interactions with their environment.

10. Which two theorists believe that development occurs through the interaction of an active person with the environment?
   a. Piaget and Freud
   b. Skinner and Bronfenbrenner
   c. Skinner and Bandura
   d. Piaget and Bandura

11. A child in Piaget's preoperational stage is able to solve problems
   a. that are concrete by using logical reasoning
   b. that are abstract by using logical reasoning
   c. using symbols
   d. through their sensory experiences and their actions

12. Of the following, Piaget has been MOST criticized for his
   a. emphasis on sexual instincts during childhood
   b. belief that children are actively involved in their development
   c. description of cognitive development
   d. belief that cognitive development occurs through an invariant sequence of coherent stages

13. Urie Bronfenbrenner's ecological approach to development contends that
   a. development is influenced by interacting environmental systems
   b. the home environment is the only really important influence on development
   c. children have a passive role in development and are unable to shape their futures
   d. the environment has a similar effect on all children

14. According to the ecological approach to development, a person's most immediate environment is the
   a. microsystem
   b. mesosystem
   c. exosystem
   d. macrosystem

15. Which of the following theories is (are) based on an organismic world view?
   a. Piaget's cognitive-developmental theory
   b. Freud's psychoanalytic theory
   c. Skinner's operant learning theory
   d. Both a and b
   e. Both b and c

PEOPLE AND THEIR IDEAS

We have reviewed lots of ideas and concepts from this chapter. Now consider the people who contributed many of these ideas. Use the matching exercise below to review the contributions of some of the more influential people discussed in this chapter. Write the appropriate letter next to the person's name.

1. Albert Bandura _____
2. Urie Bronfenbrenner _____
3. Erik Erikson _____
4. Sigmund Freud _____
5. Jean Piaget _____
6. B.F. Skinner _____
7. John Watson _____

a. Developed an ecological theory of development with different environmental systems.
b. Believed that people learn by actively processing their observations.
c. Focused attention on unconscious motivation and early childhood experiences.
d. Believed learning resulted from associating a behavior with its reinforcing or punishing consequences.
e. Focused attention on overt behaviors and believed development was solely a function of one's experiences.
f. Believed children actively constructed their own understanding of the world by interacting with the environment.
g. Believed people faced a series of life conflicts arising from the influence of social forces on the individual.

REVIEW OF THE BASIC DEVELOPMENTAL ISSUES

For this exercise, indicate each theory's position on the five basic issues in human development. Check yourself using Box 2.7 in the text.

	Freud's Psychoanalytic theory	Erikson's Neo-Freudian Psychoanalytic Theory	Learning Theory	Piaget's Cognitive-Developmental Theory	Contextual Theory
Human Nature					
Nature--Nurture					
Activity--Passivity					
Continuity--Discontinuity					
Universality--Context-Specificity					

APPLICATION QUESTIONS

By answering the following questions, you will strengthen your understanding of the material in this chapter. These questions require higher level thinking skills such as integration and application of concepts. To get you started, there is a sample answer or outline provided for the first question. This illustrates one possibility, but there are other answers you could provide that might be just as good. For the other questions, you can check yourself by referring to the text (a hint is provided), or by asking a peer or your instructor to review your answer.

1. Consider the problem of shyness. Many children and adults in our society are socially shy to a significant degree and express anxiety in many everyday, social situations. How would each of the theorists in this chapter interpret or explain the development of this condition?
    [Sample Answer provided]

2. In what ways do the learning theory explanations of development conflict with the psychoanalytic explanations of development?
    [Review the sections in the text on psychoanalytic theories (Freud and Erikson) and learning theories (Skinner and Bandura). For this question, you need to do some comparing and contrasting of the theories in order to determine where they conflict with one another.]

3. How do each of the theories address the goal of optimizing development in the example of teenage pregnancy described in this chapter? Note that in this example, optimizing development would be somehow reducing the number of teenage pregnancies.
    [Hint: Review the Boxes throughout the chapter that address the issue of teenage pregnancy Box 2.2, 2.3, 2.4, 2.5, 2.6). Try to write an answer in your own words and use the boxes to check yourself.]

4. Freud and Piaget are often considered to be the "great stage theorists" of developmental psychology. Discuss ways in which Freud and Piaget are similar in their views of development and ways in which they differ.
    [Hint: Review the sections in the text on Freud's and Piaget's theories. This is another one of those "compare and contrast" questions in which you need to relate aspects of one theory to aspects of a second theory.]

ANSWERS

Chapter Summary and Guided Review (Fill-in the blank)

1.	parsimonious		17.	anal
2.	falsifiable		18.	phallic
3.	tabula rasa		19.	Oedipus complex
4.	nature		20.	identification
5.	nurture		21.	Electra complex
6.	quantitative		22.	latency
7.	qualitative		23.	genital
8.	discontinuous		24.	defense mechanisms
9.	unconscious		25.	fixation
10.	id		26.	regression
11.	ego		27.	falsifiable
12.	superego		28.	crises
13.	psychic energy		29.	trust
14.	libido		30.	autonomy
15.	psychosexual		31.	initiate
16.	oral		32.	industry

33.	identity		45.	invariant sequence
34.	role confusion		46.	sensorimotor
35.	intimacy		47.	preoperational
36.	generativity		48.	symbols
37.	integrity		49.	concrete operations
38.	behaviorism		50.	formal operations
39.	reinforcer		51.	context
40.	punisher		52.	microsystem
41.	observational		53.	mesosystem
42.	reciprocal determinism		54.	exosystem
43.	construct		55.	macrosystem
44.	cognitive structures			

Review of Key Terms

1.	regression		26.	identity versus role confusion
2.	industry versus inferiority		27.	fixation
3.	behaviorism		28.	mesosystem
4.	concrete operations		29.	preoperational stage
5.	reciprocal determinism		30.	reinforcer
6.	operant conditioning		31.	autonomy versus shame and doubt
7.	mechanistic world view		32.	ego
8.	nature/nurture issue		33.	generativity versus stagnation
9.	activity/passivity issue		34.	intimacy versus isolation
10.	id		35.	contextual world view
11.	developmental stage		36.	formal operations stage
12.	initiative versus guilt		37.	superego
13.	Oedipus complex		38.	microsystem
14.	defense mechanisms		39.	Electra complex
15.	macrosystem		40.	eclectic
16.	tabula rasa		41.	social learning theory
17.	sensorimotor stage		42.	instinct
18.	observational learning		43.	integrity versus despair
19.	punisher		44.	psychoanalytic
20.	contextual theories		45.	universality/context-specificity issue
21.	organismic world view		46.	exosystem
22.	constructivism		47.	psychosexual stages
23.	continuity/discontinuity issue		48.	ecological approach
24.	unconscious motivation		49.	trust versus mistrust
25.	libido			

Multiple Choice Self Test

1.	A		6.	C		11.	C
2.	B		7.	A		12.	D
3.	D		8.	B		13.	A
4.	B		9.	B		14.	A
5.	A		10.	D		15.	D

1.	B		5.	F
2.	A		6.	D
3.	G		7.	E
4.	C			

Application Questions

Freud might say that shyness is used as a defense mechanism to protect the ego from anxiety caused by the superego. A shy child becomes inhibited through regression to early stages of development. Perhaps the shy child was punished for sucking his or her thumb too long in the oral stage or was punished for toilet training accidents during the anal stage. Early experiences may cause the child to develop a strong superego, which in turn leads the child to become inhibited and withdrawn in the quest to satisfy the need for perfection and acceptance in society. Whatever the specific cause, the child is not consciously aware of these motivating factors.

According to *Erikson*, a child may become shy as a result of not adequately resolving a life crisis in one of the eight psychosocial stages. For example, in the trust vs. mistrust stage, shyness could result because the parent is unresponsive to the child's needs and the child does not form a trusting relationship to others. In autonomy vs. shame and doubt, the child may not learn to be autonomous; instead, the child may feel doubtful of his/her abilities and not very comfortable trying new things. In initiative vs. guilt, the caregiver may have been too protective, inhibiting the child's initiative and interactive skills. The child may feel guilty whenever he/she tries to do something new and ends up not initiating things. As a final example, shyness might result if the child lacks proper social skills and begins to feel inferior in the Industry vs. Inferiority stage.

According to *Piaget*, children construct their own understanding of the world through their interactions with their environment. Thus, the child interprets their experiences in a way that leads the child to be shy. To avoid disequilibrium, people act in ways that are consistent with their cognitive understanding of events. The child decides that shyness is an adaptive way of interacting with their world. Perhaps the infant in the sensorimotor stage did not have adequate opportunity to explore the environment, leading to shyness because of lack of experience. Or a child in the preoperational stage who has had a bad experience may reason that all experiences are bad and withdraw from seeking new experiences.

Based on *learning theories*, people learn by forming associations between behaviors and consequences. Skinner would say that a person who is shy was either rewarded for being shy or punished for being outgoing. For example, the parent might reward the child for quiet activities like reading a book or punish child for being loud. According to Bandura, a child may model an adult who is shy and rewarded in some way.

Contextual theorists believe that development arises from the ongoing interrelationships between a changing organism and a changing world. In other words, changes in a person will affect his or her environment, and changes in the environment will affect that person. According to Bronfenbrenner, there are different environmental systems that can influence a person's development. One or more of these environments (e.g., family or peers) must be interacting with the child's own characteristics to create shyness. Maybe the child was predisposed to be shy and this, along with a family that discouraged outgoing behaviors and a peer group that was not very adventuresome, led to shyness.

CHAPTER THREE

THE GENETICS OF LIFE-SPAN DEVELOPMENT

OVERVIEW

As the title suggests, this chapter is about genetic contributions to development. This chapter does much more, though, than describe how parents pass along their genes to their children. The chapter examines how genes interact with environments to make each of us unique with respect to intellectual and psychological attributes. Interestingly, genes can influence the kinds of environments we are exposed to, and environments can affect the expression of genetic factors. Note the point made in the second half of the chapter: people do not inherit traits, they inherit predispositions for traits that may or may not arise depending on the environmental influences.

One of the most interesting findings reported in the chapter is that siblings do not become similar to one another as a result of growing up in the same family and sharing similar experiences. Instead, nonshared environmental experiences are more important in creating individual differences among family members. This may help you understand why you and your siblings are so different from one another on some basic personality characteristics.

An important lesson from this chapter concerns the logic of the methods used to study genetic and environmental influences, and the pattern of the findings. The methods, such as twin and adoption studies, can be used to demonstrate both genetic and environmental influences, not just genetic factors. You should understand the pattern of findings that would show a genetic influence, an environmental influence, and interaction effects, even if you do not know actual correlation coefficients or concordance values.

LEARNING OBJECTIVES

After reading and studying the material in this chapter, you should be able to answer the following questions.

1.   What do species heredity and evolution contribute to our understanding of universal patterns of development? What are the basic principles of Darwin's theory of evolution?

2.   What are the modern approaches to evolution?

3.   What are the basic workings of individual heredity, including the contributions of genes, chromosomes, the zygote, and the processes of mitosis and meiosis?

4.　What is the difference between genotype and phenotype?

5.　How are traits passed from parents to offspring?　What is an example of how a child could inherit a trait through each of the mechanisms?

6.　What are the general characteristics of the chromosomal abnormalities such as Down syndrome, Turner syndrome, and Klinefelter syndrome?

7.　What methods are used to assess the influences of heredity and environment on behavioral characteristics?　Describe the logic of the method, as well as strengths and weaknesses of each method.

8.　How do genes, shared environmental, and nonshared environmental factors contribute to individual differences?

9.　How do genes and environments contribute to individual differences in intellectual ability across the life span?

10.　How do genes and environments contribute to individual differences in personality and temperament across the life span?

11.　How do genes and environments contribute to differences in psychological disorders?

12.　What are three ways that genes and environments correlate to influence behavior?

13.　What tests are used to screen for genetic defects?　What defects can be identified with these tests?　What are the advantages and disadvantages of using techniques like these to test for prenatal problems?

The following summary provides an overview of the main points contained in this chapter of the text. Fill-in the blanks with terms that appropriately complete the sentence. Scattered throughout the summary are questions in parentheses. These are meant to encourage you to think actively as you are reading and connect this summary to the more detailed information provided in the text. You can answer these questions as you are filling in the blanks or you can fill-in all the blanks, then go back and reread the entire summary, addressing the questions in order to provide more depth of understanding.

SPECIES HEREDITY, EVOLUTION, AND HUMAN DEVELOPMENT
        Although people are quite different from one another, (1) _____ ensures that all members of a species share some commonalities. (*Can you provide examples of this common genetic endowment in humans?*)

Darwin's Theory of Evolution
        Charles Darwin's theory of evolution argues that our common genetic makeup has evolved through (2) _____ because genes that promote adaptation to the environment are passed on to offspring more often than genes that do not promote adaptation.

Modern Evolutionary Perspectives
        (3) _____ is the study of how the behaviors of a species have evolved over time in their natural environments. Some psychologists who test Darwinian predictions call their work (4) _____ psychology. Theorists in these fields believe we have evolved in ways that allow us to learn what environments are most adaptive. The most important goal for a member of any species is to ensure that future generations survive. Inborn behaviors emerge only when the individual has normal genes and normal (5) _____.

INDIVIDUAL HEREDITY
The Genetic Code
        Genes can contribute to differences between individuals through the process of individual heredity. At conception, a woman's egg cell is fertilized by a man's sperm, resulting in a (6) _____. This new cell has 46 threadlike (7) _____, each made up of thousands of (8) _____, or segments of DNA molecules. The single cell begins to divide through a process called (9) _____, which results in daughter cells with the same 46 chromosomes as the mother cell. The sperm and ova result from the process of (10)_____ so that they each have only 23, or half, of the original cell's chromosomes.

        Although biological siblings share the same parents, their genetic makeup is unique, partly due to the phenomenon of (11) _____ in which parts of chromosomes are exchanged during cell division. (12) _____ twins are exceptions because they develop from one zygote and so share 100% of their genes. On the other hand, (13) _____ twins result from two separate ova fertilized by different sperm, and are no more genetically similar than siblings. Siblings and fraternal twins share, on the average, half of their genes.

        Chromosomes can be seen through a powerful microscope and displayed through a photograph called a (14) _____. This display will show either two X chromosomes for a (15) _____, or one X and one Y chromosome for a (16) _____. A child's sex is determined by whether or not the sperm that fertilizes the egg carries an X or Y chromosome.

Translation of the Genetic Code
        Some gene pairs seem to be responsible for producing certain effects in a person, while

(17) _____ genes are responsible for "turning on" or "off" other genes at different times in the life span. (***Can you provide an example of gene effects that would be activated at different times across the life span?***) A person's genetic makeup is called a (18) _____, while the actual outward characteristics a person shows are part of their (19) _____.

Mechanisms of Inheritance

There are three main mechanisms of inheritance. One way to inherit is through a single pair of genes. Each gene of the pair can be either dominant or (20) _____. If one gene in the pair is (21) _____, the characteristic associated with this gene will express itself. In order for a (22) _____ trait to express itself, a person would need to receive a matched pair, one from each parent. An example of this is sickle-cell disease. Individuals who have one dominant and one recessive gene for a recessive trait are called (23) _____. They do not express the trait but can pass it on to their offspring.

Another pattern of inheritance occurs when a dominant gene in a pair does not completely mask the effects of the recessive gene. This pattern is called (24) _____. If neither gene dominates the other but both influence a trait, (25) _____ is said to be operating. (***Can you provide examples of characteristics inherited through each of these mechanisms?***)

Some traits are called (26) _____ characteristics because they are influenced by genes on the sex chromosomes, rather than on the other 22 pairs of chromosomes. (***Why are males more likely than females to inherit a trait through this mechanism?***) Many human characteristics are influenced by more than one pair of genes and so are transmitted through the mechanism of (27) _____ inheritance. (***Can you provide examples of characteristics inherited through this mechanism?***)

Mutations

Occasionally, a new gene appears that was not passed from parent to child, but results from a mutation.

Chromosome Abnormalities

Down syndrome is an example of a chromosomal abnormality that results from an extra (28) _____ chromosome. (***Why are older women at greater risk for having a child with chromosomal abnormalities such as Down syndrome?***) Turner syndrome occurs in females when cell division results in a missing (29) _____ chromosome. Males who inherit an extra X chromosome are said to have (30) _____ syndrome. (***What characteristics are associated with each of these chromosomal abnormalities?***)

STUDYING GENETIC AND ENVIRONMENTAL INFLUENCES

The field of study concerned with the extent to which genetic and environmental differences among people are responsible for differences in their traits is (31)_____. Behavior geneticists often use (32) _____ estimates, which provide information about the amount of variability between people that can be attributed to the genetic differences among those people. Even traits that are highly heritable are still influenced by environmental factors.

Experimental Breeding

One way to study the influence of genes on animal behavior is to deliberately mate animals and see whether certain traits are more or less likely following this (33) _____. (***What have researchers learned from doing these sorts of studies?***)

Twin and Adoption Studies

Experimental breeding cannot be used with humans, so researchers use twin and adoption studies to study the influences of genes and environments. (***Can you identify some cautions regarding interpretation of findings from twin and adoption studies?***) If heredity influences a trait, (34) _____ twins should be more similar on the trait than (35) _____ twins. If adopted children resemble their adoptive parents more than they resemble their biological parents on some trait, then the trait must be influenced by (36) _____ factors.

Estimating Influences

To estimate the influence of genetic and environmental factors on traits, researchers may calculate the (37) _____ rate, which indicates the percentage of pairs who both have the trait if one of them has it. They may also use (38) _____ for traits that vary numerically, such as height or intelligence.

Behavioral geneticists try to estimate how various factors contribute to individual differences observed in a trait. Some variation may occur because of (39) _____ differences, as would be evident from findings showing that identical twins score more similarly on a trait than do fraternal twins. The fact that siblings raised together in the same home score more similarly on a trait than siblings raised apart would indicate the influence of the shared (40) _____. Finding that genetically identical pairs who are raised together are not perfectly similar would indicate the influence of (41) _____ factors.

ACCOUNTING FOR INDIVIDUAL DIFFERENCES
Intellectual Abilities

Research on intellectual abilities shows the influence of genes, the shared and nonshared environment. (***Can you describe the patterns of these findings?***) Identical twins tend to become more (42) _____ to one another in mental ability after 18 months of age and tend to follow the same course of mental development. Fraternal twins tend to become less similar to one another over the years. (***Can you explain why this pattern emerges?***) Overall, research shows that the most important environmental influence is the (43) _____ component.

Temperament and Personality

The tendency to respond in predictable ways is called temperament and is considered a precursor to later personality. Individual differences in temperament during infancy seem to be related to (44) _____ differences among infants. In addition, the influence of (45) _____ environmental factors contribute to individual differences in temperament. (***What pattern of findings would support this conclusion?***) These influences help explain why siblings, who share, on average, 50% of their genes and grow up in the same home can be so different.

Psychological Disorders

Psychological problems are also influenced by genetic and environmental factors. Some individuals may be genetically predisposed to (46)_____, which involves disturbances in logical thinking and behavior. Psychological disorders are not inherited directly; people inherit (47) _____ to develop traits.

Heritability of Traits

Although all traits are influenced to some extent by genes, some traits are more heritable than others. (***Which traits are more or less heritable?***)

HEREDITY AND ENVIRONMENT: A CLOSER LOOK
Genes operate throughout a person's life span, interacting with environmental factors.

Gene/Environment Interactions
The expression of a person's genotype depends on the person' environment, and how people respond to their environment depends on their genotype.

Gene/Environment Correlations
Scarr and McCartney (1983) proposed three models for how genes and environments are correlated. In a (48) _____ genotype/environment correlation, the child as well as the child's environment are both influenced by the parents' (49) _____. In an (50) _____ genotype/ environment correlation, a child's (51) _____ triggers certain responses from other people. In an (52) _____ genotype/environment correlation, children actively seek out (53) _____ that suit their particular genotype. (*Can you provide examples of each type of genotype/ environment correlation?*) Research shows that individuals can indeed actively shape their environments, which in turn, influence them.

APPLICATIONS: GENETIC COUNSELING AND ENGINEERING
Genetic counseling provides information to parents who are concerned about the possibility of genetic birth defects. Genetic disorders that they might be tested for include (54)_____ disease, which results in degeneration of the nervous system and early death. Another disorder that parents might be concerned about is (55) _____ disease, caused by a single dominant gene and associated with motor problems, personality changes, and cognitive declines. A recessive disorder called (56) _____ results in the inability to metabolize phenylalanine, causing it to accumulate in toxic levels in the body. Left untreated, PKU results in mental retardation. However, if treated with a special diet, the worst damage can be avoided, which illustrates the interaction between genes and environment.

Future therapies might involve (57) _____ in which normal genes are substituted for ones that are defective. There are mixed feelings about the use of this sort of treatment because some ethicists are concerned about the effects of altering the genetic makeup of a population.

REVIEW OF KEY TERMS

Below is a list of terms and concepts from this chapter. Use these to complete the following sentence definitions. You might also want to try writing definitions in your own words and then checking your definitions with those in the text.

amniocentesis	Down syndrome
behavioral genetics	ethology
carrier	eugenics
chorionic villus biopsy (CVS)	evolutionary psychology
chromosome	fraternal twins
chromosome abnormalities	gene/environment correlation
codominance	gene/environment interaction
conception	gene
concordance rate	genetic counseling
crossing over	genetic engineering
dominant gene	genotype

heritability
Huntington's disease
identical twins
incomplete dominance
karyotype
Klinefelter syndrome
meiosis
mitosis
mutation
natural selection
nonshared environmental influences
phenotype
phenylketonuria (PKU)
polygenic trait
recessive gene

schizophrenia
selective breeding
sex-linked characteristic
shared environmental influences
sickle-cell disease
single gene-pair inheritance
species heredity
Tay-Sachs disease
temperament
Turner syndrome
ultrasound
X chromosome
Y chromosome
zygote

1.   A person's _____ consists of their genetic makeup.

2.   Threadlike structures containing genetic material are called _____.

3.   A fertilized egg cell is a _____.

4.   _____ is the genetic endowment common to all members of a particular species.

5.   Two individuals who develop as a result of one fertilized egg splitting in two are called _____.

6.   _____ occurs when a child receives too many or too few chromosomes at conception.

7.   Trying to improve the human race by changing the genetic makeup of the population is the practice of _____.

8.   The gene in a dissimilar pair that typically does not express itself in that person's phenotype is called the _____.

9.   The presence of the _____ determines whether the child will be male or female.

10.   Researchers who test Darwinian principles of evolution refer to their work as _____.

11.   _____ involves altering a person's genetic makeup in order to treat genetic conditions.

12.   Two individuals who developed at the same time but from two different fertilized eggs are _____.

13.   The gene in a dissimilar pair that usually expresses itself phenotypically is called the _____.

14. Cell division that results in two cells identical to the one original cell occurs through the process of _____.

15. _____ is the study of how different species evolve in their natural environments.

16. A person's _____ reflects the expression of their genotype in conjunction with environmental influences.

17. According to _____, genes that promote adaptation to one's environment will be passed to offspring more often than genes that do not promote adaptation.

18. The moment when a woman's egg is fertilized by a man's sperm is called _____.

19. _____ is a disorder involving disturbances in logical thinking, emotional expression and social behavior.

20. In a procedure called _____, fetal cells are removed from the amniotic sac by inserting a needle through the mother's abdomen in order to test chromosomal makeup.

21. The basic units of heredity are _____.

22. _____ is a chromosome disorder resulting from an extra 21st chromosome.

23. A female who receives only one X chromosome has a condition called _____.

24. A _____ refers to the interrelationship between one's genes and one's environment.

25. _____ provides information to people regarding the likelihood of genetically based problems in their unborn children.

26. A disorder resulting in dementia, emotional problems, loss of motor control, and premature death is _____.

27. Cell division that results in four cells, each with half the number of chromosomes as in the one original cell, occurs through the process of _____.

28. According to the concept of _____, the influence of our genes depends on the experiences we have, and the experiences we have depend on the genes we have.

29. A _____ is a photograph of an individual's chromosomes organized into groups.

30. Experiences that are unique to an individual are called _____.

31. _____ is a phenomenon in which parts of chromosomes are exchanged during cell division.

32. A _____ results in a change in the structure or arrangement of one or more genes, resulting in a new phenotype.

33. _____ occurs when one pair of genes determines the presence or absence of a trait.

34. A disorder in which blood cells cluster together and distribute less oxygen than normal cells is _____.

35. A male who receives an extra X chromosome has a condition called _____.

36. _____ are experiences that individuals have in common because they live in the same home environment.

37. In the inheritance pattern of _____, the dominant gene in a pair is not able to totally mask the effects of the recessive gene.

38. The _____ statistic represents the amount of variability in a trait within a large group of people that can be linked to genetic differences among those people.

39. _____ involves deliberate mating animals with certain genotypes in order to determine if it is possible to produce offspring with certain characteristics.

40. In the inheritance pattern of _____, neither gene in a pair is able to completely dominate the other and both express themselves.

41. A trait that is influenced by single genes located on the sex chromosomes is referred to as _____.

42. A characteristic that is influenced by multiple genes is called a _____.

43. Individuals who are _____ do not express a trait but can pass the trait on to their offspring.

44. _____ is a disorder in which a critical enzyme needed to metabolize phenylalanine is missing.

45. In a procedure called _____, fetal cells from the chorion are removed by inserting a catheter through the mother's vagina in order to test chromosomal makeup.

46. The _____ is a sex chromosome that, when matched with another like it, results in a female child.

47. The tendency to respond in predictable ways is part of a person's _____.

48. _____ represents the probability that one of a pair of twins will show a given characteristic, given that the other twin has the characteristic.

49. A genetic disorder that causes gradual deterioration of the nervous system is called _____.

50. A(n) _____ is a procedure to detect fetal growth and characteristics by passing sound waves over the mother's abdomen.

51. _____ refers to the scientific study of the extent to which genetic and environmental differences within a species are responsible for differences in traits.

MULTIPLE CHOICE SELF TEST

For each multiple choice question, read all alternatives and then select the best answer.

1. All children tend to walk and talk at about 12 months of age. This universal pattern of development results from
   a. the crossing over phenomenon
   b. societal expectations
   c. species heredity
   d. single gene-pair inheritance

2. A zygote
   a. merges with a sperm cell at conception to form a fertilized cell
   b. is a cell that will split and develop into fraternal twins
   c. contains only the sex chromosomes
   d. is a fertilized egg cell

3. A person's phenotype is most accurately described as
   a. a person's genetic inheritance
   b. the outcome of the interaction between a person's genotype and a particular environment
   c. the result of the union between a sperm cell and egg cell
   d. those characteristics that do not have a genetic basis

4. Suppose two people are carriers for thin lips, which is a recessive trait. Each one of their children would have a _____ chance of expressing this trait in their phenotype.
   a. 25%
   b. 50%
   c. 75%
   d. 100%

5. Incomplete dominance results when
   a. two different genes in a pair are both expressed in a compromise of the two genes
   b. one gene in a pair cannot completely mask the effects of the other gene
   c. several gene pairs contribute to the expression of a trait
   d. both parents are carriers for a particular trait

6. A person is a carrier for a genetic disorder if she/he
   a. does not show the disorder and cannot pass on the disorder to offspring
   b. does not show the disorder but can pass on the disorder to offspring
   c. shows the disorder but cannot pass on the disorder to offspring
   d. shows the disorder and can pass on the disorder to offspring

7. In X-linked traits
   a. males and females are equally likely to express the trait
   b. males are carriers of the trait but do not always express the trait
   c. females can express the trait but do so much less often than males
   d. females and males typically carry but do not express the trait

8. Down syndrome occurs when
   a. a child receives too few chromosomes
   b. a male receives an extra X chromosome
   c. there is an abnormality associated with one of the sex chromosomes
   d. a child receives an extra 21st chromosome

9. Heritability refers to
   a. the amount of variability in a group's trait that is due to genetic differences between people in the group
   b. the degree to which an individual's characteristics are determined by genetics
   c. the degree of relationship between pairs of individuals
   d. a person's genetic makeup

10. Some people have criticized the logic of twin studies because
    a. identical twins are always the same biological sex while fraternal twins are not
    b. identical twins are more likely to participate in this type of study than fraternal twins
    c. identical twins are treated more similarly than fraternal twins, making it difficult to separate environmental from genetic factors
    d. it is not always possible to accurately identify twins as fraternal or identical

11. Which of the following statements is FALSE regarding genetics and intellectual ability?
    a. Intellectual development in infancy is only weakly influenced by individual heredity and environment.
    b. Identical twins become more similar with age in their intellectual performance while fraternal twins become less similar.
    c. Both identical and fraternal twins become more similar in intellectual performance with increasing age.
    d. Genes influence the course of intellectual development.

12. With regard to individual differences in intellectual ability, research suggests that
    a. genes, shared environmental influences, and nonshared environmental influences contribute equally across the life span
    b. shared environmental influences have the greatest impact at all stages of the life span
    c. genetic influences become more influential and shared environmental influences become less influential with age
    d. shared and nonshared environmental influences become more influential and genes become less influential with age

13. The concept of an evocative genotype/environment correlation suggests that
    a. parents select environments for their children and their selection is determined by genetic factors
    b. children's genotypes trigger certain reactions from other people
    c. children seek out environments that suit their particular genotypes
    d. genotypes limit the range of possible phenotypic outcomes

14. Research shows that
    a. people directly inherit many psychological disorders
    b. people inherit predispositions to develop psychological disorders
    c. psychological disorders have no genetic basis
    d. having a parent with a psychological disorder means that the child of that person will also have the disorder

15. The goals of genetic counseling include all of the following EXCEPT
    a. Identify traits that parents might be carrying
    b. Calculate probabilities that a particular trait might be transmitted to children
    c. Make decisions for the couple about whether to terminate or continue a pregnancy
    d. Provide information about characteristics and treatment of genetic disorders

REVIEW GENETIC AND ENVIRONMENTAL CONTRIBUTIONS TO TRAITS

This exercise helps you interpret data concerning genetic and environmental contributions to human traits. Suppose you have data from groups of individuals on some psychological trait. For each of the following questions, provide hypothetical correlations in the boxes that support the desired outcome. To check yourself, use Tables 3.2 and 3.3 and the discussion of these in the sections of the chapter called "Estimating Influences" and "Intellectual Abilities."

1. What pattern of findings would show a strong genetic influence and weak environmental influence?
2. What pattern of findings would show a weak genetic influence and strong environmental influence?
3. What pattern of findings would show moderate to strong genetic AND environmental influences?

Relationship between pairs of individuals	Raised Together	Raised Apart
Identical Twins		
Fraternal Twins		
Biological Parent & Child		
Adopted Parent & Child		

APPLICATION QUESTIONS

By answering the following questions, you will strengthen your understanding of the material in this chapter. These questions require higher level thinking skills such as integration and application of concepts. To get you started, there is a sample answer or outline provided for the first question. This illustrates one possibility, but there are other answers you could provide that might be just as good. For the other questions, you can check yourself by referring to the text (a hint is provided), or by asking a peer or your instructor to review your answer.

1.   Consider a characteristic such as humor. What evidence would you need to collect to convince someone that this trait is influenced by genetic factors? What evidence would you need to show the effects of shared and nonshared environmental influences on humor?
     [Sample answer provided]

2.   How can you account for the findings that identical twins become more similar to one another in mental ability as they get older, and fraternal twins become less similar to one another in mental ability as they get older?
     [Hint: Review the section on "Intellectual Abilities" in the text.]

3.   How can you explain the intriguing finding that siblings, who share some common genetic material and who grow up in the same home, turn out to have such different personalities?
     [Hint: Review the section in the text on "Temperament and Personality," paying particular attention to the part in which this very question is posed.]

ANSWERS

Chapter Summary and Guided Review (Fill-in the blank)

1.	species heredity	21.	dominant
2.	natural selection	22.	recessive
3.	ethology	23.	carriers
4.	evolutionary	24.	incomplete dominance
5.	early experiences	25.	codominance
6.	zygote	26.	sex-linked
7.	chromosomes	27.	polygenic
8.	genes	28.	21st
9.	mitosis	29.	X
10.	meiosis	30.	Klinefelter
11.	crossing over	31.	behavioral genetics
12.	identical	32.	heritability
13.	fraternal	33.	selective breeding
14.	karyotype	34.	identical
15.	female	35.	fraternal
16.	male	36.	environmental
17.	regulatory	37.	concordance
18.	genotype	38.	correlation coefficients
19.	phenotype	39.	genetic
20.	recessive	40.	environment

41. nonshared environmental
42. similar
43. nonshared
44. genetic
45. nonshared
46. schizophrenia
47. predisposition
48. passive
49. genotypes

50. evocative
51. genotype
52. active
53. environments
54. Tay-Sachs
55. Huntington's
56. phenylketonuria (PKU)
57. genetic engineering

Review of Key Terms

1. genotype
2. chromosome
3. zygote
4. species heredity
5. identical twins
6. chromosome abnormalities
7. eugenics
8. recessive gene
9. Y chromosome
10. evolutionary psychology
11. genetic engineering
12. fraternal twins
13. dominant gene
14. mitosis
15. ethology
16. phenotype
17. natural selection
18. conception
19. schizophrenia
20. amniocentesis
21. genes
22. Down syndrome
23. Turner syndrome
24. gene/environment correlation
25. genetic counseling
26. Huntington's disease

27. meiosis
28. gene/environment interaction
29. karyotype
30. nonshared environmental influences
31. crossing over
32. mutation
33. single gene-pair inheritance
34. sickle cell disease
35. Klinefelter syndrome
36. shared environmental influences
37. incomplete dominance
38. heritability
39. selective breeding
40. codominance
41. sex-linked characteristic
42. polygenic trait
43. carriers
44. phenylketonuria (PKU)
45. chorionic villus biopsy (CVS)
46. X chromosome
47. temperament
48. concordance rate
49. Tay-Sachs disease
50. ultrasound
51. behavioral genetics

Multiple Choice Self Test

1. C
2. D
3. B
4. A
5. B
6. B

7. C
8. D
9. A
10. C
11. C

12. C
13. B
14. B
15. C

1.   *To show that humor is influenced by genetic factors, you could show that identical twins raised apart are similar to one another on some measure of humor, and more similar than fraternal twins or other siblings who are raised together. Because the only thing the identical twins raised apart have in common is their genetic makeup, any similarities among them must be due to their genetic similarity. One way to demonstrate influences of the shared environment is to show that sibling pairs raised together are more similar to one another than sibling pairs raised apart. The influence of nonshared environmental influences would be evident if identical twins raised together were dissimilar on humor.*

CHAPTER FOUR

EARLY ENVIRONMENTAL INFLUENCES
ON LIFE-SPAN DEVELOPMENT

OVERVIEW

This chapter covers a number of important environmental influences that occur early in the life span. This begins with discussion of the dramatic changes during the prenatal period and the environmental factors that can influence prenatal development. These include maternal conditions such as age, emotional state and nutritional condition, and outside factors--called teratogens--that can adversely affect development. The environment surrounding birth (the perinatal period) is also discussed, with attention to complicating factors and to the parent's experience of the birth process. Finally, the early environment of the infant is considered, including cultural differences in parent-infant interactions and the effects of the environment on low-birth-weight babies. The Application section at the end of this chapter considers environmental modifications that can improve life.

LEARNING OBJECTIVES

After reading and studying the material in this chapter, you should be able to answer the following questions.

1.   How does development proceed during the prenatal period? How does prenatal behavior of the fetus relate to postnatal behavior of the infant?

2.   How do mother's age, emotional state, and nutrition affect prenatal and neonatal development?

3.   How and when do various teratogens affect the developing fetus?

4.   What is the perinatal environment like? What hazards can occur during the birth process?

5.   What is the birth experience like from the mother's and father's perspectives, and from different cultural perspectives?

6. What are three universal goals of parenting? How do societies differ in the goals they emphasize? How and why do parenting practices differ cross-culturally?

7. To what extent are the effects of the prenatal and perinatal environments long lasting? What factors influence whether effects are lasting?

8. How can we optimize development during the prenatal and perinatal periods?

CHAPTER SUMMARY AND GUIDED REVIEW

The following summary provides an overview of the main points contained in this chapter of the text. Fill-in the blanks with terms that appropriately complete the sentence. Scattered throughout the summary are questions in parentheses. These are meant to encourage you to think actively as you are reading and connect this summary to the more detailed information provided in the text. You can answer these questions as you are filling in the blanks or you can complete all the blanks, then go back and reread the entire summary, addressing the questions in order to provide more depth of understanding.

DEVELOPMENT IN THE PRENATAL ENVIRONMENT
The prenatal environment is the physical environment of the womb.

Prenatal Stages
Conception occurs when a sperm fertilizes an egg cell, forming a single cell called a (1) _____, which begins to divide and replicate. Prenatal development is divided into three stages. The first is the (2) _____ period, which lasts from conception until implantation of the (3) _____ in the wall of the uterus.

At this point, the period of the (4) _____ begins and lasts through the eighth week of prenatal development. During this time, every major organ forms in a process called (5) _____. The layers of the embryo become distinct, with an outer layer forming the amnion and the (6) _____, which attaches to the uterine wall. Eventually, this becomes the lining of the (7) _____, a tissue that is fed by blood vessels from the mother. This tissue connects the embryo to the (8) _____, and together these structures provide nutrients and oxygen for the embryo.

The process of sexual differentiation begins during the seventh and eighth prenatal weeks with development of male testes or female ovaries from an undifferentiated tissue. The testes will then secrete (9) _____, which will stimulate development of a male internal reproduction system, or in its absence, the internal reproduction system of a female.

The third stage of prenatal development is the period of the (10) _____, which lasts from the ninth week of pregnancy until birth. At about 24 weeks, the fetus may be able to survive outside the womb, making this the age of (11) _____. The last trimester brings rapid weight gain for the fetus and rapid multiplication of (12) _____ cells. Fetal behavior becomes increasingly organized, resembling organized patterns of waking and sleeping known as (13) _____. Prenatal behavior patterns correlate with later infant patterns, demonstrating continuity in development.

The Mother's State

A number of factors associated with the prenatal environment can influence growth and development. Mothers who are younger than 17 years or older than about 40 years are more likely to experience complications. (***What is one possible reason for this increased risk associated with mother's age?***) Mothers who experience prolonged and severe (14) _____ during their pregnancies increase the risk of harm to the fetus. (***What mechanisms might explain how this factor influences fetal development?***) Maternal nutrition can also impact negatively on the developing fetus, particularly if malnutrition occurs during the (15) _____ trimester of pregnancy.

Teratogens

A teratogen is any environmental agent that can produce abnormalities in a developing fetus. (***What generalizations can be made about the effects of teratogens?***) A time when the developing embryo or fetus is particularly sensitive to environmental influences is called a (16) _____. German measles or (17) _____ is a disease that is most damaging to the developing organism during the first trimester and can cause a variety of defects. (18) _____, a sexually transmitted disease, results in similar problems but has its greatest impact on development during the middle and later stages of pregnancy. Another sexually transmitted disease is (19) _____ and can be passed from mother to infant prior to, during, or after birth.

Drugs can also impact on prenatal development. A mild tranquilizer, now off the market, called (20) _____ caused serious deformities that varied depending on when the drug was taken during pregnancy. Smoking, and even exposure to second-hand smoke, can lead to growth retardation and other developmental delays. Children whose mothers drank alcohol during pregnancy may exhibit a cluster of symptoms called (21) _____. There is no known amount of alcohol that is entirely safe to consume during pregnancy, although the severity of FAS symptoms depends on the amount of alcohol consumed. The illegal drug (22) _____ also leads to a number of prenatal and postnatal complications, including possible long-term deficits in cognitive, language, and social development. (***What other environmental conditions or maternal conditions can adversely affect prenatal development?***)

A number of environmental hazards, such as radiation and pollutants, can also adversely affect prenatal development. Some pollutants known to be hazardous have been restricted, but still exist in the environment. For example, older houses may expose children to high levels of lead in paint, and a chemical called (23) _____ still exists in some environments at unsafe levels.

THE PERINATAL ENVIRONMENT

The perinatal environment is environment surrounding birth and includes drugs administered to the mother, delivery practices, and the immediate social environment following birth. Birth consists of three stages that are, in order of occurrence, (24) _____, (25) _____, and (26) _____.

Possible Hazards

During birth, lack of adequate oxygen or (27) _____ can result in brain damage. (***What are some of the potential outcomes for an infant/child who experienced lack of oxygen at birth?***) Another birth complication can result if the fetus is not positioned in the typical head-down position, but instead is positioned feet or buttocks first, called a (28) _____ presentation. Some fetuses are delivered by a (29) _____ in which an incision is made in the mother's abdomen and uterus so that the fetus can be removed. Delivery methods and medications administered to the mother during delivery can impact on the outcome of the delivery process. Perinatal complications may also be higher for (30) _____ newborns, or those in jeopardy for some reason. To measure general well-being of an infant, the (31) _____ test is administered immediately and at five minutes after birth. (**Can you list the five characteristics assessed by this test?**)

The Mother's Experience

The cultural and social environment surrounding birth can have an impact on mother's experience of birth. Mothers who receive (32) _____ and are prepared for the birth generally have a more positive experience than other mothers.

Some research suggests that early (33) _____ between mother and infant can facilitate the beginning of attachment between them, but is not critical for the development of attachment. Many mothers show (34) _____ with their new baby--intense interest and desire to touch, hold, and interact with the baby. Some mothers may experience (35) _____, or feelings of sadness, irritability, and depression following a birth. (**What are possible explanations for these feelings, and what are the effects on the infant?**)

The Father's Experience

Like mothers, fathers experience the birth of a baby as a significant life event, and are often significantly engrossed by the baby.

THE EARLY POSTNATAL ENVIRONMENT
Culture and Early Socialization

The process by which individuals acquire the beliefs, values, and behaviors that are appropriate in their society is called (36) _____. Although what is considered appropriate varies considerably across and within cultures, all parents seem to share three general goals of parenting, which are (37) _____ to adulthood, (38) _____ self sufficiency, and (39) _____. (**Can you provide an example of each type of goal and describe how these goals might be addressed in different cultures?**) Cross-culturally, there is substantial variation in developmental goals and parenting styles. Even within cultures, parenting goals differ. Children adapt to these difference, suggesting a (40) _____ between the infant's behavior and the cultural demands.

RISK AND RESILIENCE

Even if infants experience prenatal or perinatal complications, studies show that some are (41) _____; they can get back on track and develop normally. There may be some (42) _____ factors that help prevent at-risk infants from developing problems. Success seems to depend on the child's personal resources or (43) _____ makeup as well as having a favorable postnatal (44) _____.

Low-Birth-Weight Babies

Babies may be at-risk for problems if they have low birth weights, especially if this is compounded with being (45) _____ because they are born more than three weeks before their due dates. These infants often catch up to other infants and do quite well when their mothers are attentive and responsive to them. (**What does research indicate with respect to outcomes for this group of infants?**)

APPLICATIONS: GETTING LIFE OFF TO A GOOD START

There are numerous ways that the prenatal, perinatal, and postnatal environments can be optimized.

In addition to seeking prenatal care, many couples enroll in (46) _____ classes and learn to prepare for the birth of the baby through techniques such as the (47) _____ method.

During Birth

Some couples decide to have their babies delivered at home or in a(n) (48) _____ center, which is a hospital room that provides a homelike atmosphere.

After Birth

Some parents might receive training on how to interact with their infant and elicit responses from the infant using the (49) _____ Neonatal Behavioral Assessment Scale. Providing stimulation can be particularly beneficial for at-risk infants.

REVIEW OF KEY TERMS

Below is a list of terms and concepts from this chapter. Use these to complete the following sentence definitions. You might also want to try writing definitions in your own words and then checking your definitions with those in the text.

acquired immune deficiency syndrome (AIDS)	Lamaze method
age of viability	organogenesis
alternative birth centers	perinatal environment
amnion	period of the embryo
anoxia	period of the fetus
Apgar test	placenta
artificial insemination	polychlorinated biphenyls (PCBs)
blastula	postpartum depression
breech presentation	prenatal environment
cesarean section	protective factors
chorion	resilience
cloning	rubella
critical period	socialization
engrossment	surfactant
environment	syphilis
fetal alcohol syndrome (FAS)	teratogen
germinal period	testosterone
infant states	thalidomide
in vitro fertilization (IVF)	umbilical cord

1.   During the process of _____, all major organs begin to take shape.

2.   _____ refers to the tendency to get back on track and recover from early disadvantages.

3.   _____ is the name of a mild tranquilizer that, when taken during pregnancy, results in birth defects.

4.   Symptoms in children whose mothers drank alcohol during their pregnancy are collectively referred to as _____.

5.   Organized sleep-wake patterns of babies are called _____.

6.   Chemicals known as _____ pose a threat to a developing fetus even though these substances were banned years ago.

7.   The _____ is the third prenatal period, lasting from the ninth week until birth.

8.   Personal resources and supportive environment are two types of _____ that may prevent developmental problems.

9.   Parents' interest in and desire to touch, hold, caress, and talk to their newborn baby is called _____.

10.   _____ is the process by which individuals acquire the beliefs, values, and behaviors that are important in their society.

11.   A substance that helps infants breathe by preventing the air sacs of the lungs from sticking together is _____.

12.   In a procedure called _____, sperm are injected into a woman's uterus.

13.   In a procedure called _____, sperm fertilize eggs in a laboratory and are then placed in a woman's uterus.

14.   _____ is the first prenatal period, lasting from conception to implantation of the blastula in the wall of the uterus.

15.   _____ is a membrane surrounding the amnion that attaches to the uterine lining to gather nourishment for the embryo.

16.   In the process of _____, a single cell from one organism is converted into a new organism that is a duplicate of the original.

17.   The point at about 24 weeks prenatal development when survival outside the uterus may be possible is the _____.

18.   The _____ is any experience or event that can influence an individual's development or be influenced by an individual.

19.   _____ are hospital rooms that provide a homelike atmosphere while still providing access to medical technology.

20.   The disease caused by the HIV virus that destroys the immune system is called _____.

21. A period of time during which the developing organism is particularly sensitive to environmental influences is a _____.

22. _____ is a viral infection that can cause a number of serious birth defects if contracted by the mother during the first trimester of pregnancy.

23. The primary male hormone secreted by the testes is _____.

24. _____ is a hollow ball of cells formed from the repeated cell division of the zygote.

25. _____ is any environmental agent that can produce abnormalities in a developing embryo or fetus.

26. A test used to assess the newborn's heart rate, respiration, color, muscle tone, and reflexes immediately after and five minutes after birth is the _____..

27. _____ consists of a cluster of symptoms, including feelings of sadness, irritability, resentment, and depression, that some new mothers experience shortly after a birth.

28. The physical environment of the womb is the _____.

29. _____ is a tissue connecting the mother and embryo that provides oxygen and nutrients and eliminates waste products.

30. _____ is a fluid-filled, watertight membrane surrounding the embryo.

31. _____ is a sexually transmitted disease that is most damaging during the middle and later stages of pregnancy and can result in blindness, deafness, heart problems, or brain damage.

32. In a _____, a baby is born feet or buttocks first.

33. The _____ is the environment surrounding birth, which includes influences such as delivery practices and social stimulation.

34. The _____ connects the embryo to the placenta, and contains blood vessels that nourish the fetus and eliminate wastes.

35. _____ refers to lack of adequate oxygen to the brain, which can result in brain damage.

36. _____ is the second prenatal period, lasting from implantation of the blastula to the end of the eighth week of prenatal development.

37. Some babies are delivered by _____, a surgical procedure in which an incision is made in the mother's abdomen and uterus so that the baby can be removed.

38. _____ is a method of prepared childbirth in which parents learn a set of mental exercises and relaxation techniques.

For each multiple choice question, read all alternatives and then select the best answer.

1. Research on reproductive technologies shows that children born with these procedures:
    a. are more likely to be low birth weight or premature than other children
    b. are more likely to be resentful about their atypical origins
    c. have parents who are more stressed and negative about their circumstances
    d. are equal to other groups of children in emotional adjustment and other developmental outcomes

2. The single cell that is formed by the union of a sperm cell and egg cell is called a(n)
    a. blastula
    b. embryo
    c. zygote
    d. germ cell

3. All major organs begin to form between the second and the eighth week after conception. This period of time is called the
    a. period of the embryo
    b. germinal period
    c. period of the fetus
    d. age of viability

4. The placental barrier
    a. supports the developing embryo with oxygen and nutrients from the mother
    b. blocks dangerous substances from reaching the developing embryo
    c. allows maternal blood to pass to the developing embryo
    d. is replaced by the umbilical cord at the end of the germinal period

5. Which of the following accurately represents the process of sex differentiation during the prenatal period?
    a. Sex differentiation is determined at conception by the inheritance of X and Y chromosomes.
    b. Males and females begin with different tissue at conception that evolves into different reproductive systems
    c. Sex differentiation begins around the 7th or 8th week with the development of male and female external genitalia.
    d. Males and females begin with identical tissue that can evolve into male or female reproductive systems depending on genetic and hormonal factors.

6. The presence or absence of testosterone affects the process of sexual differentiation in
    a. males only
    b. females only
    c. males and females
    d. neither males or females

7. The age of viability refers to
   a. the age at which a woman is still able to conceive
   b. the point at which a fetus has a reasonable chance of survival outside the womb
   c. the point at which the brain and respiratory system are completely formed and functional
   d. the point at which all the major organs can be identified

8. Prolonged and severe emotional strain experienced by a mother during pregnancy can result in
   a. a miscarriage
   b. prolonged and painful labor
   c. a baby who is irritable and has irregular habits
   d. all of the above

9. It is <u>most</u> important for mothers to consume ample amounts of protein, vitamins and calories during
   a. the first trimester
   b. the second trimester
   c. the third trimester
   d. before becoming pregnant

10. A critical period is a time when
    a. a fetus can survive outside the womb
    b. conception occurs
    c. the brain forms
    d. a developing organ is particularly sensitive to environmental influences

11. Mothers who contract rubella (German measles) during the first trimester of pregnancy often have children who have problems such as
    a. deafness, blindness, heart defects, and mental retardation
    b. missing or malformed limbs
    c. small head size and malformations of face, heart and limbs
    d. slow growth and low birth weight

12. Klaus and Kennell argue that emotional bonding between a mother and her newborn
    a. can occur at any time during the first three years of life
    b. is unlike any other developing relationship
    c. is necessary for later normal development to occur
    d. develops during a sensitive period 6-12 hours after birth

13. The process by which individuals acquire beliefs, values, and behavior important to adaptation to the environment is called
    a. socialization
    b. survival goal
    c. self actualization
    d. culture

14. Longitudinal studies of babies "at-risk"
    a. show that most at-risk babies continue to have problems throughout their lives
    b. show that most of these children never develop any problems regardless of their experiences
    c. show that babies at greater risk have a better prognosis because they receive more medical care than babies at less risk
    d. suggest that children can "outgrow" their problems when placed in favorable environments

15. Parents who receive "Brazelton training"
    a. learn how to elicit various responses from their infant
    b. typically have an easier time during delivery of their infant
    c. can determine right after birth if their infant is healthy
    d. can determine their infant's level of intelligence

APPLICATION QUESTIONS

By answering the following questions, you will strengthen your understanding of the material in this chapter. These questions require higher level thinking skills such as integration and application of concepts. To get you started, there is a sample answer or outline provided for the first question. This illustrates one possibility, but there are other answers you could provide that might be just as good. For the other questions, you can check yourself by referring to the text (a hint is provided), or by asking a peer or your instructor to review your answer.

1. What advice concerning prenatal care would you give to a woman who has just learned that she is two months pregnant? Provide justification for your answer.
   [Sample answer provided]

2. How do cultural variations affect infant care practices, and how do infant care practices relate to developmental outcomes?
   [Hint: Review the section on cultural factors under "The Mother's Experience" and the section on "Culture and Early Socialization."]

3. How can we structure the environment to optimize development?
   [Hint: There is information about this throughout the chapter, including things that mothers can do (or avoid) while pregnant and things that can be done after birth. Review the Application section at the end of this chapter.]

Chapter Summary and Guided Review (Fill-in the blank)

1.	zygote	26.	afterbirth
2.	germinal	27.	anoxia
3.	blastula	28.	breech
4.	embryo	29.	cesarean section
5.	organogenesis	30.	high-risk
6.	chorion	31.	Apgar
7.	placenta	32.	social support
8.	umbilical cord	33.	contact
9.	testosterone	34.	engrossment
10.	fetus	35.	postpartum depression
11.	viability	36.	socialization
12.	brain	37.	survival
13.	infant states	38.	economic
14.	stress	39.	self-actualization
15.	third (or last)	40.	goodness of fit
16.	critical period	41.	resilient
17.	Rubella	42.	protective
18.	syphilis	43.	genetic
19.	AIDS	44.	environment
20.	thalidomide	45.	premature
21.	fetal alcohol syndrome	46.	childbirth
22.	cocaine	47.	Lamaze
23.	polychlorinated biphenyls (PCBs)	48.	alternative birth
24.	contractions	49.	Brazelton
25.	delivery		

Review of Key Terms

1.	organogenesis	18.	environment
2.	resilience	19.	alternative birth centers
3.	thalidomide	20.	acquired immune deficiency syndrome
4.	fetal alcohol syndrome	21.	critical period
5.	infant states	22.	rubella
6.	polychlorinated biphenyls (PCBs)	23.	testosterone
7.	period of the fetus	24.	blastula
8.	protective factors	25.	teratogen
9.	engrossment	26.	Apgar test
10.	socialization	27.	postpartum depression
11.	surfactant	28.	prenatal environment
12.	artificial insemination	29.	placenta
13.	in vitro fertilization (IVF)	30.	amnion
14.	germinal period	31.	syphilis
15.	chorion	32.	breech presentation
16.	cloning	33.	perinatal environment
17.	age of viability	34.	umbilical cord

| 35. | anoxia | 37. | cesarean section |
| 36. | period of the embryo | 38. | Lamaze method |

Multiple Choice Self Test

1.	D	6.	C	11.	A
2.	C	7.	B	12.	D
3.	A	8.	D	13.	A
4.	A	9.	C	14.	D
5.	D	10.	D	15.	A

Application Questions

1.   *I would first note that the vast majority of pregnancies and deliveries are without complications. However, there are a number of things that a woman should be aware of that may affect prenatal development. The first three months are especially important because this is when all the major fetal organs develop (organogenesis). Diseases, such as rubella and drugs such as the prescription thalidomide or the illegal cocaine, can adversely affect the fetus, leading to long-term problems. Maternal nutrition is important, especially during the third trimester when the fetus should be putting on weight and brain development is taking place. Heavy alcohol consumption can lead to a cluster of symptoms, both physical and behavioral that can plague a child for years. Other factors can influence prenatal development, but women do not always have control of these factors, such as pollution in the air or water and their own age. Finally, these things are risk factors and do not automatically lead to developmental problems. There are large individual differences in their effects, which are influenced by the child's personal resources (e.g., genetic makeup) and the postnatal environment.*

CHAPTER FIVE

THE PHYSICAL SELF

OVERVIEW

This chapter has a great deal of useful information about physical changes across the life span. It provides an overview of the endocrine and nervous systems, which act in concert to produce physical growth and facilitate physical behavior. You will learn that there is a tremendous amount of brain growth during the prenatal period and the first two years of life. Brain development, though, is by no means "set in stone" at the end of infancy. The brain continues to be responsive to experiences, and can change to adapt to these experiences, across the life span.

This chapter covers the maturation of the reproductive system during adolescence and its changes during adulthood. The discussion of how adolescents interpret and react to the changes of puberty is particularly interesting. Physical behaviors across the life span, including motor skills, are also explored in this chapter. One of the most valuable lessons about physical behavior may be one regarding adults: healthy, active adults show little decline in physical and psychological functioning. This contradicts stereotypes of older adults as physically unfit.

LEARNING OBJECTIVES

After reading and studying the material in this chapter, you should be able to answer the following questions.

1.   How do the workings of the endocrine system contribute to growth and development across the life span?

2.   How is the nervous system organized?

3.   What are the key processes involved in early brain development?

4.   To what are extent are cells responsive to the effects of experience?

5.   What is lateralization? How does it affect behavior?

6. How does the brain change with aging?

7. What is the difference between survival and primitive reflexes? What are examples of each type of reflex? What other capabilities do newborns have?

8. How does growth proceed during infancy? What principles underlie growth?

9. How do locomotion and manipulation of objects evolve during infancy? What factors influence the development of infant's motor skills?

10. How are children's motor skills advanced relative to those of infants?

11. What physical changes occur during adolescence? What factors contribute to sexual maturity of males and females? What psychological reactions accompany variations in growth spurt and the timing of puberty?

12. What physical changes occur during adulthood?

13. How can nutrition, exercise, and changes in lifestyle affect growth and development across the life span?

CHAPTER SUMMARY AND GUIDED REVIEW

The following summary provides an overview of the main points contained in this chapter of the text. Fill-in the blanks with terms that appropriately complete the sentence. Scattered throughout the summary are questions in parentheses. These are meant to encourage you to think actively as you are reading and connect this summary to the more detailed information provided in the text. You can answer these questions as you are filling in the blanks or you can complete all the blanks, then go back and reread the entire summary, addressing the questions in order to provide more depth of understanding.

THE ENDOCRINE SYSTEM
Physical development in humans is driven by the endocrine and nervous systems. The endocrine

glands secrete chemical substances called (1) _____ directly into the bloodstream. These substances regulate growth and development. The (2) _____ gland regulates other glands and secretes (3) _____ hormone, which stimulates rapid growth and development of body cells. Growth and development are also influenced by the (4) _____ gland.

A male fetus develops male reproductive organs when a gene on his Y chromosome triggers development of (5) _____, which in turn secrete a male hormone called (6) _____. This hormone, along with others called (7) _____, stimulate the adolescent growth spurt and development of male sex organs. In females, the ovaries produce larger quantities of (8) _____, the primary female hormone, which along with progesterone, is responsible for development of female sex organs and for regulating menstrual cycles. In addition, the (9) _____ glands secrete androgen-like hormones that contribute to the maturation of bones and muscles.

THE NERVOUS SYSTEM

The nervous system is made-up of billions of nerve cells or (10) _____. Nerve cells have an axon for sending messages and (11) _____ for receiving messages. The connection point between neurons is called a (12) _____. By releasing neurotransmitters across this space, neurons can stimulate or inhibit another neuron's action. During development axons of some neurons become covered by (13) _____, which improves transmission of neural impulses.

Early Brain Development

The outer covering of the brain, the (14) _____, controls voluntary motor movements, perception, and intellectual processes. There are several important processes involved in early brain development. There is an incredible increase in the number of neurons, called (15) _____. There is migration of neurons to particular locations in the brain and (16) _____ into specialized functions. Neurons also form connections with other neurons through the process of (17) _____. Much of this activity takes place during the last prenatal trimester and the first two years of life in a period called the (18) _____. During this period, the brain also exhibits (19) _____ in response to experiences. (***How can normal and abnormal experiences affect the brain?***)

Later Brain Development

Brain growth continues beyond infancy, with increased myelination of neurons and specialization. Specialization of the two hemispheres of the cerebral cortex is called (20) _____. Specialization of the brain is evident at birth and becomes stronger throughout childhood. (***What is an example of specialization of the hemispheres?***) Brain development continues through adolescence and may be responsible for advances in adolescent thinking.

The Aging Brain

There is some degeneration of the nervous system with aging. Loss of neurons and slower transmission of signals contribute to slower information processing in older adults. The aging brain also shows (21) _____ or the ability to change in response to experiences and develop new abilities.

THE INFANT
The Newborn

Newborns can produce a number of unlearned and automatic responses to stimuli called (22) _____. (***Can you provide examples of some unlearned responses that are essential to*** *survival?*) Some (23) _____ reflexes do not seem to have functional value in our culture and typically disappear during the first year of life. (*Can you provide examples of this type of reflex? What is the significance of the presence and then the absence of these reflexes?*) Newborns also have well developed sensory systems and can learn from their experiences.

A final strength of newborns is the presence of organized patterns of daily activity such as sleep-week cycles. There are individual differences in how much time infants spend in each state, although newborns spend about (24) _____ of their time asleep and only 2-3 hours a day actively taking in their environments. Half of a newborn's sleep time is spent in active, irregular sleep called (25) _____ sleep. This percentage decreases across the life span to about 20%. (*What are possible explanations for this change across the life span?*)

Physical Growth

Physical growth during infancy is rapid and occurs in bursts. Several principles underlie the pattern of growth. Growth occurs in a (26) _____ direction, meaning from the head to the tail. As a result, the head of a newborn is more fully developed than the trunk and legs. Growth also proceeds from the center outward, or in a (27) _____ direction. (*What is an example of this principle of growth?*) According to the (28) _____ principle, physical development proceeds from responses that are global to ones that are differentiated and integrated.

Physical Behavior

The average age when half of infants have mastered a skill is the (29) _____ for the skill. Motor behaviors develop according to the cephalocaudal and proximodistal principles, so infants will be able to sit before they walk. They master (30) _____ skills using large muscle groups before (31) _____ skills that require precise motor control. (*What are some examples of how the orthogenetic principle guides the development of motor skills?*)

Most infants begin to crawl around (32) _____ months and begin to walk at about (33) _____ months. Around 9 to 12 months, infants can use a (34) _____ to pick up objects using only their thumb and one other finger. This development occurs sometime after infants have gained control of their arms and hands and thus is an example of the (35) _____ direction of development. Acquisition of motor skills is largely directed by (36) _____. Experience affects the (37) _____ at which infants progress through the sequence of motor milestones. According to the (38) _____ approach, motor development is also influenced by infants' use of feedback from different movements. (*What is an example of this process?*)

THE CHILD
Steady Growth

Growth from infancy to adolescence is slow but steady, and continues to be guided by cephalocaudal and proximodistal principles.

Physical Behavior

Children learn to control their movements in a changing environment, extending earlier skills mastered in a stationary environment. Motor skills are refined during childhood and eye/hand coordination improves. Children also have faster reaction times as they develop.

THE ADOLESCENT
Physical and Sexual Maturation

Adolescents experience rapid growth, called the (39) _____, and they experience (40) _____, which is the attainment of sexual maturity. Females typically begin their growth spurt about two years before males. (*What are the typical ages of rapid growth for males and females?*)

Puberty for girls is marked by (41) _____, their first menstruation, at about 12 or 13 years of age. For boys, the event that is typically used to mark puberty is their first (42) _____, which occurs around 13 or 14 years of age. There is large variation in the timing of physical and sexual maturation. Rate of development is largely determined by (43) _____ factors although environment also plays a role in timing of maturation, as indicated by the (44) _____ or the tendency in industrialized societies for earlier maturation and larger body size. (*What factors contribute to this trend?*)

Emotional responses to puberty are mixed for males and females, but tend to be stronger in females. (*How do pubertal changes affect parent-child relations?*) The psychological impact of being an early versus a late developer is different for males and females. Early maturing (45) _____ are often found to have advantages over their later maturing peers. (*What are some of these advantages and are they long-lasting?*) For females, early development is not necessarily an advantage, at least not before junior high school. Late-maturers of both sexes often experience some anxiety, but late-maturing (46) _____ seem to experience the most disadvantages.

Physical Behavior

Advances in strength and physical competence continue throughout adolescence. Gender differences emerge as boys' physical performance continues to increase while girls' physical performance levels off or declines. Biological differences in muscle mass may account for some of this difference, but gender-role socialization also contributes.

THE ADULT
Physical Appearance and Structure

Although physical aging occurs over most of the life span, outward signs are often not noticed until one's (47) _____. Wrinkles, thinning and graying hair, and extra weight are common physical changes in middle age. Some older adults may experience (48) _____ , extreme bone loss leaving bones fragile. (*What can be done to prevent this disease?*)

Functioning and Health

The average older adult has poorer physical functioning than younger adults, although not all older people experience declines in physical functioning. Many organ systems show a decrease in (49) _____, which is the ability to respond to demands for above-normal output. A majority of adults over the age of 65 have some sort of chronic impairment. Nonetheless, most older adults report that they are in good health.

The Reproductive System

Hormone levels fluctuate in both sexes across the life span, although hormone changes typically affect women more than men. Some women report experiencing (50) _____, a cluster of symptoms including breast tenderness and irritability just before menstruation. Both premenstrual and menstrual symptoms are affected by biological factors such as hormone changes, and by social factors. (*Can you describe some of the social factors that contribute to symptoms?*)

The end of menstrual periods occurs sometime during mid-life and is called (51) _____. The lower levels of female hormones that are produced may result in vaginal dryness and (52) _____ for many women. Some women experience psychological symptoms such as irritability and depression in connection with menopause. (*How does the experience of menopause differ cross culturally?*) In our culture, doctors often recommend (53) _____ to treat the symptoms of menopause.

Men also experience loss of reproductive capacity, but more gradually than women, during a period of time referred to as the (54) _____.

<u>Physical Behavior</u>

Changes in the brain also take place as we get older, namely, there is a loss of neurons and of functioning between neurons. Levels of neurotransmitters decline as does amount of blood flow to the brain. A number of physical behaviors are carried out at a (55) _____ pace as we get older. (*What explanation is given for this slowing of the nervous system and motor performance?*) Despite these changes, there is (56) _____ or finding ways to make up for changes due to aging.

<u>Disease, Disuse, and Abuse</u>

Chronic disease often contributes to some of the declines among older adults. In addition, declines in physical functioning may relate to (57) _____ of the body, as well as to abuses of the body.

APPLICATIONS: OPTIMIZING HEALTHY DEVELOPMENT

Nutrition can have an impact on development and functioning across the entire life span. Infants and young children who have had inadequate nutrition experience a slowing of growth but typically experience (58) _____ when their diets become adequate. Some people get too many calories and experience (59) _____. Heredity, overeating, and low activity levels all seem to contribute to obesity. Regular (60) _____ by older adults may delay physical dependence on others. Avoidance of health risks such as smoking can also delay the signs of aging.

REVIEW OF KEY TERMS

Below is a list of terms and concepts from this chapter. Use these to complete the following sentence definitions. You might also want to try writing definitions in your own words and then checking your definitions with those in the text.

adolescent growth spurt	myelin
androgens	neuron
brain growth spurt	orthogenetic principle
catch-up growth	osteoporosis
cephalocaudal principle	pincer grasp
cerebral cortex	pituitary gland
climacteric	plasticity
compensation for decline	premenstrual syndrome (PMS)
developmental norm	proximodistal principle
dynamic systems approach	puberty
endocrine gland	reaction time
estrogen	reflexes
fine motor skills	REM sleep
gross motor skills	reserve capacity
growth hormone	rites of passage
hormone replacement therapy (HRT)	secular trend
hot flashes	synapse
lateralization	synaptogenesis
menarche	testosterone
menopause	

1.   Male hormones, including testosterone, which trigger the adolescent growth spurt and development of male sex organs are collectively called _____.

2. _____ are unlearned and automatic responses to stimuli.

3. Children show mastery of _____ when they engage in movements that require precise control of their hands or feet.

4. Located at the base of the brain, the _____ is an endocrine gland that is responsible for regulating other glands and producing growth hormone.

5. According to the _____, growth proceeds in a head to tail direction.

6. Cells that have not yet been committed to a particular function and have the capacity to be shaped by experience are said to be in a state of _____.

7. _____ refers to the specialization of the left and right hemispheres of the cerebral cortex.

8. The rapid increase in growth at the end of childhood is the _____.

9. _____ refers to the period of rapid brain development starting with the last trimester of pregnancy and lasting until a child's second birthday.

10. The _____ is the tendency for earlier maturation and larger body size in industrialized societies over time.

11. _____ is a disease resulting from a loss of minerals, which causes deterioration of bone tissue.

12. Some women experience _____, a cluster of symptoms including breast tenderness, a bloated feeling, irritability and moodiness that occur just before menstruation.

13. _____ is secreted by the pituitary gland and stimulates growth and development of body cells.

14. _____ occurs after a growth deficit and gets a person back on his/her genetically programmed growth course.

15. Some women may experience _____, which are sudden, brief, and unpredictable sensations of warmth that may be followed by a cold shiver.

16. A(n) _____ is a ductless gland that secretes hormones directly into the bloodstream.

17. A female hormone secreted by the ovaries that stimulates development of female sex organs and regulates menstrual cycles is _____.

18. The _____ is the convoluted outer covering of the brain that controls motor, sensory-perceptual, and intellectual processes.

19. According to the _____, growth proceeds from the central portions of the body to the extremities.

20. The _____ is evident when children use their thumb in opposition to one other finger in order to pick up and manipulate objects.

21. The point when a person reaches sexual maturity and acquires secondary sexual characteristics is called _____.

22. A _____ is the basic cell of the nervous system that transmits and receives signals.

23. A _____ represents the average age when half of all infants can master a particular skill.

24. _____ is defined as a girl's first menstrual period.

25. The period of time during which males and females experience declines in their reproductive capacity is the _____.

26. The space between the axon of one neuron and the dendrites of another neuron is the _____.

27. _____ is active, irregular sleep that includes rapid eye movements and is associated with brain wave activity that resembles wakefulness.

28. _____ is a waxy substance that covers the axon of some neurons and facilitates transmission of neural impulses.

29. Women experience _____ when their menstrual periods end sometime during mid-life.

30. The ability of an organ system to respond to a request for excess output is known as its _____.

31. The testes secrete a male hormone called _____.

32. The process of forming connections among neurons is _____.

33. According to the _____, growth proceeds from being global and undifferentiated to being increasingly specific, differentiated, and integrated.

34. Children use their _____ when they run or otherwise make movements that involve large muscle groups.

35. According to the _____, children use sensory feedback to their movements to develop more sophisticated behavior patterns.

36. The speed with which people can respond to a task is their _____.

37. Rituals that mark the transition from childhood to adulthood are called _____.

38. Some women take _____ to reduce the symptoms associated with menopause.

39. Older adults often find ways to makeup or adapt to losses in their physical functioning through a process called _____.

MULTIPLE CHOICE SELF TEST

For each multiple choice question, read all alternatives and then select the best answer.

1. Which structure is considered the "master gland" of the endocrine system?
   a. thyroid gland
   b. hypothalamus
   c. adrenal gland
   d. pituitary gland

2. Which of the following is NOT a key developmental process of early brain growth?
   a. proliferation of neurons
   b. migration of neurons to select locations
   c. isolation of neurons into unique positions
   d. differentiation of neurons into specialized functions

3. The brain growth spurt, a period of rapid brain development, occurs
   a. during the prenatal period and the first two years after birth
   b. during the prenatal period only
   c. during infancy and childhood
   d. during puberty

4. Which of the following is TRUE regarding early brain development?
   a. Neurons continue to be produced until puberty.
   b. Neurons are rapidly forming connections with other neurons.
   c. The function of each neuron is determined at conception.
   d. The ultimate location of neurons is flexible throughout infancy and childhood.

5. Plasticity ensures that the brain
   a. can recover from any sort of damage
   b. receives the maximum benefits from stimulation throughout the life span
   c. is not influenced by adverse environments
   d. is responsive to individual experiences

6. Lateralization is a process by which
   a. one hemisphere takes over for the other's functions after brain damage has occurred
   b. specialization of the functions of the left and right hemisphere occurs
   c. neurons in the brain develop rapidly
   d. neurons are covered by a myelin sheath

7. As the body ages from childhood to adulthood, the brain
   a. develops more neurons
   b. begins to form a myelin sheath around many neurons
   c. grows longer dendrites that may form new connections with other neurons
   d. releases large quantities of neurotransmitters

8.   The primitive reflexes
     a.   are essential to survival
     b.   disappear sometime during infancy
     c.   include rooting, sucking, and swallowing
     d.   protect the infant from various adverse conditions

9.   The cephalocaudal principle predicts that:
     a.   growth of the brain and spinal cord will be the last to occur
     b.   growth will proceed from bones and cartilage to internal organs
     c.   growth will proceed from head to tail
     d.   growth will proceed from the midline to the extremities

10. Based on the cephalocaudal principle of growth, infants typically can _____ before they can
     _____.
     a.   stand; roll over
     b.   roll over; control their arms or hands
     c.   walk backward; walk up steps
     d.   sit; walk

11. Which of the following hormone(s) trigger the adolescent growth spurt?
     a.   progesterone
     b.   androgens
     c.   activating hormones
     d.   thyroxine

12. Regarding the timing of maturation:
     a.   Sheila, who matures early, is likely to be more popular than Mary, who matures late.
     b.   Bill, who matures late, is likely to be more academically skilled than Mark, who matures
          early
     c.   Tom, who matures early, is likely to be confident and poised relative to Steve, who
          matures late.
     d.   Mike, who matures "on time" is likely to be viewed most favorably by his parents and
          teachers, relative to other boys in his class who mature early or late.

13. The secular trend refers to
     a.   earlier maturation and decreased body size from generation to generation
     b.   later maturation and decreased body size from generation to generation
     c.   historical changes in life expectancy from generation to generation
     d.   earlier maturation and increased body size from generation to generation

14. The apparent decline of physical performance of females by the end of adolescence
     a.   is a myth not supported by any data
     b.   results largely from socialization differences between males and females
     c.   results from an overall decline in the proportion of muscle mass relative to fat
     d.   is similar to the decline that occurs in males

15. Menopause is a time when
    a. women no longer ovulate or menstruate
    b. most women experience mood swings for extended periods of time
    c. women continue to ovulate but do not menstruate
    d. women experience an increase in hormone levels

APPLICATION QUESTIONS

By answering the following questions, you will strengthen your understanding of the material in this chapter. These questions require higher level thinking skills such as integration and application of concepts. To get you started, there is a sample answer or outline provided for the first question. This illustrates one possibility, but there are other answers you could provide that might be just as good. For the other questions, you can check yourself by referring to the text (a hint is provided), or by asking a peer or your instructor to review your answer.

1. Suppose you are in charge of writing a newsletter for adults who are approaching retirement age. In one issue of the newsletter, you want to write an informative article on physical changes that these adults might experience as they age. What would this article say?
   [Sample answer provided]

2. Now write the same article but for a different readership: Parents with a newborn infant. What changes in motor skills can they anticipate that their child will go through as she or he progresses through infancy, childhood, and adolescence?
   [Hint: There is information about this throughout the chapter, but especially in the sections on "The Infant," "The Child," and "The Adolescent." You will need to integrate material from several subsections of these three sections.]

3. What evidence is there that lateralization takes place at an early age, yet still allows for plasticity in brain function across the life-span?
   [Hint: There is information about this in several sections, including "Early Brain Development," "Later Brain Development," and "The Aging Brain."]

ANSWERS

Summary and Guided Review (Fill-in the blank)

1.	hormones	31.	fine motor
2.	pituitary	32.	seven
3.	growth	33.	twelve
4.	thyroid	34.	pincer grasp
5.	testes	35.	proximodistal
6.	testosterone	36.	maturation
7.	androgens	37.	rate
8.	estrogen	38.	dynamic systems
9.	adrenal	39.	growth spurt
10.	neurons	40.	puberty
11.	dendrites	41.	menarche
12.	synapse	42.	ejaculation
13.	myelin	43.	genetic
14.	cerebral cortex	44.	secular trend
15.	proliferation	45.	males
16.	differentiation	46.	males
17.	synaptogenesis	47.	40's
18.	brain growth spurt	48.	osteoporosis
19.	plasticity	49.	reserve capacity
20.	lateralization	50.	premenstrual syndrome
21.	plasticity	51.	menopause
22.	reflexes	52.	hot flashes
23.	primitive	53.	hormone replacement therapy
24.	70%	54.	climacteric
25.	REM	55.	slower
26.	cephalocaudal	56.	compensation for decline
27.	proximodistal	57.	disuse
28.	orthogenetic	58.	catch-up growth
29.	developmental norm	59.	obesity
30.	gross motor	60.	exercise

Review of Key Terms

1.	androgens	13.	growth hormone
2.	reflexes	14.	catch-up growth
3.	fine motor skills	15.	hot flashes
4.	pituitary gland	16.	endocrine gland
5.	cephalocaudal principle	17.	estrogen
6.	plasticity	18.	cerebral cortex
7.	lateralization	19.	proximodistal principle
8.	adolescent growth spurt	20.	pincer grasp
9.	brain growth spurt	21.	puberty
10.	secular trend	22.	neuron
11.	osteoporosis	23.	developmental norm
12.	premenstrual syndrome (PMS)	24.	menarche

25.	climacteric	33.	orthogenetic principle
26.	synapse	34.	gross motor skills
27.	REM sleep	35.	dynamic systems approach
28.	myelin	36.	reaction time
29.	menopause	37.	rites of passage
30.	reserve capacity	38.	hormone replacement therapy (HRT)
31.	testosterone	39.	compensation for decline
32.	synaptogenesis		

Multiple Choice Self Test

1.	D	6.	B	11.	B
2.	C	7.	C	12.	C
3.	A	8.	B	13.	D
4.	B	9.	C	14.	B
5.	D	10.	D	15.	A

Application Questions

1.	*Worried about a few physical changes as you approach retirement? Well, it's not as bad as you may have heard. Sure, you have a few wrinkles, some gray hair, and a little extra weight around the middle. It will probably take you longer to do the things you sped through as a young adult. For women, menopause may mean hot flashes and vaginal dryness, making intercourse more painful. Old age may also bring a loss of bone mass, or osteoporosis, which can lead to fractures and seriously erode quality of life. Unfortunately, statistics indicate that a majority of older adults have some sort of chronic impairment, such as arthritis. Despite this, a majority of older adults report that their health is actually quite good, suggesting that they take impairments in stride or find ways to work around them.*

The good news is that if you take care of yourself and remain healthy and active, you can look forward to a satisfying old age. Older adults who are disease free perform just as well on many physical tasks as younger adults. Many older adults perform tasks more slowly because they are out of shape; continuing to exercise may reduce this disadvantage of aging. In many ways, the saying, "use it or lose it," applies to the physical functioning of older adults.

CHAPTER SIX

PERCEPTION

OVERVIEW

You should take note of the point at the beginning of this chapter: sensation and perception are at the very heart of human functioning. Without sensation and perception, there would be no meaningful cognitive activity or social interactions, no enjoyable walks through the neighborhood, and no ability to appreciate music or food. The centrality of sensation and perception makes it important to understand changes in these processes across the life span.

Many significant changes in perceptual processes occur during infancy, with few changes during childhood, adolescence, and early adulthood. During middle and older adulthood, there are again some notable changes in perceptual processes. Thus, for the sections on "The Infant" and "The Adult," there is weighty coverage of vision, hearing, taste, smell, touch, temperature, and pain. Additionally, the section on infants discusses several ingenious, yet simple, methods of assessing infants' perceptual abilities. The section of the chapter on children concentrates on the development of attentional processes, which are so important to perception, and on reading, which requires complex perceptual processing.

LEARNING OBJECTIVES

After reading and studying the material in this chapter, you should be able to answer the following questions.

1.   What are the views of empiricists and nativists on the nature/nurture issue as it relates to sensation and perception?

2.   How are perceptual abilities of infants assessed?

3.   What are the infants' visual capabilities? What sorts of things do infants prefer to look at?

4.   How is the visual cliff used to assess depth perception? What do we know about infants' depth perception?

5.   What does is mean to say that the infant is an intuitive theorist?

6.   What are the auditory capabilities of infants? What do we know about infants' abilities to perceive speech?

7.   What are the taste and smell capabilities of infants? To what extent are infants sensitive to touch, temperature and pain?

8.   To what extent can infants integrate their sensory experiences? What is an example of cross-modal perception?

9.   What role do early experiences play in development of perceptions? What factors contribute to normal visual perception?

10.   How does culture influence one's perceptions?

11.   What changes occur in attention from infancy to adulthood?

12.   What perceptual capabilities are involved in learning to read?

13.   What changes occur in visual capabilities and visual perception during adulthood?

14.   What changes in auditory capabilities and speech perception occur during adulthood?

15.   What changes occur in taste and smell, and in sensitivity to touch, temperature and pain during adulthood?

16.   How can hearing impaired persons be helped with their hearing loss?

CHAPTER SUMMARY AND GUIDED REVIEW

The following summary provides an overview of the main points contained in this chapter of the text. Fill-in the blanks with terms that appropriately complete the sentence. Scattered throughout the summary are questions in parentheses. These are meant to encourage you to think actively as you are reading and connect this summary to the more detailed information provided in the text. You can answer these questions as you are filling in the blanks or you can complete all the blanks, then go back and reread the entire summary, addressing the questions in order to provide more depth of understanding.

The process by which sensory receptors detect stimuli and transmit it to the brain is called (1) _____. The process of interpreting this information is called (2) _____. These processes are at the center of human understanding.

ISSUES OF NATURE AND NURTURE

One issue concerning perceptual development is whether infants are born with knowledge or need to acquire all knowledge through their senses. The (3) _____ took the latter position and believed that infants began life as blank slates. This position represents the (4) _____ side of the nature/nurture issue. The (5) _____ argued that infants are born with knowledge, which represents the (6) _____ side of the nature/nurture issue.

THE INFANT
Assessing Perceptual Abilities

Infants' perceptual capabilities are often assessed with a technique called (7) _____, which measures decreased responding to a stimulus that has been presented repeatedly. (*Can you explain the rationale of this approach?*) Another technique is to present two stimuli to infants and measure their (8) _____, which shows that they can discriminate the two stimuli. In some instances, infants can be operantly conditioning to respond in a particular way when a particular stimulus is presented; their response to a second stimulus can then be measured to determine whether they perceive the stimuli to be similar or different.

Vision

A newborn's ability to perceive visual detail, or (9) _____, is poor. This may result from problems with (10) _____, which refers to the changing shape of the lens of the eye to bring objects at varying distances into focus. Young infants can visually detect differences in stimuli and prefer to look at (11) _____ stimuli such as faces. (*Is the apparent preference for faces <u>really</u> a preference for faces? Why or why not?*) Young infants tend to be attracted to patterns that have (12) _____ or light-dark transitions, stimuli that move, and stimuli that are moderately complex. In general, infants prefer to look at what they can see well.

At around 2 months of age, infants begin to visually explore the entire field of a figure or form, rather than just an exterior border of the figure. They also begin to prefer (13) _____ faces over scrambled facial features. This might suggest that infants are beginning to form (14) _____ for familiar objects.

Another aspect of visual perception is perception of (15) _____ or three-dimensional space. Infants develop (16) _____, which is the tendency to perceive an object as its same size despite changes in the retinal image of the object as its distance from the eyes changes. Depth perception has been assessed using an apparatus called the (17) _____, which has an apparent drop-off. Early research showed that infants of crawling age perceived depth, demonstrated by their avoidance of the drop-off. A major limitation of this assessment technique was that infants needed to be able to be crawling. (***How has the visual cliff been used to test younger infants?***)

An important perceptual task for infants is learning to distinguish one object from another. To organize the world of objects, infants use (18) _____ as a cue to establish the boundaries of objects. In addition, infants seem to be equipped with organized systems of knowledge, called (19) _____, that help them understand their world.

Hearing

Newborns' auditory capabilities are fairly well developed. Infants are able to discriminate basic speech sounds, or (20) _____, early in life. In fact, unlike adults, infants can discriminate speech sounds of languages not spoken in the home. Familiarity with voices begins to develop prenatally, and newborns are able to recognize their mothers' voices. (***Can you describe how this has been studied?***) Infants can also discriminate between rhythmic music and nonrhythmic noise soon after birth.

Taste and Smell

The sense of taste and the sense of smell, or (21) _____, are well developed at birth. Infants show distinct taste preferences and those that are breast-fed can recognize their mothers on the basis of smell.

Touch, Temperature, and Pain

Newborns are sensitive to tactile stimulation and may respond with reflexes if touched in certain areas. Newborns are also sensitive to temperature and to pain. The intensity of a painful experience can be communicated by the quality of an infant's (22) _____.

Integrating Sensory Information

Putting together information from different senses can help an infant make sense of the world. Some senses seem to be integrated earlier than other senses. For example, touch and vision, as well as vision and hearing, seem to be linked very early.

The ability to recognize through one sense modality an object that is familiar through another sense modality is called (23) _____. (***Can you provide an example of this?***) Cross-modal perception of all forms does not reliably occur until 4-6 months of age.

Influences on Early Perceptual Development

The presence of such significant early perceptual capabilities suggests that (24) _____ plays a role in perceptual development. Early experiences are also necessary for normal development. Infants need to be exposed to a variety of (25) _____ stimulation for neurons in the visual areas of the brain to develop normally. Infants also need to be exposed to movement in their environment, especially if they are not able to move. Infants actively seek and explore their environments, which means that they typically expose themselves to appropriate sensory experiences. (***What three phases of exploratory behavior do infants go through?***) Finally, the way we perceive and interpret sensory experiences varies across cultures. (***What are some examples of these variations?***)

THE CHILD
The Development of Attention

Although much of sensory and perceptual development is complete by the end of infancy, children need to develop better (26) _____, the selective focusing of perception and cognition on some particular aspect of the environment. Attention span increases during childhood and attention becomes more (27) _____. (*What evidence is there to support this conclusion?*) In addition, visual search becomes more (28) _____ or exhaustive during childhood.

Learning to Read

Learning to read is a complex perceptual task that begins when children equate reading with storytelling. Children must also learn that the symbols on a page represent words and they must be able to decode the letters and translate them into sounds. Learning to read depends on recognizing the (29) _____ of letters so that they can be distinguished from one another. In order to learn how letters correspond to sounds, children must acquire (30) _____, the understanding that words can be broken down into basic units of sound, or phonemes. Serious problems with reading might indicate (31) _____, which shows up in a variety of ways depending on the child. (*What causes this reading disability in at least some cases?*) Research suggests that the best approach to teaching reading is based on (32) _____, or a code-oriented approach.

THE ADOLESCENT

Attention span continues to increase during adolescence as those parts of the brain involved in attention become fully myelinated. Adolescents also become more efficient at ignoring (33) _____ information so that they can focus their attention more effectively. Adolescents tend to use more efficient strategies for scanning visual displays.

THE ADULT

Sensory and perceptual capabilities gradually decline with age. There are increases in (34) _____, which means that a higher level of stimulation is needed for sensory detection as we age. Older people may also have trouble processing sensory information.

Vision

A number of changes occur within the eye as we age. Many adults experience a loss of near vision starting in their 40's, which is a sign of a condition called (35) _____. The ability to clearly see details, known as (36) _____, normally decreases with age. Significant decreases, however, are usually associated with pathological conditions. One such condition is (37) _____, in which the lens of the eye becomes opaque and limits the amount of light entering the eye. In another condition, (38) _____, there is increased fluid pressure in the eye, which can eventually lead to blindness. Older people also tend to be less sensitive to dim light, and the process of adjusting to low light levels, (39) _____, does not function as well for older people. Older people may have trouble detecting the details of (40) _____ objects and typically have a smaller field of vision. (*What are some implications of these changes in visual capabilities?*)

Research shows that older adults perform worse on visual search tasks than younger adults, particularly when there are numerous distractions. Older adults have the greatest difficulties processing visual information in situations that are (41) _____ and (42) _____, but have few problems with familiar or simple tasks.

Hearing

Hearing problems are often associated with aging. One common problem is decreased sensitivity to high-frequency sounds, a condition called (43) _____. Older adults seem to have more trouble with speech perception than younger adults, especially under poor listening conditions, such as a great deal of (44) _____. As with visual perception, older adults perform better on auditory tasks that are familiar or meaningful to them.

Taste and Smell

Sensory thresholds for some tastes increase with age. Taste for (45) _____ substances does not seem to change markedly across the life span. Sensitivity to odors and the ability to discriminate between them are highest from childhood to middle adulthood and then decline in old age. Decreases in taste and smell can affect recognition of different foods, although losses in the sense of (46) _____ seems to contribute more to problems of food recognition.

Touch, Temperature, and Pain

Sensitivity to touch and changes in temperature decrease with age. Sensitivity to pain seems to both increase and decrease in older adults. Older adults are less likely to report mild forms of pain, but were likely to report stronger forms of pain stimulation as being particularly strong.

The Adult in Perspective

The most serious age changes in perception occur with vision and hearing. Most older adults suffer some losses, although overall levels are fairly good.

APPLICATIONS: AIDING PEOPLE WITH HEARING IMPAIRMENTS

To improve the speech perception of infants and young children with hearing problems, hearing (47) _____ and (48) _____ training have been used. Children who are profoundly deaf may benefit from advanced amplication produced from a (49) _____; benefits are greatest when this occurs before age five. In addition to hearing aids, the (50) _____ can be structured to facilitate better hearing among older adults.

REVIEW OF KEY TERMS

Below is a list of terms and concepts from this chapter. Use these to complete the following sentence definitions. You might also want to try writing definitions in your own words and then checking your definitions with those in the text.

attention	olfaction
cataracts	perception
cochlear implant	phoneme
contour	phonological awareness
cross-modal perception	presbycusis
dark adaptation	presbyopia
distinctive feature	sensation
dyslexia	sensory threshold
empiricist	size constancy
glaucoma	visual accommodation
habituation	visual acuity
intuitive theories	visual cliff
nativist	

1.	A _____ is a critical attribute of people or objects that allows for differentiation between items.

2.	The process of _____ produces changes in the shape of the lens to bring objects at varying distances into focus.

3.	Someone who believes that infants enter the world with knowledge that permits them to perceive meaningful patterns in the world is a(n) _____.

4.	The tendency to perceive an object as its same size despite changes in the retinal image of the object as its distance from the eyes changes is called _____.

5.	The detection of stimuli by the sensory receptors and the transmission of this information to the brain is the process of _____.

6.	Sense of smell, which is mediated by receptors in the nasal passage, is also called _____.

7.	The _____ is an apparatus with an apparent drop-off that is used to assess early depth perception.

8.	The point at which a minimum level of stimulation can be detected by a sensory system is its _____.

9.	Decreased responding to a stimulus that has been presented repeatedly is _____.

10.	The basic unit of speech is a _____.

11.	The process of _____ involves the interpretation of sensory input.

12.	The ability to recognize through one sensory modality an object that is familiar through another is called _____.

13.	_____ refers to the dark and light boundaries or transitions of a perceptual pattern.

14.	A _____ is a device that permits amplification of sound by directly stimulating the auditory nerve with electrical impulses.

15.	The process of _____ selectively focuses perception and cognition on some aspect of the environment.

16.	The sharpness of the visual system, or its ability to perceive detail, is _____.

17.	The process of adjusting to lowered levels of light is called _____.

18.	Understanding that spoken words can be broken down into basic sound units is called _____.

19. A decreased ability to focus on objects that are close to the eye occurs in the condition of

_____.

20. _____ is a fairly common form of reading disability.

21. Opaque or cloudy areas in the lens of the eye that decrease the amount of light reaching the retina result in _____.

22. A person who believes that infants enter the world with no knowledge of the world, and learn everything through their senses is a(n) _____.

23. Increased fluid pressure in eye is a symptom of _____.

24. Problems in hearing that result from aging, such as decreased sensitivity to high-frequency sounds, are called _____

MULTIPLE CHOICE SELF TEST

For each multiple choice question, read all alternatives and then select the best answer.

1. Sensation refers to _____ of stimuli while perception refers to _____ of this information.
   a. detection; interpretation
   b. sense; the value
   c. interpretation; detection
   d. recognition; the use

2. Nativists argue that a child is
   a. born knowing nothing and learns through interaction with the environment
   b. born with knowledge and is very similar to an adult in terms of perceptual ability
   c. influenced intellectually by genetics, maturation and the environment
   d. learns mainly through cultural experiences

3. Suppose you repeatedly present a stimulus until an infant loses interest in it. This technique is known as
   a. visual accommodation
   b. color discrimination
   c. visual acuity
   d. habituation

4. Which of the following is TRUE about young infants' visual capabilities?
   a. Infants are not able to perceive color until sometime during the second half of the first year.
   b. Infants as young as two months can detect details of a patterned stimulus as well as adults.
   c. Infants are fairly good at detecting differences in brightness levels of stimuli.
   d. Infants' visual systems are at their peak performance.

5.   Newborns appear to have a preference for viewing human faces. This probably reflects
       a.   an innate ability to recognize faces
       b.   a preference for patterned stimuli with contour and some complexity
       c.   the fact that infants will learn to look at what they have been reinforced for in the past
       d.   the fact that infants can focus only on faces

6.   At around 2 or 3 months of age, infants prefer to look at "normal" faces as opposed to faces that
       have been distorted in some way. This suggests that
       a.   infants cannot really detect a difference between them
       b.   infants have organized their perceptions according to Gestalt principles
       c.   infants prefer the simplest form or pattern
       d.   infants are developing mental representations of what a normal face looks like

7.   Very young infants are most visually attracted to
       a.   a highly complex stimulus
       b.   a moderately complex stimulus
       c.   a colorful stimulus
       d.   a black and white stimulus

8.   The visual cliff is an apparatus used to determine
       a.   depth perception
       b.   size constancy
       c.   visual acuity
       d.   visual accommodation

9.   Two-month-olds tested on the visual cliff typically show a slower heart rate on the deep side
       than on the shallow side of the cliff. This suggests that two-month-olds
       a.   are afraid of falling off the apparent cliff
       b.   detect a difference between the two sides of the visual cliff
       c.   perceive size constancy
       d.   have learned to avoid potential drop-offs

10.   Normal hearing in young infants is different from normal hearing in adults in that infants
       a.   are better able to hear soft sounds and whispers
       b.   have more difficulty discriminating between speech sounds
       c.   are unable to localize sound
       d.   can distinguish between all speech sounds, including those not used in the language of
              adults around them

11.   The point at which a dim light can still be detected is termed
       a.   dark adaptation
       b.   sensory threshold
       c.   visual accommodation
       d.   visual acuity

12. An infant who sucks on an object and then recognizes this object visually is showing evidence of
   a. selective attention
   b. habituation
   c. cross-modal perception
   d. recognition of the object's distinctive features

13. Research findings with animals suggest that, in order for normal perceptual development to occur, infants
   a. must be able to actively move through their environment
   b. must be able to watch movement in the environment
   c. must be exposed to patterned stimulation
   d. Both B and C

14. Most age related hearing problems originate in the
   a. hearing center of the brain
   b. auditory nerves and receptors
   c. structures of the middle ear
   d. outer ear membrane

15. When speaking to people who are hard of hearing, the speaker should
   a. elevate the voice--shout if necessary
   b. talk directly into the person's ear so they can hear better
   c. repeat what she has just said instead of rewording the misunderstood statement
   d. make sure the hearing impaired person can see him/her

APPLICATION QUESTIONS

By answering the following questions, you will strengthen your understanding of the material in this chapter. These questions require higher level thinking skills such as integration and application of concepts. To get you started, there is a sample answer or outline provided for the first question. This illustrates one possibility, but there are other answers you could provide that might be just as good. For the other questions, you can check yourself by referring to the text (a hint is provided), or by asking a peer or your instructor to review your answer.

1. In light of their sensory and perceptual abilities, what do young infants know about the people and world around them?
   [Sample answer provided]

2. Discuss the likely outcomes for an infant born with congenital cataracts that preclude any sort of visual stimulation.
   [Hint: Review the section in the text on "Influences on Early Perceptual Development."]

3. What sensory and perceptual changes can an older adult expect? What implications do these changes have with respect to an older adult's lifestyle?
   [Hint: Review the sections in the text under "The Adult."]

4.   Based on what you know from this chapter about perceptual capabilities and preferences, what recommendations would you make for designing an infant's nursery? What recommendations would you make for an older adult's living quarters?
[Hint: Think of the applications of the material in the sections that cover infants' sensory capabilities, particularly their vision and hearing. Likewise, consider the applications of the material covered in "The Adult."]

ANSWERS

Chapter Summary and Guided Review (Fill-in the blank)

1.	sensation	26.	attention
2.	perception	27.	selective
3.	empiricists	28.	systematic (or detailed)
4.	nurture	29.	distinctive features
5.	nativists	30.	phonological awareness
6.	nature	31.	dyslexia
7.	habituation	32.	phonics
8.	preferential looking	33.	irrelevant
9.	visual acuity	34.	sensory thresholds
10.	visual accommodation	35.	presbyopia
11.	patterned	36.	visual acuity
12.	contour	37.	cataracts
13.	normal	38.	glaucoma
14.	mental representations (or schemata)	39.	dark adaptation
15.	depth	40.	moving
16.	size constancy	41.	novel
17.	visual cliff	42.	complex
18.	common motion	43.	presbycusis
19.	intuitive theories	44.	background noise
20.	phonemes	45.	sweet
21.	olfaction	46.	smell
22.	cries	47.	aids
23.	cross-modal perception	48.	auditory
24.	nature	49.	cochlear implant
25.	patterned	50.	environment

Review of Key Terms

1.	distinctive feature	10.	phoneme
2.	visual accommodation	11.	perception
3.	nativist	12.	cross-modal perception
4.	size constancy	13.	contour
5.	sensation	14.	cochlear implant
6.	olfaction	15.	attention
7.	visual cliff	16.	visual acuity
8.	sensory threshold	17.	dark adaptation
9.	habituation	18.	phonological awareness

19.	presbyopia	22.	empiricist
20.	dyslexia	23.	glaucoma
21.	cataracts	24.	presbycusis

Multiple Choice Self Test

1.	A	6.	D	11.	B
2.	B	7.	B	12.	C
3.	D	8.	A	13.	D
4.	C	9.	B	14.	B
5.	B	10.	D	15.	D

Application Questions

1.   *Infants actually know a lot more than previously thought. They can recognize their mother's voice, and if they are breast-fed, they can recognize her by smell. They can see people and objects that are close to them, particularly if what they are looking at has sharp light-dark contrasts or bold patterns. This means that infants can see their parents' faces fairly well when parents are interacting with them. Infants seem to like looking at human faces more than other patterned stimuli, but this seems to be because the features of faces are interesting. Show them a picture of a scrambled face, and they will look at it almost as long as they look at a "normal" face. Objects in the environment that move are interesting to infants, as long as the movement is not too fast. Finally, infants like to look at things that are somewhat, but not overly, complex. As they mature, they prefer increasing complexity. The bottom line is that infants like to look at things that they can see well.*

CHAPTER SEVEN

COGNITION AND LANGUAGE

OVERVIEW

This is a big chapter, both literally and figuratively. It covers Piaget's theory of cognitive development, which is considered to be one of the major developmental theories. To master this theory, you will need to understand *what* develops, as well as *how* this development occurs in the Piagetian perspective. "What" develops are the cognitive schemes or structures and this growth is reflected in children's progression through Piaget's four stages of development. The "how" of development occurs through the processes of organization and adaptation, and is motivated by cognitive disequilibrium.

In addition to the *what* and *how*, you need to have some sense of how the theory has fared in light of the decades of research that have been conducted on children's thinking. Piaget's theory stops short of being a life span theory; Piaget did not propose any new stages beyond formal operations in adolescence. As discussed in the chapter, though, other researchers have looked at cognitive changes during adulthood.

Another significant theorist to emerge in this area is Vygotsky, who viewed cognitive development as a product of social interactions and the child's sociocultural context. The textbook provides discussion of Vygotsky's contributions and how they differ from Piaget's.

The other major component of this chapter is language development. You will need to understand the various components of language that children need to master in order to learn language. You will also need to understand the developmental course of language. Finally, how do theorists account for the fact that children learn language with little formal instruction? The textbook covers the three major theoretical perspectives on language development--learning theory perspective, Chomsky's nativist perspective, and the social interactionist perspective--and also considers whether there is support for a critical period for language acquisition.

LEARNING OBJECTIVES

After reading and studying the material in this chapter, you should be able to answer the following questions.

1.   How do organization, adaptation, and disequilibrium guide development?

2.   What are examples of assimilation and accommodation?

3.   What are the major achievements of the sensorimotor stage?

4.   What are the characteristics and limitations of preoperational thought?

5.   What are the major characteristics and limitations of concrete operational thought?

6.   What are the main features of formal operational thought?

7.   In what ways might adult thought be more advanced than adolescent thought?

8.   What are the limitations and challenges to Piaget's theory of cognitive development?

9.   What is Vygotsky's perspective on cognitive development?

10.   How do Vygotsky and Piaget differ in their ideas about cognition and language?

11.   What components of language must children master?

12.   What is the typical developmental course of language development?

13.   How do learning, nativist, and interactionist perspectives explain the acquisition of language? Which explanation is best supported by research?

14.   Can cognitive functioning be improved with training? Explain.

The following summary provides an overview of the main points contained in this chapter of the text. Fill-in the blanks with terms that appropriately complete the sentence. Scattered throughout the summary are questions in parentheses. These are meant to encourage you to think actively as you are reading and connect this summary to the more detailed information provided in the text. You can answer these questions as you are filling in the blanks or you can complete all the blanks, then go back and reread the entire summary, addressing the questions in order to provide more depth of understanding.

PIAGET'S APPROACH TO COGNITIVE DEVELOPMENT

Piaget was interested in the common mistakes that children of different ages made and believed that these responses reflected different stages of thinking. He used a question-and-answer technique called the (1) _____ to determine the process of children's thinking. This method allows for flexibility but is not standardized for all children.

What is Intelligence?

According to Piaget, intelligence is a basic life function that helps an organism adapt to its environment. Further, organisms are actively involved in their own development. As knowledge is gained, people form (2) _____, or cognitive structures, which are organized patterns of action or thought that allow us to interpret our experiences. Infants' schemes are action-oriented, while preschool-age children develop symbolic schemes. Older children can manipulate symbols in their heads to solve problems.

How Does Intelligence Develop?

Schemes develop through two innate processes. One is (3) _____ in which children combine existing schemes into more complex schemes. (*What is an example of this process?*) The second process is (4) _____, which refers to the process of adjusting to the demands of the environment. This adjustment occurs through (5) _____, by which new experiences are interpreted in terms of existing schemes, and through (6) _____, in which existing cognitive schemes are modified to account for new experiences. (*What are examples of each of these processes?*) When we encounter new experiences, the conflict between new information and old understanding creates (7) _____, which stimulates cognitive growth.

Major cognitive changes are organized into four distinct stages. Thinking in each stage is qualitatively different from thinking in the other stages. Progress through the stages occurs in an (8) _____, or unchanging order for all children, although *rate* of progress may vary from child to child.

THE INFANT

According to Piaget, infants are in the (9) _____ stage, which has six substages and is dominated by behavioral schemes.

Substages of the Sensorimotor Stage

Through the six substages, infants gradually switch from relying on innate reflexes to using mental symbols to guide future behavior. Piaget referred to the ability to use one thing to represent objects or experiences as the (10) _____.

The Development of Object Permanence

One of the important achievements of the sensorimotor stage is (11) _____, or the understanding that objects continue to exist even though not directly experienced. Infants in substage four (8-12 months) will search for a concealed object if they watched while it was hidden, but if the object is then hidden in a new location, infants in this substage typically make the (12) _____ error. Not until substage six (18-24 months) are infants capable of mental representation and following invisible displacements of objects. Recent research suggests that infants have a rudimentary understanding of object permanence earlier than Piaget claimed. (***Why is object permanence an important concept for infants to develop?***)

THE CHILD
The Preoperational Stage
       According to Piaget, preschool-age children are in the preoperational stage of cognitive development where children use symbolic reasoning but not logical reasoning. Children in this stage lack (13) _____, the understanding that certain properties of a substance or object remain the same despite superficial changes in appearance. There are several reasons for this. They lack the cognitive operation called (14) _____, which means they have trouble focusing on two or more dimensions of a problem at the same time. Instead, preoperational children engage in (15) _____ where they focus on a single aspect of the problem when more are relevant. In addition, preoperational children lack (16) _____ or the process of mentally reversing an action. Preoperational children also have trouble with (17) _____ or the processes of change from one state to another and so their thought is static. (***Try writing responses to one of the conservation problems that demonstrate each of these concepts from a preoperational child's perspective.***)
       Piaget also believed that preoperational children were (18) _____ because of their tendency to view the world from their own perspective and their trouble recognizing other points of view. Preoperational children have difficulty relating subclasses of objects to the whole class of objects because they tend to center on the most perceptually salient feature of the task, and so they have trouble solving (19) _____ problems.
       Piaget seems to have underestimated what the preschool age child can do. Recent research suggests that they understand simple conservation concepts and classification systems, and they are not as egocentric as Piaget claimed. Nonetheless, preschool children rely more on their perceptions to solve tasks than older children do.

The Concrete Operations Stage
       School-age children (roughly 7 to 11 years) are in Piaget's third stage of cognitive development-- concrete operations. They have mastered the logical operations that were absent from preoperational thought (***What are these mental operations?***). This allows concrete operational children to solve conservation tasks. They can also mentally order items along a quantifiable dimension, an operation called (20) _____ , and have mastered (21) _____, a cognitive operation that allows children to recognize the relationships among elements in a series. (***What are examples of problems that children can solve by applying each of these operations?***) Finally, concrete operational children can solve (22) _____ problems because they understand that subclasses are included in a whole class.

THE ADOLESCENT
The Formal Operations Stage
       According to Piaget, adolescents are entering the stage of formal operations. Like concrete operational children, adolescents can reason logically about objects. In addition, they can apply their mental actions to ideas, extending their reasoning to non-concrete, or (23) _____ concepts. This facilitates (24) _____ reasoning.
       Formal operational thinkers also use systematic problem-solving strategies, rather than trial-and-

error approaches often used by children in earlier stages. One type of reasoning that formal operational thinkers might use is (25) _____, where individuals reason from general ideas to specific implications of these ideas.

Implications of Formal Thought

Mastery of formal operational thought takes place over several years and is often quite slow. There are several implications of formal operational thought. On the positive side, formal operational thought may be related to achieving a sense of identity and to advances in moral reasoning. On the other hand, formal operational thought may lead to a period of confusion or rebellion because of all the questions about life that formal operational thinkers can generate. Specifically, formal operational adolescents may experience (26) _____ where they have trouble separating their own thoughts and emotions from those of others. According to Elkind, this emerges in two forms. One is the (27) _____, which involves confusing your own thoughts with those of a hypothetical audience. (*Can you provide an example of this phenomenon?*) A second form is the (28) _____, which is a tendency to think that your thoughts or feelings are unique and that others cannot possibly experience the same thoughts or feelings.

THE ADULT

Piaget believed that formal operational thought was mastered by most 15-18 year olds, however more recent research suggests otherwise.

Limitations in Cognitive Performance

Many adults do not reason at the formal operational level. Although average intelligence contributes to formal operational thought, formal education is an important factor as well (*Can you explain why this is the case?*). Further, we tend to apply formal operational thought to areas with which we have some expertise and knowledge.

Growth Beyond Formal Operations?

Despite the fact that formal operational thought is not completely mastered by all adults, some researchers believe that Piaget did not go far enough with cognitive development and have proposed growth beyond formal operations, that is, (29) _____. One suggestion is that adults are more likely than adolescents to use (30) _____ thinking, which means that they believe that knowledge depends on the subjective perspective of the person with the knowledge. (*What does Perry's work with college students indicate about changes in thought throughout college?*). Adults may also be better able to uncover and resolve contradictions between ideas, and to think about entire systems of ideas.

Aging and Cognitive Skills

Cross-sectional studies with older adults suggest that they perform poorly on concrete and formal operational tasks. Older adults may approach tasks using different styles of thinking that are useful in everyday life, but not on laboratory-type tests.

PIAGET IN PERSPECTIVE
Piaget's Contributions

Piaget's contributions to developmental psychology are enormous. His theory has stimulated a tremendous amount of research and his insights about development--such as active involvement in one's own development and sequencing of cognitive development--continue to guide our understanding of children's thinking.

Challenges to Piaget

Piaget's contributions must be viewed in the context of various challenges to the theory. One criticism of Piaget is that he (31) _____ the cognitive abilities of young children. Piaget has also been criticized for blurring the distinction between competence and (32)_____. Some researchers do not believe that development is best characterized by a series of broad, coherent (33) _____ or qualitative changes in thinking. Piaget has also been criticized for describing development but not really (34) _____ development. Other researchers have criticized Piaget for not giving enough attention to the role of (35)_____ influences on cognitive development.

VYGOTSKY'S SOCIOCULTURAL PERSPECTIVE

Vygotsky developed a theory of cognitive development that emphasizes the sociocultural context of development and the influence of social interactions.

Culture and Thought

Culture and historical context shape what people know and how they think.

Social Interaction and Thought

Social interactions that foster cognitive growth typically take place in the zone of (36)_____ development. This is the difference between what learners can do (37) _____ and what they can do with assistance. Vygotsky believed that children learned through (38) _____ as they interacted with more skilled thinkers or problem solvers.

Language and Thought

According to Vygotsky, the primary means of passing on successful problem solving strategies is through (39) _____. Vygotsky noted that young children often talked to themselves when working on a problem and he believed this (40) _____ guided the child's thoughts and behaviors. Through social interactions, (41) _____ speech is transformed into (42) _____ speech, and eventually this becomes (43)_____ speech. (***How is this different from Piaget's view of early speech and thought?***)

MASTERING LANGUAGE

Mastering language is accomplished at a young age despite its complex nature.

What Must be Mastered

Language is a system of symbols that can be combined using agreed-on rules to produce messages. The sound system of language is its (44) _____. The meaning of language is its (45) _____ aspect. Children must come to understand that the symbols of a language represent things or ideas. The rules specifying how to combine symbols meaningfully make up the (46) _____ of language. Rules specifying how to use language appropriately in different contexts make up the (47) _____ of language. (***What is an example of this?***)

The Course of Language Development

Prelinguistic vocalizations begin at birth with several distinct cries. By the end of the first month, infants begin (48) _____, or repeating vowel-like sounds, and by 3 or 4 months of age, infants combine vowel and consonant sounds to produce (49) _____. These early utterances are the same across all cultures until about six months of age when experience begins to alter them. (***What evidence shows that experience has an impact on babbling?***) Infants can understand the meanings of many words before they can (50)_____ the words.

At about one year, infants produce their first meaningful words, often called (51)_____ because when combined with gestures or intonation, these single words can convey the meaning of an entire sentence. The pace at which language develops escalates around 18 months of age during a (52) _____. Young children often err in their speech by using fairly specific words to refer to a general class of objects, which is an (53) _____. (***Can you provide an example of this?***) Young children may also err by using a general word too narrowly, which is an (54) _____. (***Can you provide an example?***)

Around 18 to 24 months, infants typically begin to combine two or more words into simple sentences called (55) _____ speech. These early sentences may be best described in terms of a (56) _____, which focuses on the semantic relations between words. The language of preschool-age children is developing rapidly with their ability to use symbols. Their understanding of grammatical rules is often evident in the mistakes they make. For example, children often over apply rules they have learned to cases that are irregular, an error called (57) _____. Chomsky proposed that language be described in terms of (58)_____, which consists of rules of syntax for transforming basic sentences into other forms. (***Can you provide an example of one of these rules?***) School-age children refine their pronunciation skills, and produce longer and more complex sentences. They also develop an ability to think about language and use language in ways not possible at younger ages. There are also increases in vocabulary across most of the life span.

How Language Develops

There are several theoretical explanations of how children come to learn language. The (59)_____ perspective claims that children learn language the same way they learn everything else--through observation, imitation, and reinforcement. This perspective seems to best explain how children acquire the development (60) _____ and phonology of language, but not the development of the rules of (61) _____. (***What evidence supports this explanation of language acquisition?***)

The (62) _____ perspective proposes that humans have an inborn mechanism, called a (63) _____, that allows children to infer the rules governing the speech they hear and then apply these rules to their own speech. (***What evidence supports this explanation of language acquisition?***) This theory may explain (64) _____ developments but has difficulty with other aspects of language acquisition. (***What are the two major problems with this perspective?***)

The (65) _____ perspective acknowledges that both the learning and nativist perspectives have some valuable aspects. Innate capacities and the language environment interact to influence language development. These theorists emphasize how the social interactions between infants and adults contribute to language and cognitive developments. Adults typically converse with infants using (66) _____, a simplified speech that is spoken slowly and in a high-pitched voice. Adults may also respond to a child's vocalization by using (67)_____, or a more complete expression of what the child said. (***What other things do adults do to facilitate language development?***)

Children seem to learn language with apparent ease, while adults often have great difficulty learning a language. This suggests that there might be a (68) _____ for language acquisition. Research supports the idea of a sensitive period, but does not clearly show when this period ends.

Below is a list of terms and concepts from this chapter. Use these to complete the following sentence definitions. You might also want to try writing definitions in your own words and then checking your definitions with those in the text.

A, not B, error
accommodation
adaptation
adolescent egocentrism
assimilation
babbling
centration
child-directed speech
class inclusion
clinical method
concrete operations stage
conservation
cooing
decentration
egocentrism
expansion
formal operations stage
functional grammar
genetic epistemology
guided participation
holophrase
horizontal décalage
hypothetical-deductive reasoning
imaginary audience
intonation
language
language acquisition device (LAD)

morphology
object permanence
organization
overextension
overregularization
personal fable
phonology
postformal thought
pragmatics
preoperational stage
private speech
relativistic thinking
reversibility
scheme (schema)
semantics
sensorimotor stage
seriation
symbolic capacity
syntax
telegraphic speech
transformational grammar
transformational thought
transitivity
underextension
vocabulary spurt
zone of proximal development

1.   Children are _____ when they repeat consonant-vowel combinations.

2.   _____ is the tendency to view the world from one's own perspective and to have trouble recognizing other points of view.

3.   _____ is a method of learning through interaction with others who provide aid and support.

4.   A single word that, when combined with gestures or intonation, conveys the meaning of an entire sentence is called a _____.

5.   According to Piaget, the inborn tendency to combine existing schemes into new and more complex schemes is _____.

6.   The rules for forming words are the _____ of language.

7.   Young children have a tendency to use fairly specific words to refer to a general class of objects or events, an error known as _____.

8.   Understanding that objects continue to exist even when those objects are no longer directly experienced is called _____.

9.   Adolescents sometimes create an _____ when they confuse their own thoughts with the thoughts of a hypothetical audience.

10.   _____ is an inborn tendency to adjust to the demands of the environment.

11.   Parents often use _____ when they provide comments that are more complete follow-up expressions of a thought expressed by a child.

12.   The _____ is often made by 8 to 12 month old infants who successfully find an object hidden at one location and then continue to search at this hiding location after watching the object being hidden at a second location.

13.   Cognitive development that may emerge after formal operations is referred to as _____.

14.   The process of interpreting new experiences in terms of existing cognitive structures is called _____.

15.   _____ is the ability to understand changes from one state to another.

16.   An infant's repetition of vowel-like sounds in association with positive affective states is called _____.

17.   Young children sometimes use a general word too narrowly, an error called a(n) _____.

18.   The _____ is an inborn mechanism for acquiring language that allows children to infer rules governing others' speech and then use these rules to produce their own speech.

19.   The _____ is the difference between what one can do independently and what one can do with assistance .

20.   _____ is a form of simplified speech used by adults when speaking to young children.

21.   In Piaget's _____ stage of cognitive development, children can logically reason about physical objects and experiences.

22.   The rules of syntax specifying how to transform basic sentences into other forms are called _____.

23. Children use _____ when they construct two or three word sentences that contain only critical content words.

24. The process of mentally "undoing" an action is called _____.

25. _____ speech is not directed toward another person but helps direct the speaker's thoughts and behaviors.

26. Infants' understanding of the world is constructed through their senses and actions in Piaget's _____ stage of cognitive development.

27. During the _____ there is a dramatic increase in language acquisition.

28. _____ is the process of modifying existing cognitive structures in order to understand or adapt to new experiences.

29. The analysis of early language in terms of the semantic relations between words is called the _____ of language.

30. Piaget used the _____, an interview technique in which a child's response to each question determines the next question.

31. The _____ of language refers to the relationship between words or symbols and what they represent or mean.

32. _____ reasoning occurs when specific implications are derived from general ideas or hypotheses, and are then systematically tested.

33. In Piaget's _____ stage of cognitive development, children can reason logically about hypothetical and abstract ideas.

34. A _____ is an organized pattern of thought or action used to interpret our experiences.

35. _____ is a problem differentiating one's own thoughts and feelings from those of other people.

36. The ability to use images, words, or gestures to represent objects and experiences emerges with the development of _____.

37. A cognitive operation called _____ allows children to mentally order items along a quantifiable dimension.

38. The _____ refers to the tendency to think that you and your thoughts and feelings are unique.

39. _____ is the system of rules specifying how to combine words to form sentences.

40. Children can reason using symbols but do not reason logically in Piaget's _____ stage of cognitive development.

41. _____ is a cognitive operation that allows children to recognize the relationship among elements in a series.

42. _____ consists of a system of symbols that can be combined according to agreed-on rules to create messages.

43. Understanding that certain properties of a substance or object remain the same despite superficial changes in appearance is called _____.

44. _____ are the rules specifying how language is to be used appropriately in different social contexts.

45. _____ is the system of speech sounds of a language.

46. Children sometimes over-apply grammatical rules to irregular nouns and verbs, an error known as _____.

47. The tendency to focus on a single aspect of problem when more aspects are relevant is called _____.

48. _____ is an understanding that knowledge depends on the subjective perspective of the person with the knowledge.

49. _____ is the understanding that subclasses are included in a whole class.

50. The ability to focus on two or more dimensions of a problem at one time is called _____.

51. Piaget called the study of how we come to know reality _____.

52. Variations in pitch, loudnes, and timing of words or sentences are components of _____.

53. The term _____ represents Piaget's recognition that different cognitive skills related to the same stage of cognitive development may emerge at different times.

MULTIPLE CHOICE SELF TEST

For each multiple choice question, read all alternatives and then select the best answer.

1. An example of accommodation is
   a. believing that all four-legged animals with fur are dogs
   b. realizing that a cat fits into a different category than a dog
   c. the confusion that a child experiences when new events challenge old schemas
   d. a child who sees a cat and refers to it as a dog

2. Which of the following statements best characterizes Piaget's position on the nature-nurture issue?
   a. The environment is primarily responsible for providing children with cognitive skills.
   b. Innate mechanisms are primarily responsible for determining intelligence.
   c. Ideas are not innate or imposed by others, but are constructed from experiences.
   d. Some cognitive skills result from innate characteristics while others are influenced only by environmental experiences.

3. Throughout the sensorimotor stage, infants change from
   a. focusing on symbols to using simple mental operations
   b. an egocentric perspective to one that considers other viewpoints
   c. relying on reflexes for understanding their world to mentally planning how to solve simple problems
   d. focusing on sensory information to focusing on motoric information for gaining knowledge about their world

4. Which of the following is an example of object permanence?
   a. visually tracking a moving object
   b. searching for a shoe under the bed because this seems like a likely hiding place
   c. searching for a toy where the child just watched it being hidden
   d. using goal directed behavior to systematically check all possible hiding locations for a toy

5. Which of the following responses to a conservation problem indicates that the child has reversibility of thought?
   a. The amount of water in the two cups is the same because even though one is taller, the other one is wider.
   b. The amount of water in the two cups looks about the same, so I'd say they were equal.
   c. I didn't see you spill any water, so the amounts are the same.
   d. If you'd pour the water back into the original container, you'd see it has the same amount of water as the other container.

6. Research on Piaget's description of preoperational thought has found that
   a. when task demands are reduced, young children can successfully solve some problems at a more sophisticated level.
   b. when task demands are reduced, it has little impact on performance because children do not yet have the cognitive capabilities to solve the problem.
   c. Piaget was correct in his description of <u>when</u> certain abilities emerged, but was not always accurate in his description of what underlying thought was required for these abilities.
   d. Piaget overestimated what most preschool-age children can do.

7. Formal operational children are different from concrete operational children in that
   a. formal operational children can deal with possibilities
   b. formal operational children focus on realities
   c. concrete operational children systematically test all possible solutions to a problem
   d. concrete operational children are more likely to be egocentric.

8. Piaget has been criticized by modern developmentalists who suggest that
   a. Piaget was somewhat pessimistic concerning the timing of cognitive abilities in adolescents
   b. Piaget was overly optimistic concerning the abilities of infants and young children
   c. development is a gradual process rather than a stagelike process
   d. development is stagelike but stages follow a different pattern than what Piaget suggested

9. Research by Perry with college students suggests that their thinking progresses from:
   a. assuming that truth is absolute to understanding that truth is relative
   b. uncertainty about the "correctness" of answers to absolute certainty about the correctness
   c. considering all possible options to selecting a single answer
   d. being able to think logically about ideas to thinking logically about multiple sets of ideas

10. Research with older adults solving Piagetian tasks shows that
    a. nearly all are reasoning at the formal operational level
    b. older adults perform worse than younger adults on many concrete operational tasks
    c. older adults perform similarly to younger adults on all Piagetian tasks
    d. older adults are more egocentric than younger adults and tend to use transductive reasoning

11. In comparing Piaget's perspective to Vygotsky's perspective, which of the following is TRUE?
    a. Piaget believed that knowledge was constructed through independent exploration of the world while Vygotsky believed that social interactions were needed for development of more advanced thinking.
    b. Both believed that language development was independent of cognitive development.
    c. Vygotsky believed that private speech was not a developmentally important phenomenon, while Piaget used it as evidence of egocentrism.
    d. Piaget and Vygotsky both proposed that children progress through major stages in reaching mature cognitive understanding of the world.

12. Vygotsky used the term zone of proximal development to refer to:
    a. the influence that thought and language have on one another
    b. the child's approximate level of cognitive skill on a particular task
    c. the difference between what someone can do independently and what they can do with another person's help
    d. the point at which the child progresses from one level of understanding to another

13. Phonology refers to the _____ of language, while semantics refers to the _____ of language.
    a. sound system; meaning
    b. rules for forming sentences; meaning
    c. meaning; rules for how to use language
    d. rules for combining sounds; rules for forming sentences

14. Calling all four-legged animals "doggie" is an example of
    a. overregularization
    b. underextension
    c. overextension
    d. telegraphic speech

15. Learning theorists argue that language is acquired through
    a. biologically programmed learning capacities
    b. imitation of others' language and reinforcement for recognizable speech
    c. cognitive understanding of speech sounds and their relationship to real objects and actions
    d. a device that allows children to sift through language and generate rules that govern the language

COMPARE THE MAIN IDEAS OF PIAGET AND VYGOTSKY

This exercise will help you compare Piaget's views on cognitive development with those of Vygotsky. Use Table 7.2 in the text to check your answers.

	PIAGET	VYGOTSKY
1. Is cognitive development universal or context specific?		
2. What sorts of activities lead to cognitive growth?		
3. Is knowledge best constructed individually or with others?		
4. How do cognitive development and language relate to one another?		
5. Are peers or adults more important in the development of cognition?		
6. What is the relationship between learning and development?		

We have reviewed lots of ideas and concepts from this chapter. Now consider the people who contributed many of these ideas. Use the matching exercise below to review the contributions of some of the more influential people discussed in this chapter. Write the appropriate letter next to the person's name.

1. Noam Chomsky _____
2. David Elkind _____
3. Rochel Gelman _____
4. William Perry _____
5. Jean Piaget _____
6. Lev Vygotsky _____

a. Developed a theory of children's thinking that focused on a people's adaptations to their environment and their active construction of reality.
b. Demonstrated that young children understand number concepts and simple conservation tasks.
c. Noted that adolescents are often egocentric because they have trouble distinguishing their own thoughts from those of others.
d. Argued that humans have an inborn mechanism for acquiring language (the "LAD").
e. Found that college students move from absolutist thinking to relativistic thinking during the college experience.
f. Developed a theory of cognitive development that incorporated a person's culture and social context.

APPLICATION QUESTIONS

By answering the following questions, you will strengthen your understanding of the material in this chapter. These questions require higher level thinking skills such as integration and application of concepts. To get you started, there is a sample answer or outline provided for the first question. This illustrates one possibility, but there are other answers you could provide that might be just as good. For the other questions, you can check yourself by referring to the text, or by asking a peer or your instructor to review your answer.

1. Apply Piaget's description of cognitive development to a social issue such as divorce, birth of a new sibling, or adoption. What would a child's understanding of one these events be in each of Piaget's four stages of cognitive development?
[Sample answer provided]

2. Piaget's theory has stimulated a tremendous amount of research on cognitive development over the past 30 years. Considering what we have learned from this research, how would Piaget's theory need to be updated to account for the findings that have emerged since the theory was developed?
[Hint: Read the "Challenges to Piaget" section in the text, as well as the research on Piaget's theory that was discussed in sections on "The Infant," "The Child," "The Adolescent," and "The Adult."]

3. Suppose you need to design a program to teach 6-year-old children a new academic skill. How

would you approach this from Piaget's perspective? How would you approach this from Vygotsky's perspective? How would the two programs be similar or different?
[Hint: Review the sections in the text on Piaget's and Vygotsky's theories, and read the "Applications: Improving Cognitive Functioning" section.]

4. Consider how deafness affects the language development of children. Questions to think about include: Do you need to hear speech to develop speech? More generally, do you need to be exposed to a language (spoken or unspoken) in order to develop a language? What is the relationship between thought and language? Is language an important basis for thought (Is it a _necessary_ basis for thought)?
    [Hint: Read the Box on "Language Acquisition among Deaf Children" in the text.]

ANSWERS

Chapter Summary and Guided Review (Fill-in the blank)

1.	clinical method	33.	stages
2.	schemes	34.	explaining
3.	organization	35.	social
4.	adaptation	36.	proximal
5.	assimilation	37.	independently
6.	accommodation	38.	guided participation
7.	disequilibrium	39.	language
8.	invariant	40.	private speech
9.	sensorimotor	41.	social
10.	symbolic capacity	42.	private
11.	object permanence	43.	inner
12.	A, not b	44.	phonology
13.	conservation	45.	semantic
14.	decentration	46.	syntax or grammar
15.	centration	47.	pragmatics
16.	reversibility	48.	cooing
17.	transformations	49.	babbling
18.	egocentric	50.	produce or express
19.	class inclusion	51.	holophrases
20.	seriation	52.	vocabulary spurt
21.	transitivity	53.	overextension
22.	class inclusion	54.	underextension
23.	abstract	55.	telegraphic
24.	hypothetical	56.	functional grammar
25.	hypothetical-deductive	57.	overregularization
26.	adolescent egocentrism	58.	transformational grammar
27.	imaginary audience	59.	learning
28.	personal fable	60.	semantics
29.	postformal	61.	syntax
30.	relativistic	62.	nativist
31.	underestimated	63.	language acquisition device (LAD)
32.	performance	64.	syntactic

65. interactionist
66. motherese

67. expansion
68. critical period

Review of Key Terms

1. babbling
2. egocentrism
3. guided participation
4. holophrase
5. organization
6. morphology
7. overextension
8. object permanence
9. imaginary audience
10. adaptation
11. expansion
12. A, not B, error
13. postformal thought
14. assimilation
15. transformational thought
16. cooing
17. underextension
18. language acquisition device (LAD)
19. zone of proximal development
20. child-directed speech
21. concrete operations
22. transformational grammar
23. telegraphic speech
24. reversibility
25. private
26. sensorimotor
27. vocabulary spurt

28. accommodation
29. functional grammar
30. clinical method
31. semantics
32. hypothetical-deductive
33. formal operations
34. scheme
35. adolescent egocentrism
36. symbolic capacity
37. seriation
38. personal fable
39. syntax
40. preoperational
41. transitivity
42. language
43. conservation
44. pragmatics
45. phonology
46. overregularization
47. centration
48. relativistic thinking
49. class inclusion
50. decentration
51. genetic epistemology
52. intonation
53. horizontal décalage

Multiple Choice Self Test

1.	B	6.	A	11.	A
2.	C	7.	A	12.	C
3.	C	8.	C	13.	A
4.	C	9.	A	14.	C
5.	D	10.	B	15.	B

People and their Ideas

1.	D	3.	B	5.	A
2.	C	4.	E	6.	F

1.	*Considering adoption, children in the sensorimotor stage most likely would not understand the concept because they are just experiencing the beginning of thought at the end of this stage.*

A preoperational child might be able to tell people, "I'm adopted," but they wouldn't really understand what this meant. For one thing, they have static thought and focus on end results. They would only know that they ended up with the people they call Mom and Dad, but not really grasp the process that led to this. In addition, preoperational children exhibit centration, which allows them to focus on only a single aspect of a problem. They might be able to focus on where babies come from, but not integrate this with other concepts that occur with adoption. Another difficulty for the preoperational child is class inclusion. This child would have trouble understanding that adoption is one "classification" of ways a parent can "get" a child, but that most children are not gotten this way. Also, children in preoperations are egocentric, so they would have trouble understanding the perspective of other people involved (e.g., the mother who gave them up for adoption). Finally, preoperational children can't understand that they are the children of their biological mother and their adoptive mother; they center on one or the other.

The concrete operational child would be better able to comprehend adoption because of their increased powers of logical reasoning. For instance, concrete operational children can decenter, so they can focus on more than one aspect of the problem. They would also understand that adoption is one of several ways that children end up in a particular family. Not until formal operations, though, would adolescents gain a better understanding of why they were adopted. They could consider all the abstract issues that go into adoption decisions and reason about possibilities (e.g., what might have happened if they had not been adopted). On the negative side, formal operational children could devise hypothetical reasons for why their biological parents did not want to raise them and this might create some anguish. They may also be interested in knowing more about their biological parents, as this information might allow them to systematically test various theories they have constructed about their circumstances.

CHAPTER EIGHT

LEARNING AND INFORMATION PROCESSING

OVERVIEW

The first part of this chapter provides an overview of three major learning paradigms: classical conditioning, operant conditioning, and observational learning. Many of you may recall being introduced to these concepts in an introductory psychology course. Now you will learn how these learning processes change across the life span. For example, can infants be conditioned? Does age place any restrictions on a person's ability to learn through one of these processes?

The second part of this chapter focuses on learning and memory. The information processing model is used to describe how information is moved in and out of the memory stores. You will learn that young children and older adults have trouble with some learning and memory tasks. To understand these difficulties in learning and memory, four hypotheses are explored. These involve changes in: 1) basic capacities, 2) memory strategies, 3) metamemory, and 4) knowledge base. These provide a useful way to organize much of the research on developmental changes in learning and memory.

LEARNING OBJECTIVES

After reading and studying the material in this chapter, you should be able to answer the following questions.

1.   How does classical conditioning work? What is a good example of classical conditioning?

2.   How does operant conditioning work? What is a good example of operant conditioning? What factors influence the success of operant conditioning?

3.   What is the distinction between negative reinforcement and punishment?

4.   How does learning take place through observation?

5.   Can young infants learn? In what ways? What is the evidence?

6.   How do basic learning capacities change with age?

7.   What is the general orientation of the information-processing model to cognition? What are the specific components of the model?

8.   How do researchers assess infant memory? What information can infants typically remember? What are the limitations of infants' memory?

9.   What are four major hypotheses about why memory improves with age? Which of these hypotheses is (are) supported by research?

10.   How do problem solving capacities change during childhood?

11.   What developments occur in the information processing abilities of adolescents?

12.   In what ways do memory and cognition change during adulthood? What are the strengths and weaknesses of older adults' abilities? What factors help explain the declines in abilities during older adulthood?

13.   How can memory be improved?

CHAPTER SUMMARY AND GUIDED REVIEW

The following summary provides an overview of the main points contained in this chapter of the text. Fill-in the blanks with terms that appropriately complete the sentence. Scattered throughout the summary are questions in parentheses. These are meant to encourage you to think actively as you are reading and connect this summary to the more detailed information provided in the text. You can answer these questions as you are filling in the blanks or you can complete all the blanks, then go back and reread the entire summary, addressing the questions in order to provide more depth of understanding.

BASIC LEARNING PROCESSES
Classical Conditioning
        Learning is a relatively permanent change in behavior that results from one's

(1) _____. One form of learning is (2) _____, where a stimulus that initially had no effect on an individual comes to elicit a response through its association with a stimulus that already produces the desired response. A stimulus that elicits the desired response without prior learning experiences is the (3) _____ stimulus. A stimulus that produces the desired response only after being associated with a stimulus that always elicits the response is the (4) _____ stimulus. An unlearned response to an unlearned stimulus is the (5) _____ response, while a learned response to a conditioned stimulus is the (6) _____ response. (*Can you provide an example of classical conditioning that is not in the text?*) Research with the classical conditioning paradigm shows that many (7) _____ responses are learned this way. Classically conditioned responses can be unlearned through the same process, called (8) _____.

Operant (Instrumental) Conditioning

Another basic form of learning is operant conditioning, where behaviors or responses become more or less probable depending on their consequences. One possible consequence is (9) _____, where something administered following a behavior strengthens that behavior. Behaviors could also be strengthened by removing something negative following the behavior, a process called (10) _____. (*Can you provide an example of this?*) Decreasing the strength of a behavior is accomplished either by adding something unpleasant following a behavior, which is called (11) _____, or removing something positive, which is (12) _____. [Hint: To remember whether reinforcement or punishment is positive or negative, think of the action being performed. When something is added to the situation, it is positive (reinforcement or punishment) and when something is removed from the situation, it is negative (reinforcement of punishment).] (*Can you describe ways to make the use of punishment effective?*)

Sometimes, a behavior is followed by no consequences, which eventually leads to (13) _____ because the behavior is not being reinforced. Reinforcing a behavior every time it occurs is providing (14) _____ reinforcement. Reinforcing only some instances of a behavior is providing (15) _____ reinforcement, which tends to result in slower extinction if the reinforcements are provided on an (16) _____ schedule. (*Why is this the case?*)

Observational Learning

The third form of learning described in this chapter is observational learning, which results from observing the behavior of other people. Learning a behavior does not necessarily mean an individual will (17) _____ the behavior. (*How did Bandura's bobo doll study illustrate the process of observational learning, in particular, the role of reinforcement in the observational learning process?*) The process of (18) _____ reinforcement means that if the learner observes the model getting reinforced for his or her actions, the learner will be more likely to perform the behavior. (*Can you describe the cognitive processes that are involved in observational learning?*)

Stability and Change in Learning

Research suggests that newborns can learn through classical and operant conditioning, and possibly through observational learning. However, they are limited in their capacities. (*Can you provide evidence of each type of learning in newborns?*) Infants' ability to learn through classical conditioning is limited to a few reflexes and takes many trials. Operant learning is similarly restricted to a few behaviors already familiar to the infant. Changes in observational learning are evidenced by the infant's ability to imitate a response after a delay, a phenomenon called (19) _____. As they get older, infants can also imitate (20) _____ of novel actions. Adults show some changes in learning, requiring additional trials or more time. Otherwise, learning through classical conditioning, operant conditioning, and observation continue across the life span.

THE INFORMATION PROCESSING APPROACH

The three forms of learning just described are part of the behavioral approach to learning. Another approach to learning is the information processing perspective, which uses a (21) _____ analogy to understand learning. A popular information-processing model proposes that information coming into the information-processing system (i.e., the person) is held briefly in a (22) _____. If the person pays attention to this information, it will be moved into (23) _____, also called working memory. Information to be remembered for any length of time must somehow be moved into (24) _____ memory.

In order to remember something, it must first get "into the system" through (25) _____. Then it goes into (26) _____, or the holding of information in long-term memory. When the information is needed, it must be (27) _____ from long-term memory. Retrieval of information by reproducing it without cues uses (28) _____, which is more difficult than indicating whether or not the information has been previously experienced, which uses (29) _____ memory. Between these two forms of retrieval is (30) _____ _____ recall where some sort of hint is given. Using the information-processing system to achieve a goal or make a decision is (31) _____. To be able to do this, the information-processing system includes a number of executive (32) _____ to monitor and plan.

THE INFANT
Early Memory

Assessing infant memory is often done by repeatedly presenting them with a stimulus until they no longer respond to it, a process called (33) _____. (**What is another method to assess infant memory?**) Infants will likely have trouble with retrieval of information unless they are provided with sufficient (34) _____ to aid retrieval. Evidence of pure recall memory comes when infants show (35) _____ _____ imitation and also when they can solve object permanence tasks.

Infantile Amnesia

The lack of memory for events during infancy is called infantile amnesia. Research suggests that children are at least (36) _____ years old before they can remember a significant event. (**What are some of the theories about why we experience infantile amnesia?**)

THE CHILD
Learning and Memory

Although the basic learning processes are present during infancy, learning and memory clearly improve during childhood. There are four main hypotheses about why this improvement occurs.

Do basic capacities change? One possibility is that basic capacities change. For example, some neo-Piagetian theorists propose that working memory space increases during childhood. However, research does not show that total capacity changes, although children do get more efficient at using the space they have as many processes become (37) _____ and require little effort.

Do memory strategies change? Another possibility for the improvement in learning and memory is that memory strategies improve with age. Although young children can deliberately remember when they are highly motivated, their memory strategies are not always very effective. One strategy is to use (38) _____, or repeating the items to be remembered. Another strategy is (39) _____, or classifying items to be remembered into meaningful groups. A third strategy is to use (40) _____, or creating meaningful links between the items to be remembered. Rehearsal typically develops first, followed by use of organization and finally by spontaneous use of elaboration in adolescence. Even when effective memory strategies are used, appropriate (41) _____ strategies must also be employed for successful recall.

Does knowledge about memory change? A third explanation for the improvement in learning and memory is that knowledge about memory and other cognitive processes changes with age. Knowledge of memory and memory processes is called (42) _____ and does improve with age. (*Can you provide evidence that shows growth in this skill?*) However, these improvements are not always found to be strongly associated with increases in memory.

Does knowledge of the world change? A fourth possibility is that increased knowledge of the world in general, or (43) _____, leads to improvements in memory. There is research evidence that children who have an extensive knowledge base in a particular area can outperform adults who are novices in the same area.

Problem Solving

Problem solving capacities also change during childhood. Siegler uses a (44)_____ approach to determine what information children take in and what rules they generate to solve a problem. Siegler's research shows that 3-year-olds guess; that is, they use no strategies. By age 4 or 5, most children are rule governed, but the type of rule used changes with age and children have trouble integrating multiple pieces of information. Even by age 20, only 30% of participants use the correct rule to solve the problem.

THE ADOLESCENT

During adolescence, some new learning and memory strategies, such as elaboration, emerge. Adolescents' use of strategies is more deliberate, selective, and spontaneous than younger children's. Adolescents know more in general, so their (45) _____ expand, and they also show improvements in their understanding of their learning and memory processes, or their (46) _____.

THE ADULT
Developing Expertise

During adulthood, developing expertise in a field facilitates memory and problem solving within this field. (*In what ways can this affect memory and problem solving?*) Expertise, though, is fairly (47) _____ because it does not improve memory in other areas.

Learning, Memory, and Aging

Self-reports suggest that memory declines with age. Declines in memory are slight and usually do not occur until one's 60's or 70's. Also, since much of the research in this area has used (48) _____ designs, the apparent declines could be due to other factors related to cohort differences. Not all adults experience memory problems and not all tasks create memory difficulties for older adults.   Older adults tend to have trouble with (49) _____ tasks because they are slower than younger adults to learn and retrieve information. They also have trouble on tasks that are (50) _____ or have little relevance to them. Tasks requiring rarely used skills and tasks requiring (51) _____ memory rather than recognition memory are also problematic for older adults. Age differences are small on tasks of (52) _____ memory, which occurs unintentionally and without conscious deliberation. Age differences are larger on (53) _____ memory tasks that require deliberate processing.

Possible explanations for the learning and memory declines observed in older adults are basically the same as those considered for young children's performance. Unlike young children, older adults know much about the world, so they do not have deficient (54)_____. Metamemory problems also do not seem to contribute greatly to memory declines in older adults. Older adults do not always spontaneously use effective strategies. They also need to devote more space than younger adults to short-term or (55) _____ memory, which leaves less space to devote to other purposes.

(*What might account for declines in short-term memory capacity?*) It is also possible that the declines in memory observed for older adults compared to younger adults are due to generational or (56)_____ differences. Older adults tend to be less educated and may not be as motivated to perform as younger adults. Overall, the (57) _____ in which a task is performed affects memory and learning performance. When older adults are tested in the laboratory, the context of remembering is usually quite different from the everyday contexts in which they normally learn and remember.

Problem Solving and Aging

Older adults also seem to perform more poorly than young adults on problem solving tasks. On a twenty-questions task, asking (58) _____ questions is most efficient. Older children and young adults use this strategy, but older adults do not unless the task is altered to make it more familiar to them.

REVIEW OF KEY TERMS

Below is a list of terms and concepts from this chapter. Use these to complete the following sentence definitions. You might also want to try writing definitions in your own words and then checking your definitions with those in the text.

classical conditioning
conditioned response (CR)
conditioned stimulus (CS)
constraint-seeking questions
continuous reinforcement
counterconditioning
cued recall memory
deferred imitation
elaboration
encoding
executive control processes
explicit memory
extinction
implicit memory
infantile amnesia
information-processing approach
knowledge base
long-term memory
metacognition
metamemory
method of loci
negative punishment

negative reinforcement
observational learning
operant conditioning
organization (as memory strategy)
partial reinforcement
positive punishment
positive reinforcement
problem solving
recall memory
recognition memory
rehearsal
retrieval
rule assessment approach
sensory register
short-term memory
storage
time out
unconditioned response (UCR)
unconditioned stimulus (UCS)
vicarious reinforcement
working memory

1.   A form of learning in which behaviors or responses become either more or less probable depending on their consequences is called _____.

2.   The memory strategy of _____ involves repeating items to be remembered.

3.   Decreasing the likelihood of future responses by administering something unpleasant is called
      _____.

4.   _____ is memory that occurs unintentionally.

5.   The ability to imitate an action after some delay is called _____.

6.   _____ is the act of getting information out of long-term memory when it is needed.

7.   _____ is a memory strategy that involves classifying items to be remembered into
      meaningful groups.

8.   Memory that requires individuals to indicate whether they have previously experienced a
      stimulus is _____.

9.   _____ is a learned response to a conditioned stimulus.

10.   To increase the likelihood of a behavior in the future, we could use _____ by
      administering a pleasant stimulus following the behavior.

11.   _____ is a memory store that temporarily stores a limited amount of information and
      allows active use of this information.

12.   We can decrease the likelihood of future responding with _____ or removing
      something pleasant from the situation.

13.   The memory strategy of _____ involves creating meaningful links between the items
      to be remembered.

14.   Reinforcing a behavior every time it occurs is _____.

15.   _____ is a memory store that is relatively permanent and holds our knowledge of the
      world and our past experiences.

16.   Our knowledge of our own memory and memory processes is called _____.

17.   Creating a mental map of space and using this image as a memory device is the
      _____.

18.   _____ is a form of learning in which a stimulus that initially had no effect on an
      individual comes to elicit a response through its association with a stimulus that already
      produces the desired response.

19.   _____ is the process of getting information into the information-processing system,
      and processing it.

20.   Applying classical conditioning principles to extinguish a conditioned response is using
      _____.

21.   _____ is a type of memory that requires individuals to reproduce a previously
      encountered stimulus without cues.

22. In classical conditioning, a stimulus that elicits the desired response without learning experiences is the _____.

23. Our lack of memory for the first few years of life is called _____.

24. In _____, a behavior is eliminated by removing its reinforcing consequences.

25. Holding information in long-term memory is referred to as _____.

26. Using the information-processing system to achieve a goal or make a decision is known as _____.

27. A person's _____ is their knowledge of a content area.

28. _____ are the information processing tools that plan and monitor problem solving and decision making.

29. In classical conditioning, the _____ produces the desired response only after it is associated with a stimulus that always elicits the response.

30. _____ results from observing the behavior of other people.

31. _____ memory is intentional and deliberate.

32. In the process of _____, children are influenced by observing another person receive reinforcement.

33. The _____ approach to cognition uses a computer analogy and emphasizes mental processes involved in attention, perception, memory, and decision making.

34. _____ refers to knowledge about the mind and cognitive processes that might be used.

35. _____ is a problem solving strategy that rules out several possible solutions rather than just one.

36. With _____, only some instances of a behavior are rewarded.

37. The _____ holds a very brief, but literal image or record of stimuli.

38. Any stimulus that increases the likelihood of a behavior occurring in the future when it is removed following the behavior is _____.

39. In classical conditioning, an unlearned response to an unconditioned stimulus is the _____.

40. The _____ is an analysis of problem solving ability that determines what information is encoded and what rules are generated by the problem solver.

41.   Providing a hint to facilitate retrieval is _____.

42.   Many parents use _____ to discipline their children by removing them from a situation in which their misbehavior is reinforced.

43.   Short-term memory is also referred to as _____.

MULTIPLE CHOICE SELF TEST

For each multiple choice question, read all alternatives and then select the best answer.

1.   You turn on the can opener to open the dog's food and the dog comes running into the room. In this example, food is the _____; the sound of the can opener is the _____; and running into the room in response to the sound is the _____.
   a.   unconditioned stimulus; conditioned stimulus; unconditioned response
   b.   conditioned stimulus; unconditioned stimulus; conditioned response
   c.   unconditioned stimulus; conditioned stimulus; conditioned response
   d.   conditioned stimulus; conditioned response; unconditioned response

2.   A stimulus can serve as reinforcement or as punishment depending on whether it
   a.   is pleasurable or not (negative) for the subject receiving it
   b.   increases or decreases the frequency of the behavior it follows
   c.   occurs before or after the behavior in question
   d.   is administered or taken away from the person

3.   Which of the following is an example of negative reinforcement?
   a.   Giving a child dessert as a reward for eating his/her vegetables at dinner
   b.   Paying a child for each "A" received on his or her report card
   c.   A parent stops nagging a child when the child finally cleans his or her room
   d.   Cutting a child's television viewing by 30 minutes each time the child misbehaves

4.   Which of the following is <u>necessary</u> in order to learn through observation?
   a.   Observing the model get a reward or punishment for his/her actions
   b.   Being provided with an opportunity to imitate the model's actions immediately after the observation
   c.   Hearing the model describe the consequences of his/her actions
   d.   Observing and remembering the model's actions

5.   Partial reinforcement
   a.   is the best way to initially teach a child an unfamiliar behavior
   b.   is a good way to maintain behaviors over a long period of time
   c.   allows a child to accurately predict when a behavior will be reinforced
   d.   leads to extinction of most responses

6. In order to effectively use punishment as a deterrent to bad behavior a parent should
   a. delay punishment until both parents can address the behavior together with the child
   b. speak quietly so the child does not feel intimidated
   c. explain the inappropriateness of the behavior and the reasons for punishment
   d. punish the behavior when it is extreme but not necessarily punish when the behavior is mild or moderate

7. Which of the following is NOT true regarding infants' abilities to learn?
   a. Infants need many trials in order to learn simple behaviors.
   b. Infants can be conditioned as long as the responses are already familiar to them.
   c. Even newborns can be conditioned.
   d. The easiest way for young infants to learn is through observation.

8. Research on imitation suggests that
   a. young infants can show imitation but this may be a reflex-like action
   b. infants of all ages reliably show imitation
   c. young infants reliably imitate novel acts but older infants have lost this ability
   d. imitation is not evident at all until about 8-12 months of age

9. Taking an essay exam is an example of _____, while taking a multiple choice exam uses _____ memory.
   a. long term memory; short term
   b. recall; reconstruction
   c. recall; recognition
   d. recognition; long term memory

10. Habituation occurs when an infant
    a. stops responding to a repeatedly presented stimulus
    b. is conditioned to respond to a familiar stimulus
    c. learns to respond to a desired stimulus
    d. turns in the direction of a novel stimulus

11. Memory strategies tend to develop in order, with _____ appearing first, followed by _____, and then _____.
    a. organization; elaboration; rehearsal
    b. organization; rehearsal; elaboration
    c. rehearsal; elaboration; organization
    d. rehearsal; organization; elaboration

12. Siegler's research on children's use of rules on the balance beam problem shows that
    a. most children master the correct rule by age 8
    b. even the youngest children, age 3, use logical rules to solve the problem
    c. children master a single rule, applying it to all tasks, before moving on to another rule
    d. children progress from guessing to trying several rules to selection of correct rules

13. One difference between the memory strategy use of preadolescents and adolescents is that adolescents
    a. randomly select a strategy
    b. use fewer strategies to remember important information
    c. remember more irrelevant information than younger children
    d. are better able to distinguish the more relevant points from the irrelevant points

14. Which of the following statements accurately describes memory performance of adults?
    a. Memory systematically declines throughout adulthood.
    b. Memory declines may occur after age 60 and are typically slight.
    c. Memory does not change from adolescence through middle adulthood, but after this, memory declines quite rapidly.
    d. Older adults experience no memory declines because they use more memory strategies than younger adults.

15. Research on expertise shows that
    a. experts do not know any more than nonexperts but are able to organize their knowledge more effectively
    b. it depends on domain-specific knowledge and strategies
    c. experts spend more time thinking through all possible options on a problem before selecting the correct one
    d. expertise generalizes from one area to another, so experts tend to be good on multiple tasks

REVIEW CLASSICAL AND OPERANT CONDITIONING PRINCIPLES

This exercise will help ensure that you understand the basic principles of classical and operant conditioning.

Operant Conditioning
What are the consequences of administering or withdrawing positive and negative stimuli? Write in the label and provide an example. Use Figure 8.2 in the text to check your answers.

	Positive Stimulus	Negative Stimulus
Administered		
Withdrawn		

Classical Conditioning
Suppose an infant likes to eat applesauce, but one day there is a very noxious odor present when the baby is fed the applesauce, which makes her nauseous. The next time she is offered applesauce, she refuses to have anything to do with it. Using the diagram below, indicate how classical conditioning would account for the infant's behavior. You should note the stimuli and responses from the example, as well

as the label of these (e.g., unconditioned or conditioned stimulus/response). Use Figure 8.1 in the text to check yourself.

Preconditioning Phase

_____   →→→→   _____
Neutral Stimulus   ???

_____   →→→→   _____
Unconditioned Stimulus   ???

Conditioning Phase

_____
Neutral Stimulus

_____   →→→→   _____
Unconditioned Stimulus   ???

Postconditioning Phase

_____   →→→→   _____
????   ???

_____   →→→→   _____
Unconditioned Stimulus   ???

PEOPLE AND THEIR IDEAS

We have reviewed lots of ideas and concepts from this chapter. Now consider the <u>people</u> who contributed many of these ideas. Use the matching exercise below to review the contributions of some of the more influential people discussed in this chapter. Write the appropriate letter next to the person's name.

1.   Albert Bandura   _____
2.   Robert Siegler   _____
3.   B. F. Skinner   _____
4.   John Watson and Rosalie Raynor   _____

a.   Showed the powerful effects of a behavior's consequences on future behavior.
b.   Demonstrated that infant's emotional responses could be classically conditioned.
c.   Demonstrated that learning could occur in the absence of any direct consequences to the learner.

d.   Used an information processing analysis to document children's use of rules on a problem solving task.

APPLICATION QUESTIONS

By answering the following questions, you will strengthen your understanding of the material in this chapter. These questions require higher level thinking skills such as integration and application of concepts. To get you started, there is a sample answer or outline provided for the first question. This illustrates one possibility, but there are other answers you could provide that might be just as good. For the other questions, you can check yourself by referring to the text, or by asking a peer or your instructor to review your answer.

1.   Use several different learning principles to describe ways you might reduce a child's temper tantrums. [Sample answer provided.]

2.   How could you use learning principles to change a child's television viewing habits? [Hint: Review the sections in the chapter on basic learning processes as well as the sample answer for application question one.]

3.   What practical suggestions regarding the memory and problem solving skills of older adults would be helpful to someone who works with older adults?
[Hint: Review the sections in the text on "The Adult," particularly Explaining Declines in Old Age, and the Application section on Improving Memory.]

4.   In what ways are the memory, learning, and problem solving skills of young children and older adults similar?
[Hint: Review the sections on "The Child" and "The Adult" and consider the four hypotheses about how learning and memory change with age.]

5.   As children's eyewitness testimony in court proceedings has increased, we have seen more research on children's reliability as witnesses. Based on what you know about memory development from this chapter, what conclusions and suggestions can you make regarding use of children as witnesses?
[Hint: Review the section on "The Child," with attention to strengths and weaknesses of children's memory.]

ANSWERS

Chapter Summary and Guided Review (Fill-in the blank)

1.	experience	9.	positive reinforcement
2.	classical conditioning	10.	negative reinforcement
3.	unconditioned	11.	positive punishment
4.	conditioned	12.	negative punishment
5.	unconditioned	13.	extinction
6.	conditioned	14.	continuous
7.	emotional	15.	partial
8.	counterconditioning	16.	unpredictable

17.	perform	38.	rehearsal
18.	vicarious	39.	organization
19.	deferred imitation	40.	elaboration
20.	sequences	41.	retrieval
21.	computer	42.	metamemory
22.	sensory register	43.	knowledge base
23.	short-term	44.	rule assessment
24.	long-term	45.	knowledge bases
25.	encoding	46.	metacognition
26.	storage	47.	domain specific
27.	retrieved	48.	cross-sectional
28.	recall	49.	timed
29.	recognition	50.	unfamiliar
30.	cued	51.	recall
31.	problem solving	52.	implicit
32.	control processes	53.	explicit
33.	habituation	54.	knowledge bases
34.	cues	55.	working
35.	deferred	56.	cohort
36.	two	57.	context
37.	automatized	58.	constraint-seeking

Review of Key Terms

1.	operant conditioning	23.	infantile amnesia
2.	rehearsal	24.	extinction
3.	positive punishment	25.	storage
4.	implicit memory	26.	problem solving
5.	deferred imitation	27.	knowledge base
6.	retrieval	28.	executive control processes
7.	organization	29.	conditioned stimulus (CS)
8.	recognition memory	30.	observational learning
9.	conditioned response (CR)	31.	explicit
10.	positive reinforcement	32.	vicarious reinforcement
11.	short-term memory	33.	information-processing
12.	negative punishment	34.	metacognition
13.	elaboration	35.	constraint-seeking questions
14.	continuous reinforcement	36.	partial reinforcement
15.	long-term memory	37.	sensory register
16.	metamemory	38.	negative reinforcement
17.	method of loci	39.	unconditioned response (UCR)
18.	classical conditioning	40.	rule assessment approach
19.	encoding	41.	cued recall memory
20.	counterconditioning	42.	time out
21.	recall memory	43.	working memory
22.	unconditioned stimulus (UCS)		

1.	C	6.	C	11.	D
2.	B	7.	D	12.	D
3.	C	8.	A	13.	D
4.	D	9.	C	14.	B
5.	B	10.	A	15.	B

People and Their Ideas

1.	C	3.	A
2.	D	4.	B

Application Questions:

1.   *Children could be reinforced when they do not have a temper tantrum. For example, parents could wait until the child is being good and give him/her a hug and some praise, which would be positive reinforcement. Or they could tell the child that because he/she had been very good, he/she does not have to take out the trash, a dislike chore, which would be using negative reinforcement. Once a temper tantrum occurs, a parent could try ignoring it, hoping that it will be extinguished through lack of reinforcement (i.e, the parent doesn't give the child any rewarding attention for the tantrum). If this doesn't work, a parent might have to use punishment. They could do this by spanking or yelling at the child, which is positive punishment, or they could take away something the child really likes, such as his or her favorite TV show, which would be negative punishment.*

CHAPTER NINE

INTELLIGENCE AND CREATIVITY

OVERVIEW

Much of the research and theory in this chapter focuses on intelligence. The discussion begins by considering the meaning of intelligence: is it one ability or many? If it consists of multiple abilities, what are these? Next, the most common tests for measuring IQ are discussed, including the Stanford-Binet and Wechsler scales. The next sections each examine a major age group--infants, children, adolescents, and adults--and discuss developmental changes in intelligence. In particular, the stability and continuity of IQ scores are considered, as are the potential uses of IQ scores.

Genetic and environmental factors that influence IQ scores are discussed in this chapter. Recall that genetic influences on intelligence were discussed earlier in the text (Chapter 3 on Genetics), and it might be useful for you to review the evidence for genetic contributions that was presented in the earlier chapter. The section in this chapter focuses on environmental factors, including the home, social class, and culture.

A discussion of the extremes of intelligence--mental retardation and giftedness--is also included in this chapter. Finally, creativity is discussed, including its definition and measurement, and whether or not we can identify developmental changes in creativity.

LEARNING OBJECTIVES

After reading and studying the material in this chapter, you should be able to answer the following questions.

1.   How do psychometric theorists define intelligence?

2.   What is the difference between fluid and crystallized intelligence?

3.   How does Gardner define intelligence?

4.   What is Sternberg's triarchic theory of intelligence?

5.   How do the Stanford-Binet and Wechsler intelligence tests compare and contrast to one another?

6.   What is the dynamic assessment approach to intelligence testing?

7.   How is infant intelligence measured? To what extent is infant intelligence related to later intelligence?

8.   Are IQ scores stable during childhood? What factors contribute to gains and losses in IQ scores?

9.   How well do IQ scores predict school achievement? To what extent is IQ related to occupational success?

10.   How do IQ and mental abilities change with age?

11.   What factors predict declines in intellectual abilities in older adults?

12.   To what extent does wisdom exist in older adults?

13.   What evidence shows genetic influence on IQ scores? What other factors influence IQ scores?

14.   How are mental retardation and giftedness defined? What are the outcomes for individuals who are mental retarded or gifted?

15.   What is creativity? How does it change across the life span?

16.   How can intellectual performance be improved across the life span?

CHAPTER SUMMARY AND GUIDED REVIEW

The following summary provides an overview of the main points contained in this chapter of the text. Fill-in the blanks with terms that appropriately complete the sentence. Scattered throughout the summary are questions in parentheses. These are meant to encourage you to think actively as you are reading and connect this summary to the more detailed information provided in the text. You can answer these questions as you are filling in the blanks or you can complete all the blanks, then go back and reread the entire summary, addressing the questions in order to provide more depth of understanding.

WHAT IS INTELLIGENCE

The Psychometric Approach

The psychometric approach views intelligence as a trait or set of traits that vary among people and can be measured. A statistical procedure called (1) _____ has been used by psychometricians to identify clusters of tests or test items that are strongly related to one another, but unrelated to other items. Spearman used factor analysis to study intelligence and concluded that a (2) _____ factor contributed to performance on many different tasks. Thurstone identified seven distinct (3) _____ mental abilities, and Guilford proposed that intelligence consists of as many as 120 different mental abilities. Guilford's (4) _____ model focused on the contents, operations, and products of intelligence. Cattell and Horn propose that intelligence consists of two major dimensions. The ability to solve novel problems is (5) _____ intelligence and the ability to use knowledge acquired through experiences is (6) _____ intelligence.

Gardner's Theory of Multiple Intelligence

More recently, Gardner proposed that there are multiple intelligences, including at least seven distinct abilities. (***Can you give examples or list the different abilities?***) Evidence that someone can be good in one ability but poor in another comes from individuals with the (7) _____.

Sternberg's Triarchic Theory

Sternberg's triarchic theory emphasizes three aspects of intelligent behavior. According to this model, intelligent behavior depends on the (8) _____ in which it is displayed and so can be expected to vary from one culture or subculture to another. Intelligent behavior is also affected by the (9) _____ that one has with a situation or task. The intelligent response to a task the first time it is encountered may differ from what is considered intelligent after many encounters with the same task. The increased efficiency that comes with familiarity and practice with a task reflects (10) _____. Administering an intelligence test to two groups of people that has items familiar to one group but not to the other introduces (11) _____ and makes it unfair to compare performances of the two groups. The third aspect of Sternberg's triarchic model includes the information-processing (12) _____, or strategies.

HOW IS INTELLIGENCE MEASURED?

The Stanford-Binet Test

Binet and Simon designed the first intelligence test, assessing intelligence as a child's (13) _____ from the level of age-graded problems that a child could solve. The revised version of this original test, the Stanford-Binet, calculates a child's intelligence quotient or IQ by comparing the child's mental age on the test to his/her chronological age. The standards of typical performance or (14) _____ are based on a large and representative sample of people from different backgrounds.

Intelligence and Creativity

The Wechsler Scales

The Wechsler Scales of intelligence separate IQ into a verbal and a (15) _____ component. (*Why might it be helpful to consider these two components separately?*)

The Distribution of IQ Scores

If a large number of IQ scores are plotted on a graph, they form a (16) _____, which shows that more people score around the mean of 100 and fewer people score at the extremes of the curve.

Intelligence Testing Today

A new approach to assessing intelligence is (17) _____, which attempts to determine how well children learn new material with instruction. Feuerstein's Learning Potential Assessment Device focuses on children's (18) _____ to learn rather than what they have already learned. (*Can you explain how administration of Feuerstein's test is different from the Stanford-Binet or Wechsler?*) One of the concerns with traditional IQ tests is that they measure a person's performance at a particular point in time, and do not measure the person's underlying (19) _____.

THE INFANT
Developmental Quotients

Infant intelligence is typically measured with the (20) _____ Scales of Infant Development. This test includes a motor scale and a mental scale, which are used to assign a (21) _____. A third component of the test is an infant behavioral record. Bayley scores can be used to chart developmental progress and low scores may indicate mental retardation.

Infant Intelligence and Later Intelligence

Scores on the Bayley do not accurately predict later IQ, possibly because the infant tests and IQ tests measure qualitatively different abilities. Another possibility is that intelligence during infancy is highly influenced by universal (22) _____ processes. Starting around the age of two, these forces lessen and individual differences become more apparent. Recent research suggests that later IQ may be better predicted by performance on some measures of infant (23) _____, such as speed of habituation and preference for novelty. (*Why might this be a better predictor?*)

THE CHILD
How Stable are IQ Scores during Childhood?

Starting at age 4, there is a fairly strong relationship between IQ scores obtained at different times throughout childhood. However, although group scores are fairly stable, scores of individual children can fluctuate quite substantially. (*What do these findings suggest?*)

Causes of Gain and Loss

One reason for fluctuating IQ scores is an unstable environment. The (24) _____ hypothesis suggests that intellectual development of children from impoverished environments is diminished and this effect builds over time so that children's intelligence actually seems to decline. (*Is there any research support for this hypothesis?*)

THE ADOLESCENT
Continuity between Childhood and Adulthood

Intelligence continues to grow during early adolescence, but levels off in late adolescence. This may be related to basic brain changes. Individual performance on IQ tests tends to be more stable at this age and predicts adult IQ performance quite well.

IQ and School Achievement

IQ scores are often used to predict school achievement and they are fairly accurate in doing this. Prediction is more accurate for high school grades than for college grades. (*Why is this the case?*)

THE ADULT
IQ and Occupational Success

In adults, there is a relationship between IQ scores and occupational status. Specifically, the more prestigious jobs are filled with people who, overall, have higher IQs than people in less prestigious jobs. IQ scores are also related to measures of actual job performance.

Change in IQ with Age

Early cross-sectional research on intelligence across the life span indicated that IQ scores steadily decreased from about age 20 on. However, subsequent (25) _____ research indicates that IQ does not decline across early and middle adulthood, and only modest declines in IQ occur in old age. One major factor contributing to these different findings is (26) _____ or generational effects. Sequential studies of changes in intelligence show that some gains in intelligence are made throughout middle adulthood, and declines typically occur only late in life. (*Do you remember how sequential designs eliminate the weaknesses inherent to cross-sectional and longitudinal designs?*) This research also indicates that (27) _____ intelligence declines earlier and more sharply than (28) _____ intelligence. On the Wechsler adult test, IQ scores on the (29) _____ scale decline earlier than IQ scores on the (30) _____ scale. In addition, performance on (31) _____ tests declines in old age and may reflect a general slowing of the adult's information processing ability. However, declines in intellectual performance are not universal.

Predictors of Decline

For individuals who do experience a decline in intellectual performance, poor (32) _____ is often the culprit. People tend to experience a (33) _____ a few years before they die. Another factor contributing to declining intellectual performance is lack of a (34) _____ lifestyle.

Potential for Wisdom

A person who has exceptional insight about life is often considered to have wisdom. Research indicates that (35) _____ is more relevant than age to the development of wisdom. (*What qualities are thought to indicate wisdom?*) In general, wisdom is not common among older adults.

FACTORS THAT INFLUENCE IQ SCORES
Genes

Differences in IQ scores across the life span are influenced by genetic factors, as evidenced by the results of twin studies and adoption studies. (*What pattern of results from these studies would demonstrate a genetic influence on IQ scores?*)

Home Environment

Research shows that at least ten environmental factors are associated with low IQ scores. These include being a member of a minority group and receiving little positive affection from one's mother. (*What are other risk factors for low IQ?*) An instrument for measuring the amount and type of intellectual stimulation in a child's home is the (36) _____. Scores on this inventory predict children's cognitive functioning fairly well. In particular, (37) _____ involvement with the child, provision of appropriate (38) _____ materials, and opportunities for various types of stimulation were strongly related to the child's cognitive functioning. Research suggests that the best predictor of a child's IQ at age two is (39) _____. Later, quality of home environment significantly predicts IQ.

Social Class Differences

IQ scores are affected by the socioeconomic status of the child's family, such that children who come from disadvantaged backgrounds score lower than children from middle-class homes. According to the (40) _____, average IQ scores have increased around the world. (***What factors might account for this phenomenon?***)

Racial and Ethnic Differences

A great deal of controversy has surrounded the finding that children of different racial and ethnic backgrounds score lower on IQ tests than white Anglo-American children. There are several possible reasons for this. One is (41) _____ in testing because the tests are more appropriate for children from white, middle-class backgrounds. In an attempt to eliminate or reduce this possibility, (42) _____ IQ tests have been developed. Differences between racial and ethnic groups are still apparent on these tests.

Another possibility is that minority children are not as highly (43) _____ in testing situations as white, middle-class children. Related to this, research shows that African American children perform poorly when they believe that tests may be measuring qualities associated with negative stereotypes of African Americans.

A third possibility is that there are (44) _____ differences between ethnic and racial groups that contribute to observed differences on IQ tests. There are, in fact, genetic differences (45) _____ groups, but these differences do not translate into differences (46) _____ groups.

A fourth explanation for average group differences is environmental variation. Support for this explanation comes from the finding that the IQ scores of black children increase when these children are adopted into white, middle-class homes. This suggests that children, regardless of their racial background, do better when they grow up in intellectually (47) _____ environments, with responsive parents and exposure to the culture of the test.

THE EXTREMES OF INTELLIGENCE
Mental Retardation

Individuals who are diagnosed with mental retardation show below average intellectual functioning and impairments in (48) _____. (***What are the different levels of mental retardation?***) Retardation that is due to some identifiable biological cause is termed (49) _____ retardation and usually accounts for the more severe and profound cases of retardation. (***What are examples of this type of mental retardation?***) Retardation that is due to a combination of low genetic potential and poor environment is (50) _____ retardation and usually results in mild retardation.

Giftedness

Individuals who have high IQ scores or show special abilities are considered gifted. Terman's longitudinal of gifted children dispelled a number of myths about gifted individuals. In short, gifted individuals are not the social misfits or weaklings that many people believed them to be. As adults, children from Terman's study were generally healthy, happy, and productive.

CREATIVITY AND SPECIAL TALENTS

What is Creativity?

Individuals who can produce novel responses or works are considered to be high in creativity. This involves (51) _____ thinking, or the ability to come up with a variety of ideas or solutions to a problem. Creativity is often measured by the total number of different ideas that one can generate in response to a problem, or (52) _____. IQ tests typically measure (53) _____ thinking, which involves coming up with the one "correct" answer to a problem.

Creativity in Childhood and Adolescence

Children who are creative tend to show more freedom, originality, humor, violence, and playfulness, and engage in more pretend play than children who are not creative. Creativity seems to be related to a child's (54) _____. Performance on tests of creativity tends to increase throughout childhood and adolescence. Individuals who have creative talent are likely to achieve accomplishments if they are highly (55) _____ and grow up in a nurturing environment.

Creative Achievement in Adulthood

Creative output seems to increase throughout early adulthood and declines only in older adulthood. This pattern varies, though, depending on the field of work. According to one theory, people may have a certain limit on their creative potential. Creativity involves generating the ideas, or (56) _____, and executing the ideas to produce creative output, which is (57) _____. Individuals may generate ideas at different rates, accounting for differences in creativity across different fields as well as differences related to age.

APPLICATIONS: BOOSTING INTELLECTUAL PERFORMANCE ACROSS THE LIFE SPAN

Early Intervention for Preschool Children

One of the best known early intervention programs is (58) _____. Although these programs produced initial gains in IQ, the gains were short-lived. (***What are some of the long-term benefits of early intervention programs?***)

Enrichment for Low-IQ Adolescents

According to Feuerstein, low IQ adolescents are not picking up as much from their experiences as other learners. The solution it to provide a (59) _____ who will structure and interpret the environment for them while teaching them cognitive strategies to do well.

IQ Training for Aging Adults

Research with older adults shows that training can recapture lost skills or improve current skills.

REVIEW OF KEY TERMS

Below is a list of terms and concepts from this chapter. Use these to complete the following sentence definitions. You might also want to try writing definitions in your own words and then checking your definitions with those in the text.

automatization	cumulative-deficit hypothesis
convergent thinking	developmental quotient (DQ)
creativity	divergent thinking
crystallized intelligence	dynamic assessment
cultural-familial retardation	factor analysis
culture bias	fluid intelligence

Flynn effect
giftedness
HOME inventory
ideational fluency
intelligence quotient (IQ)
mental age (MA)
mental retardation
normal distribution

organic retardation
psychometric approach
savant syndrome
structure-of-intellect model
terminal drop
test norms
triarchic theory of intelligence
wisdom

1.   The increase in average IQ scores that has occurred over the course of the 20th century is termed the _____.

2.   _____ allows us to use our minds to solve novel problems.

3.   _____ is retardation that is caused be some combination of low genetic potential and a poor environment

4.   The _____ provides an index of an infant's performance on developmental tasks relative to other infants the same age.

5.   The rapid decline in intellectual abilities that often occurs within a few years before dying is called the _____.

6.   The _____ is a theoretical perspective that views intelligence as a trait or set of traits on which people differ and these differences can be measured.

7.   Intelligence tests typically measure _____ , or thinking that produces a single answer to question or problem.

8.   _____ is the ability to use knowledge acquired through specific learning and life experiences.

9.   The ability to produce novel responses or words is referred to as _____ .

10.   The _____ proposes that impoverished environments inhibit intellectual growth, and these negative effects accumulate over time.

11.   On an intelligence test, the _____ is level of age-graded problems that a child can solve.

12.   Sternberg's _____ is an information-processing theory that emphasizes the context, experience, and information-processing components of intelligent behavior.

13.   _____ are standards of typical performance on a test as reflected by average scores and the range of scores around the average.

14.   Creativity tests often measure _____, the type of thinking that produces a variety of solutions to a problem when there is no one right answer.

15. _____ refers to the total number of different ideas that one can generate when asked to think of all the possible solutions to a problem or question.

16. The process of _____ refers to the increased efficiency of information-processing that comes with familiarity and practice.

17. People with _____ either have high IQ scores or show special abilities in areas valued by society.

18. Retardation that is due to some identifiable biological cause associated with hereditary factors, diseases, or injuries is called _____.

19. _____ is a statistical procedure used to identify clusters of tests or test items that are related to one another but are unrelated to other items.

20. An index of a person's performance on an intelligence test relative to their chronological age is a(n) _____.

21. _____ is the notion that IQ tests favor children from certain cultural backgrounds, namely white middle-class backgrounds.

22. Guilford's _____ proposes that intelligence consists of as many as 120 different intellectual abilities.

23. A person who has an extraordinary talent but who is otherwise mentally retarded is diagnosed with _____.

24. Individuals with _____ perform significantly below average on intelligence tests and show deficits in adaptive behavior skills during the developmental period.

25. The _____ is an instrument for measuring the amount and type of intellectual stimulation in a child's home environment.

26. _____ is a technique that evaluates how well children learn new material with instruction.

27. Some older adults are believed to show _____, or sound judgment and advice about important life issues.

28. The _____ is a bell-shaped distribution with most scores falling close to the average score.

For each multiple choice question, read all alternatives and then select the best answer.

1.   Which of the following is an example of crystallized intelligence?
      a.   remembering unrelated word pairs (e.g., dog-couch)
      b.   solving verbal analogies
      c.   realizing the relationship between geometric figures
      d.   solving word comprehension problems (e.g, what does "participate" mean?)

2.   The _____ emphasizes the importance of context, experience and information-processing components in defining intelligent behavior.
      a.   triarchic theory of intelligence
      b.   psychometric approach to intelligence
      c.   factor analysis approach
      d.   structure-of-intellect model

3.   Sternberg's contextual component of intelligence suggests that intelligence
      a.   depends on expectations of particular cultures
      b.   is consistent across different contexts
      c.   varies with the amount of experience a person has
      d.   consists of general and specific mental abilities

4.   If someone achieves a score of 100 on the Stanford-Binet intelligence test, it means that this person
      a.   scored higher than approximately 68% of the population
      b.   is somewhat below average in intelligence
      c.   has the same chronological (CA) and mental age (MA) levels
      d.   could answer all the questions appropriate for 10-year-olds

5.   The Bayley Scale of Infant Development is a useful indicator of
      a.   childhood intelligence
      b.   whether or not the child is gifted
      c.   a child's developmental progress through major milestones
      d.   problem solving abilities that the child possesses

6.   Feuerstein's Learning Potential Assessment Device measures
      a.   what children have learned
      b.   infant intelligence
      c.   children's abilities to learn by observing an adult solve the task
      d.   children's potential to learn new things with minimal guidance

7.   Correlations between scores on infant intelligence tests and scores on later intelligence tests show that
      a.   infants who score high typically score high as children and adolescents
      b.   infant intelligence scores can predict later intelligence for those who score around the mean of 100
      c.   there is little relationship between infant intelligence and later intelligence
      d.   infant intelligence scores can predict childhood intelligence but not adult intelligence

8.   Correlations of IQ measured during early and middle childhood with IQ measured during adolescence and young adulthood indicate that for individuals, IQ scores
a.   are quite stable
b.   can fluctuate quite a bit
c.   generally increase with age
d.   generally decrease with age

9.   The cumulative-deficit hypothesis suggests that
a.   lack of intellectual stimulation produces an overall deficit in intelligence that is stable over time
b.   lack of intellectual stimulation depresses intellectual growth more and more over time
c.   lack of intellectual stimulation early in life is less damaging than lack of intellectual stimulation later in life
d.   parents with low IQ scores will have children with low IQ scores

10.   The relationship between IQ and occupational status indicates that
a.   IQ scores are more likely to predict job preference than job performance
b.   people with high IQ scores do not work in low status occupations
c.   people with high IQ scores are more likely to work in high status occupations than people with low IQ scores
d.   there is no relationship between these two factors

11.   Which of the following describes how intellectual abilities change with age?
a.   Overall, intellectual abilities decline significantly with age.
b.   Crystallized intelligence declines with age more than fluid intelligence.
c.   Fluid intelligence declines with age more than crystallized intelligence.
d.   No decline in intelligence occurs with age.

12.   Declines in intellectual performance among older adults may occur because of all of the following EXCEPT:
a.   unstimulating life styles
b.   slower response times
c.   poor health
d.   lack of sufficient knowledge base

13.   Research on ethnic and racial differences in IQ scores shows that differences
a.   do not really exist
b.   result from genetic differences between racial groups
c.   can be reduced with the appropriate environmental intervention
d.   do exist but cannot be reduced or eliminated

14.   Mental retardation is defined by:
a.   deficits in intelligence and difficulties with adaptive behavior, both evidenced during the developmental period
b.   abnormal brain development
c.   inability to function at grade-level in school
d.   low scores on standardized intelligence tests that become increasingly poor over time

15.   With respect to creativity in adulthood,
    a.   creative endeavors decrease throughout adulthood
    b.   creative endeavors increase in young adulthood and then usually peak and remain steady
            in middle adulthood
    c.   creative endeavors are at their peak during college years and early adulthood
    d.   creative endeavors decline significantly for older adults in all fields

PEOPLE AND THEIR IDEAS

We have reviewed lots of ideas and concepts from this chapter. Now consider the <u>people</u> who
contributed many of these ideas. Use the matching exercise below to review the contributions of some of
the more influential people discussed in this chapter. Write the appropriate letter next to the person's
name.

1.   Nancy Bayley   _____
2.   Alfred Binet   _____
3.   Raymond Cattell and John Horn   _____
4.   Reuven Feuerstein   _____
5.   Howard Gardner   _____
6.   J. P. Guilford   _____
7.   Robert Sternberg   _____
8.   Lewis Terman   _____
9.   David Wechsler   _____

a.   Constructed the first modern intelligence test.
b.   Developed a theory of intelligence that emphasizes three elements of intelligent behavior:
        context, experience, and information-processing skills.
c.   Proposed two broad aspects of intelligence: fluid intelligence and crystallized intelligence
d.   Proposed that intelligence consisted of as many as 180 different abilities, organized by
        contents, operations, and products.
e.   Developed a theory of intelligence focused on the ways in which people are smart, rather
        than on how smart they are. The theory proposes seven distinct intellectual abilities.
f.   Constructed intelligence tests that provide verbal and performance scores along with a full-scale
        IQ score.
g.   Designed a test to assess an infant's development relative to other infants of the same age.
h.   Developed a test that assesses what children <u>can</u> learn rather than what they have learned.
i.   Conducted longitudinal research with gifted children, dispelling many common myths about
        giftedness.

APPLICATION QUESTIONS

By answering the following questions, you will strengthen your understanding of the material in this
chapter. These questions require higher level thinking skills such as integration and application of
concepts. To get you started, there is a sample answer or outline provided for the first question. This
illustrates one possibility, but there are other answers you could provide that might be just as good. For
the other questions, you can check yourself by referring to the text, or by asking a peer or your instructor
to review your answer.

1.	In order to make the most accurate prediction about later IQ based on <u>infant</u> measures, what information or test would you want to have access to? Justify your answer.
	[Sample answer provided.]

2.	Discuss evidence that supports the conclusion that IQ scores are influenced by genetic factors. Discuss evidence that supports the conclusion that IQ scores are influenced by environmental factors.
	[Hint: Review the section in this chapter on "Factors that influence IQ scores." Also go back and review the section in Chapter Three on "Intellectual Abilities," which describes data that support genetic influences on intelligence.]

3.	It has been noted that there may be culture bias in intelligence testing, resulting in certain groups of people scoring lower or higher than other groups of people. Another finding regarding intelligence tests is that they are relatively accurate at predicting academic success and job performance. What conclusions can be logically drawn from these two seemingly disparate findings?
	[Hint: You need to integrate your understanding of these two pieces of information. Review the sections of the chapter on "IQ and school achievement," "IQ and occupational success," and "Culture bias." Then consider how you could synthesize these findings to arrive at a logical conclusion.]

ANSWERS

Chapter Summary and Guided Review (Fill-in the blank)

1.	factor analysis	24.	cumulative-deficit
2.	general	25.	longitudinal
3.	primary	26.	cohort
4.	structure-of-intellect	27.	fluid
5.	fluid	28.	crystallized
6.	crystallized	29.	performance
7.	savant syndrome	30.	verbal
8.	context	31.	timed
9.	experience	32.	health
10.	automatization	33.	terminal drop
11.	culture bias	34.	stimulating
12.	components	35.	expertise
13.	mental age	36.	HOME inventory
14.	test norms	37.	parental
15.	performance	38.	play
16.	normal distribution	39.	mother's IQ
17.	dynamic assessment	40.	Flynn effect
18.	potential	41.	culture bias
19.	competence	42.	culture fair
20.	Bayley	43.	motivated
21.	developmental quotient	44.	genetic
22.	maturational	45.	within
23.	attention	46.	between

47.	stimulating	54.	home environment
48.	adaptive behavior	55.	motivated
49.	organic	56.	ideation
50.	cultural-familial	57.	elaboration
51.	divergent	58.	Project Head Start
52.	ideational fluency	59.	mediator
53.	convergent		

Review of Key Terms

1.	Flynn effect	15.	ideational fluency
2.	fluid intelligence	16.	automatization
3.	cultural/familial retardation	17.	giftedness
4.	developmental quotient (DQ)	18.	organic retardation
5.	terminal drop	19.	factor analysis
6.	psychometric approach	20.	intelligence quotient (IQ)
7.	convergent thinking	21.	culture bias
8.	crystallized intelligence	22.	structure-of-intellect model
9.	creativity	23.	savant syndrome
10.	cumulative-deficit hypothesis	24.	mental retardation
11.	mental age (MA)	25.	HOME inventory
12.	triarchic theory of intelligence	26.	dynamic assessment
13.	test norms	27.	wisdom
14.	divergent thinking	28.	normal distribution

Multiple Choice Self Test

1.	D	6.	D	11.	C
2.	A	7.	C	12.	D
3.	A	8.	B	13.	C
4.	C	9.	B	14.	A
5.	C	10.	C	15.	B

People and Their Ideas

1.	G	4.	H	7.	B
2.	A	5.	E	8.	I
3.	C	6.	D	9.	F

Application Questions

1.   *I would want to have access to a measure of infant attention, such as how quickly an infant becomes bored with a stimulus (speed of habituation) or the extent to which an infant prefers a novel stimulus rather than a familiar one (preference for novelty). These sorts of measures show how quickly an infant processes information. The faster they process information, the more quickly they learn, and the brighter they will be later on.*

The Bayley DQ scores don't correlate very well with later IQ scores, probably because the Bayley measures motor skills and behaviors. While these may be important measures during infancy of whether an infant is "on track," they are not important components of later intelligence. Intelligence tests focus on verbal and quantitative reasoning, not motor skills.

Another useful measure to collect during infancy might be scores on the HOME Inventory. This provides an estimate of how stimulating the home is, and is related to later performance on IQ tests. Infants and young children who grow up in homes that provide stimulation and interaction with parents typically score higher on measures of intelligence.

Finally, it might also help to know the IQ score of the infant's mother. Maternal IQ predicts infant's IQ, although it is less useful as children get older, suggesting that environmental factors begin to influence intelligence.

CHAPTER TEN

SELF-CONCEPTIONS AND PERSONALITY

OVERVIEW

How do perceptions of ourselves develop and change over the life span? How do personalities emerge and change? This chapter addresses these sorts of questions about self-conceptions and personality. A sense of self emerges during infancy and becomes more established during childhood. Children think of themselves and others in fairly concrete terms, whereas adolescents and adults think more abstractly.

The beginnings of personality are evident in an infant's temperament. You will learn that some aspects of personality are fairly stable from childhood on, but other aspects change in response to changes in a person's social environment. This chapter also covers Erikson's theory of psychosocial development. Erikson believed that personality evolved over the entire life span as people are confronted with different crises that can be resolved in positive or negative ways. Erikson's eight stages are introduced at the beginning of the chapter and then elaborated throughout the chapter.

LEARNING OBJECTIVES

After reading and studying the material in this chapter, you should be able to answer the following questions.

1.   How do psychoanalytic, psychometric (trait), and social learning theories explain personality development?

2.   How does self-concept emerge during infancy? How does self-concept change across the life span?

3.   How has infant temperament been categorized? How do these temperament styles interact with caregiver characteristics? How does temperament relate to later personality?

4.   What changes occur in the development of children's and adolescent's self-esteem? What factors influence self-esteem?

5.	What is the focus of each of Erikson's psychosocial stages? What factors can influence how each crisis is resolved?

6.	What factors influence the development of identity during adolescence?

7.	How does personality change during adulthood? Why do people change or remain the same?

8.	How can self-esteem be improved throughout the life span?

CHAPTER SUMMARY AND GUIDED REVIEW

The following summary provides an overview of the main points contained in this chapter of the text. Fill-in the blanks with terms that appropriately complete the sentence. Scattered throughout the summary are questions in parentheses. These are meant to encourage you to think actively as you are reading and connect this summary to the more detailed information provided in the text. You can answer these questions as you are filling in the blanks or you can complete all the blanks, then go back and reread the entire summary, addressing the questions in order to provide more depth of understanding.

CONCEPTUALIZING THE SELF

	An organized set of attributes, motives, values, and behaviors unique to an individual is that person's (1) _____. Personalities are often described in terms of (2) _____ that are thought to be relatively consistent across situations and times. Your perception of your traits and attributes is your (3) _____ and your feeling about the characteristics that make up your self concept is (4) _____.

Theories of Personality Development

	According to Freud, personality forms in infancy and early childhood and changes very little after this. Erikson believed that personality continued to grow and change across the life span. (*In what other ways are Freud and Erikson different?*) According to the (5) _____ approach, personality is a set of traits that can be measured. Statistical procedures called (6) _____ are used to identify distinct groups of personality traits. Research suggests that personality can be described in terms of the (7) _____ dimensions of neuroticism, extraversion, openness to experience, agreeableness, and conscientiousness. Social learning theories propose that personality is strongly influenced by (8) _____ factors and can change when these factors change. (*How are stage theory views of personality different from non-stage theory views of personality?*)

THE INFANT
The Emerging Self

	One of the first signs that infants recognize themselves as distinct individuals is when they recognize themselves in a mirror. (***When does this understanding emerge?***) Infants begin to form a (9) _____ self and classify themselves along dimensions such as age and gender. The ability to recognize self depends in part on (10) _____ development and also on social experiences. Our understanding of self is also influenced by social interactions and reflects how others people respond to us, a concept known as the (11) _____ self. (*Can you describe how other people might affect our self-concept and self-esteem?*)

Temperament

Temperament is the tendency to respond in predictable ways to events. Some researchers have focused on three dimensions of temperament that are partly influenced by genetic factors. These are emotionality, activity, and (12) _____. In addition, Kagan has studied (13) _____, or the tendency to be shy and restrained with unfamiliar people or situations. Again, there seems to be a genetic influence on this characteristic as well as stability across time.

Another way of classifying infant temperament is using categories that are based on five dimensions including mood, regularity of habits, and adaptability. About 40% of the infants studied were classified as (14) _____, meaning that they had regular habits, were typically happy and content, and were adaptable to new experiences. About 10% of the infants were considered (15) _____ because they were active, irritable, did not have regular habits, and responded negatively to new experiences. About 15% of the infants were (16) _____ and were inactive, somewhat moody, and had somewhat regular habits. Whether or not infant temperament persists into childhood and adulthood may depend on (17) _____ between the individual and environment. (*Can you describe how this might lead to change or to consistency of temperamental characteristics?*)

THE CHILD
Elaborating on a Sense of Self

Preschool children's self-concepts tend to be (18) _____ and physical. School-age children can describe their inner traits and begin to compare their abilities to those of companions. This leads to (19) _____ where children use comparisons to evaluate themselves.

Self-Esteem

Self-esteem is also developing during childhood. Research indicates that children have well-defined feelings about themselves and are able to distinguish between their competencies in different areas, indicating that self-esteem is (20) _____.

Influences on Self-Esteem

In general, some children have higher self-esteem than others because they are more competent and they receive more positive feedback from others. High self-esteem is fostered by parents who are warm and democratic. (*How does feedback from others contribute to the development of high or low self-esteem?*)

The Personality Stabilizes

A number of important personality dimensions do not stabilize until childhood, although some aspects of early temperament do carry over to later personality. Traits that persist seem to be those that are valued by (21) _____, while those that disappear or change may conflict with cultural norms.

THE ADOLESCENT
Self-Conceptions

The self-concepts of adolescents become more psychological and (22) _____, and they are more self-aware than younger children. Adolescents' descriptions of themselves are also more differentiated and more coherent or (23) _____ than those of younger children.

Self-Esteem

For a small group of adolescents, there is a drop in self-esteem, particularly among girls with multiple stressors. For most adolescents, their self-esteem when they leave adolescence is about the same as when they entered adolescence.

Forming a Sense of Identity

Erikson believed that adolescents are faced with the important psychosocial task of identity versus (24) _____. There are several developmental trends in achieving a sense of identity. Adolescents who have not experienced a crisis of identity and have not made a commitment to an identity are in the (25) _____ status, while adolescents who have not experienced a crisis but have made a commitment fall into the (26) _____ status. Adolescents who have faced a crisis (or are currently facing one) but have not yet made a commitment fall into the (27) _____ status. Adolescents who have faced a crisis about who they are and what they believe in, and who have made a commitment, have achieved (28) _____ status. (***What gender differences exist in identity formation?***)

Identity formation is influenced by cognitive development and by relationships with parents. (***What kinds of parent-adolescent relationships are associated with each of Marcia's identity statuses?***) It is also affected by experiences outside the home and the broader cultural context. (***How do each of these factors influence identity formation?***)

THE ADULT
Self-Perceptions

Self-esteem and descriptions of self do not vary across adulthood. Older adults' evaluations of their ideal selves are closer to their evaluation of their real selves than those of younger adults. Individuals also change their (29) _____ of evaluation over time, as well as their comparison group.

Continuity and Discontinuity in Personality

In addressing whether personality is stable across adulthood, two questions arise. One question is whether an individual's (30) _____ within a group on some personality trait remains the same, which is the stability of individual differences. A second question is whether there is stability in the (31) _____ levels of some personality trait within a group. Longitudinal research has focused on five major dimensions of personality. With respect to the first question, individual rankings on these dimensions of personality are fairly stable across time. (***Can you provide a concrete example of what this means for a specific individual?***) With respect to the second question, cross-sectional research suggests that older adults have different personalities than younger adults. However, these results may reflect (32) _____ or generational effects, suggesting that the (33) _____ context in which people develop affects their personalities.

Personality does show some growth from adolescence to middle adulthood, but there is little systematic change in personality from middle adulthood to later adulthood. The personalities of some people remain stable, while those of other people change across the life span. Personalities may remain stable because of the influence of (34) _____ factors or because childhood experiences continue to impact on personality throughout the life span. It is also possible that personalities remain stable because (35) _____ remain stable. Changes in the environment might explain why some personalities change, and maturation and aging might also contribute to change. Change may also occur when there is a poor fit between the person and his/her environment.

<u>Psychosocial Growth</u>

According to Erikson, infants confront the conflict of (36) _____ versus (37) _____. Toddlers must achieve a sense of (38) _____ or risk feeling shame and doubt. Preschool children and kindergartners struggle with the conflict of (39) _____ versus (40) _____ while school-age children must master (41) _____ or possibly develop feelings of inferiority. As already noted, adolescents face the task of developing an identity. Young adults face the psychosocial task of (42) _____ versus (43) _____. Research supports Erikson's claim that individuals' must achieve a sense of (44) _____ before being able to develop true intimacy. (***How might the relationship between identity and intimacy differ for men and women?***) Middle-age adults are concerned with the psychosocial crisis of (45) _____ versus (46) _____ as they work to produce something lasting and important for future generations. Finally, older adults face the psychosocial conflict of (47) _____ versus (48) _____. Elderly adults may engage in a process of (49) _____ where they reflect on unresolved issues in order to come to terms with their lives.

APPLICATIONS: BOOSTING SELF-ESTEEM

For those children and adults who have low self-esteem, there are a variety of techniques for improving it. Training can improve skills that children believe are weak or can help them re-evaluate the skills they have. Counseling can provide support that is otherwise missing. Some older adults may have lower self-esteem because of the negative messages about aging in our society and prejudice against elderly people, or (50) _____. Self-esteem may be improved by training elderly adults to attribute their difficulties to the (51) _____ rather than to (52) _____.

REVIEW OF KEY TERMS

Below is a list of terms and concepts from this chapter. Use these to complete the following sentence definitions. You might also want to try writing definitions in your own words and then checking your definitions with those in the text.

activity
ageism
autonomy versus shame and doubt
behavioral inhibition
big five
categorical self
difficult temperament
diffusion status
easy temperament
emotionality
ethnic identity
false self behavior
foreclosure status
generativity versus stagnation
goodness of fit
identity
identity achievement status
identity versus role confusion

industry versus inferiority
initiative versus guilt
integrity versus despair
intimacy versus isolation
life review
looking-glass self
moratorium period
moratorium status
personality
self-concept
self-regulation
self-esteem
slow-to-warm-up temperament
social comparison
sociability
temperament
trust versus mistrust

1. The process of _____ takes into account how one compares to others, and uses that information to judge one's self.

2. An identity status called _____ is when a person has not experienced a crisis and has not reached a commitment.

3. Having a clear sense of who you are, where you are heading, and where you fit into society refers to having a(n) _____.

4. The psychosocial conflict of _____ occurs when a young child tries to accept more grown-up responsibilities that she/he may not be able to handle.

5. A(n) _____ is achieved when a person has experienced a crisis and has made a commitment to certain goals.

6. The psychosocial conflict of _____ usually occurs during elementary school when children need to acquire important academic and social skills.

7. Classification of one's self along dimensions such as age and sex shows development of a(n) _____.

8. A person's _____ is reflected in his/her tendency to respond in predictable ways to events.

9. _____ is an identity status in which a person has not experienced a crisis but has made a commitment.

10. Your understanding of yourself, including unique attributes or traits, is your _____.

11. A _____ is the process of reflecting on unresolved conflicts of the past in order to come to terms with your self and derive new meaning from the past.

12. The psychosocial conflict of _____ faces young adults who must develop strong friendships and intimate relationships.

13. _____ is the first psychosocial conflict in which infants must develop a basic sense of trust.

14. Your feelings about the characteristics that make up your self constitute your _____.

15. Adolescents experience the psychosocial conflict of _____ when they must develop a sense of who they are socially, sexually, and professionally.

16. The _____ refers to the fact that our understanding of self is a reflection of how other people view us and respond to us.

17. Older adults face the psychosocial conflict of _____ during which they must assess their life and find it meaningful.

18. _____ is an identity status in which a person is currently experiencing a crisis or actively addressing identity issues and has not yet made a commitment.

19. _____ is defined as an organized combination of attributes, motives, values, and behaviors that is unique to each individual.

20. The psychosocial conflict of _____ involves being productive in one's work and with one's family.

21. The major dimensions of personality are collectively referred to as the _____.

22. During the psychosocial conflict of _____, toddlers must learn some independence.

23. _____ refers to prejudice against elderly people.

24. The degree to which a child's temperament is compatible with the expectations and demands of his/her environment is reflected in the _____ between child and environment.

25. Acting out of character or playing a part that is not one's true self constitute _____.

26. Infants who are generally content, adaptable to new experiences, keep regular habits, and tolerant of frustrations of discomforts are classified with a(n) _____.

27. A dimension of temperament that reflects the degree to which a baby is sluggish is _____.

28. Infants who are inactive, moody, moderately regular in their habits, and take some time to adapt to new situations are classified with a(n) _____.

29. _____ is the tendency to be very shy or restrained in unfamiliar settings.

30. A dimension of temperament that reflects how reactive babies are to events is _____.

31. _____ refers to a sense of personal identification with the values and traditions of a particular ethnic group.

32. Infants who are active, irritable, irregular in their habits, not very adaptable to new situations, and easily frustrated are classified with a(n) _____.

33. Society provides a _____ for most adolescents so that they can experiment with different roles in order to find their identity.

34. The ability to recognize one's self in a mirror or photo is _____.

35. The degree to which one is interested in and responsive to people is reflected in the personality trait of _____.

For each multiple choice question, read all alternatives and then select the best answer.

1. Self-esteem refers to a person's
    a. cognitive understanding of self
    b. perception of his or her abilities and traits
    c. overall evaluation of his or her worth as a person
    d. knowledge of who they are

2. According to Erik Erikson, personality
    a. develops in the first five or six years after birth and changes little after this
    b. develops and changes throughout the life span
    c. development is complete in adolescence once a sense of identity has been achieved
    d. is formed in childhood and only changes later in life under extreme environmental conditions

3. Someone who adheres to social learning theory would believe that
    a. personality develops through a series of systematic stages that are similar for all people
    b. personality is shaped by the environment during childhood, but once it is formed, changes very little in response to environmental changes
    c. some aspects of personality are determined only by genetic factors while other are determined only by environmental factors
    d. personality traits are only consistent across the life span if the person's environment remains the same

4. Infants with a spot of rouge on their noses who recognize themselves in a mirror will
    a. reach for the nose of their mirror image
    b. reach for their own nose
    c. look behind the mirror
    d. begin to cry indicating that they are confused

5. An infant who is classified as "slow-to-warm-up"
    a. follows a somewhat regular schedule, is inactive, and somewhat moody
    b. follows a somewhat regular schedule, is active, and tolerates frustrations fairly well
    c. follows a regular schedule, appears content, and is adaptable to new experiences
    d. does not follow a regular schedule, is inactive, and reacts very negatively to new experiences

6. Research on behavioral inhibition suggests that
    a. whether one is inhibited as a toddler determines whether one will be shy as an adult
    b. inhibited toddlers are more likely to turn out to be shy children than uninhibited toddlers
    c. inhibited toddlers were securely attached as infants
    d. inhibited children show the same patterns of physiological arousal to events as uninhibited children

7. A child who can compare her abilities to those of her companions is likely to be in Piaget's
    _____ stage of cognitive development.
    a. sensorimotor
    b. preoperational
    c. concrete operational
    d. formal operational

8. When Harter's self-perception scale was administered to children in third through ninth grades, it
    was found that
    a. only the oldest children had well-defined self-concepts
    b. children typically did not distinguish between their competencies in different areas
    c. children showed a "halo effect" by evaluating themselves high in all areas
    d. children's ratings of themselves were consistent with how others rated them

9. According to Erikson, a third grader who has problems with reading and math may develop a
    sense of
    a. doubt
    b. guilt
    c. inferiority
    d. role confusion

10. Adolescents who have experienced a crisis involving identity but have not resolved the crisis or
    made a commitment are classified in Marcia's _____ status.
    a. diffusion
    b. moratorium
    c. foreclosure
    d. identity achievement

11. An adolescent who says "My parents taught me that abortion is wrong and so I just would not
    consider having an abortion or voting for someone who supports abortion." This statement
    reflects which identity status?
    a. diffusion
    b. moratorium
    c. foreclosure
    d. identity achievement

12. Longitudinal research on the major dimensions of personality suggests that
    a. they are relatively consistent over time in adults
    b. they change considerably over time in adults
    c. they are strongly correlated with infant temperament
    d. they cannot be reliably measured in adults

13. Findings from cross-sectional research that, as a group, adult personalities change systematically
    over time, may reflect
    a. the fact that personality is affected by the historical context in which it develops
    b. changes in the way personality has been measured over the years
    c. the fact that personality begins to disintegrate as we age
    d. the fact that people grow more similar as they get older

14. Older adults face Erikson's psychosocial conflict of
    a.   integrity versus stagnation
    b.   generativity versus stagnation
    c.   intimacy versus despair
    d.   integrity versus despair

15. Compared to adults who do not achieve a firm sense of identity, those adults who <u>do</u> achieve a sense of identity are
    a.   equally likely to form genuine intimacy with another person
    b.   more likely to form genuine intimacy with another person
    c.   are less likely to form intimate relationships because they feel very good about themselves as individuals
    d.   more likely to form many pseudo intimate relationships but no intimate relationships

REVIEW ERIKSON'S PSYCHOSOCIAL STAGES

For each of Erikson's psychosocial stages, indicate the approximate age period when the conflict is experienced and the central issue or conflict that must be resolved. Check your answers using Table 10.1 in the text.

STAGE	AGE RANGE	CENTRAL ISSUE OR CONFLICT
Trust v. mistrust		
Autonomy v. shame and doubt		
Initiative v. guilt		
Industry v. inferiority		
Identity v. role confusion		
Intimacy v. isolation		
Generativity v. stagnation		
Integrity v. despair		

REVIEW THE FOUR IDENTITY STATUSES

For this exercise, consider the area of career identity. For each of the four identity statuses, note whether or not a crisis has been experienced (Yes or No) and whether or not a commitment has been made (Yes or No). Also provide an example related to career identity for each type of status. Check your answers by referring to Table 10.3 in the text.

TYPE OF IDENTITY STATUS	Crisis?	Commitment?	Example
Diffusion			
Moratorium			
Foreclosure			
Identity Achievement			

APPLICATION QUESTIONS

By answering the following questions, you will strengthen your understanding of the material in this chapter. These questions require higher level thinking skills such as integration and application of concepts. To get you started, there is a sample answer or outline provided for the first question. This illustrates one possibility, but there are other answers you could provide that might be just as good. For the other questions, you can check yourself by referring to the text (a hint is provided), or by asking a peer or your instructor to review your answer.

1. Taking into consideration everything you have read about personality, how would you summarize the findings on stability of personality characteristics across the life span? [Sample answer provided.]

2. Based on research, what could you tell parents who are concerned about their infant's or toddler's temperament (perhaps it is a difficult temperament, or the infant is inhibited)? [Hint: Review the section of the chapter on "Temperament," paying particular attention to the discussion of "Goodness of Fit."]

3. How does self-esteem change across the life span, and what factors influence self-esteem in positive or negative directions? [Hint: Review the sections throughout the chapter on self-esteem and the Application on "Boosting Self-Esteem" at the end of the chapter.]

Chapter Summary and Guided Review (Fill-in the blank)

1.	personality	27.	moratorium
2.	traits	28.	identity achievement
3.	self-concept	29.	standards
4.	self-esteem	30.	ranking
5.	psychometric	31.	average
6.	factor analysis	32.	cohort
7.	big five	33.	historical
8.	environmental	34.	hereditary (or genetic)
9.	categorical	35.	environments
10.	cognitive	36.	trust
11.	looking-glass	37.	mistrust
12.	sociability	38.	autonomy
13.	behavioral inhibition	39.	initiative
14.	easy	40.	guilt
15.	difficult	41.	industry
16.	slow-to-warm-up	42.	intimacy
17.	goodness of fit	43.	isolation
18.	concrete	44.	identity
19.	social comparison	45.	generativity
20.	multidimensional	46.	stagnation
21.	society	47.	integrity
22.	abstract	48.	despair
23.	integrated	49.	life review
24.	role confusion	50.	ageism
25.	diffusion	51.	environment
26.	foreclosure	52.	aging

Review of Key Terms

1.	social comparison	17.	integrity versus despair
2.	diffusion status	18.	moratorium status
3.	identity	19.	personality
4.	initiative versus guilt	20.	generativity versus stagnation
5.	identity achievement status	21.	big five
6.	industry versus inferiority	22.	autonomy versus shame and doubt
7.	categorical self	23.	ageism
8.	temperament	24.	goodness of fit
9.	foreclosure status	25.	false self behavior
10.	self-concept	26.	easy temperament
11.	life review	27.	activity
12.	intimacy versus isolation	28.	slow-to-warm-up temperament
13.	trust versus mistrust	29.	behavioral inhibition
14.	self-esteem	30.	emotionality
15.	identity versus role confusion	31.	ethnic identity
16.	looking-glass self	32.	difficult temperament

33. moratorium period

34. self-recognition

35. sociability

Multiple Choice Self Test

1.	C	6.	B	11.	C
2.	B	7.	C	12.	A
3.	D	8.	D	13.	A
4.	B	9.	C	14.	D
5.	A	10.	B	15.	B

Application Questions

1. *The beginnings of personality emerge during infancy with temperament characteristics. Some of these characteristics persist beyond infancy if there is "goodness of fit" between the child's characteristics and the demands of the environment. Social experiences shape temperament into what we think of as a child's personality. Components of this personality tend to persist over time if the traits are valued by society and are consistent with gender roles expectations. In terms of the "big five" personality traits, there is a good deal of stability in these throughout adulthood. Thus, a young adult who is extraverted is likely to be extraverted as an older adult. An older adult who is not very open to new experiences was probably not very open as a younger adult. Correlations, though, between scores on personality measures are not perfect, indicating that there is some change over time. In particular, research shows that personalities are still forming throughout adolescence and early adulthood, and become more established sometime during one's thirties.*

CHAPTER ELEVEN

GENDER ROLES AND SEXUALITY

OVERVIEW

Most students find this chapter particularly interesting, perhaps because gender issues are so central to our lives. The first and larger part of this chapter is devoted to discussion of gender roles across the life span. This includes a description of several theoretical explanations of how gender role behaviors are acquired: Money and Ehrhardt's biosocial theory, Freud's psychoanalytic theory, social learning theory, and the cognitive theories. Pay particular attention to how these theories can be integrated to best explain gender typing, and to the evidence that supports the theories.

The second part of the chapter covers developmental issues related to sexuality. This includes expressions of sexuality during infancy and childhood, with discussions of children's knowledge about sex, their sexual behavior, and the sexual abuse of children. This section also covers the sexual orientation, behavior and morality of adolescents, and changes in sexuality during adulthood.

LEARNING OBJECTIVES

After reading and studying the material in this chapter, you should be able to answer the following questions.

1.   What are gender norms and stereotypes? How do they play out in the behaviors of men and women?

2.   What actual psychological differences exist between males and females?

3.   How does Eagly's social role hypothesis explain gender stereotypes?

4   How do gender role stereotypes influence infants' behavior and treatment?

5.   How do children acquire gender role stereotypes? In what ways do children exhibit gender-typed behavior?

6. What theoretical explanations account for gender-typed behaviors? How well supported are these theories?

7. How do gender roles change throughout adulthood?

8. What is androgyny? To what extent is it useful?

9. How are infants are affected by their sex? What do we know about infant sexuality?

10. What do children know about sex and reproduction? How does sexual behavior change during childhood?

11. What factors contribute to the development of sexual orientation? What are adolescents' sexual attitudes and behavior today?

12. What changes occur in sexual activity during adulthood?

SUMMARY AND GUIDED REVIEW

The following summary provides an overview of the main points contained in this chapter of the text. Fill-in the blanks with terms that appropriately complete the sentence. Scattered throughout the summary are questions in parentheses. These are meant to encourage you to think actively as you are reading and connect this summary to the more detailed information provided in the text. You can answer these questions as you are filling in the blanks or you can complete all the blanks, then go back and reread the entire summary, addressing the questions in order to provide more depth of understanding.

MALE AND FEMALE

Males and females differ in a number of ways. They differ genetically because they have different (1) _____, which trigger release of different levels of (2) _____. Males and females also differ because societies expect them to adopt different patterns of behavior, or (3) _____, specifying how they should act as males or females. Gender-role (4) _____ are society's expectations of what males and females should be like, and these create gender-role (5)_____, or overgeneralizations about what males and females are like.

Children learn their biological sex and acquire the behaviors and values that society considers appropriate for members of that sex through a process of (6) _____.

Gender Norms and Stereotypes

Girls in our society have traditionally been encouraged to adopt an (7) _____ role that involves being nurturant, kind, cooperative, and sensitive to other's needs. Boys have been encouraged to adopt an (8) _____ role that involves being dominant, independent, assertive, and competitive. Stereotypes about women's and men's roles continue to exist, although women describe themselves as having more masculine traits than they did in the past.

Actual Gender Differences

A classic review of gender research revealed only four psychological differences between males and females. Females have greater (9) _____ ability than males. Beginning in adolescence, males outperform females on tests of (10) _____ ability and (11) _____ reasoning. As early as two years of age, males tend to be more (12) _____ than females. Some researchers disagree with this summary of gender differences, arguing in some cases that there are more real differences between males and females, and in other cases arguing that there are no "real" gender differences. (*What other gender differences have been supported by more recent research?*) Findings of psychological sex differences are based on averages for males and females and do not apply to all individuals. Many differences that we think exist between males and females are based on (13) _____. In addition, Eagly's (14) _____ hypothesis suggests that the roles played by men and women in society help create our stereotypes about gender.

THE INFANT
Differential Treatment

Our society begins to treat males and females differently at birth. Adults interact differently and interpret reactions differently when they believe they are interacting with a male infant rather than a female infant.

Early Learning

By age 2 1/2 to 3, children show that they have acquired (15) _____ because they know whether they are male or female. Even before this time, children are beginning to act in ways that society finds gender appropriate.

THE CHILD

At about the same time that young children acquire gender identity, they begin to learn (16) _____, or society's ideas about what males and females are like. They also acquire gender-typed behaviors.

Acquiring Gender Stereotypes

Children as young as 2½ years already hold stereotypical beliefs about boys' and girls' activities. Children around 6 or 7 years believe that these stereotypes are absolute while older children are more flexible in their thinking about gender-role stereotypes. (*Why is there this developmental difference in thinking about gender-role stereotypes?*)

Gender-Typed Behavior

Young children prefer toys that society deems gender-appropriate and they develop a preference for same-sex playmates, with increased gender (17) _____ into separate groups of boys and girls during elementary school. Boys are under more pressure than girls to behave in gender-appropriate ways. (*Can you explain why this is true?*)

THE ADOLESCENT
Adhering to Gender Roles
     Adolescents tend to adhere more strictly to gender roles than do younger children. (***Why is this the case?***) In the process of gender (18) _____, increased pressure among adolescents to conform to gender roles magnifies differences between males and females.

Theories of Gender-Role Development
     There are several theories that try to explain the development of gender roles. Money and Ehrhardt proposed a (19) _____ theory that focuses on the interaction of biological and social influences. According to this theory, several critical events contribute to gender-role development. One is receiving an X or Y chromosome, and the second event is the release of (20) _____, which stimulates the development of a male internal reproductive system. A third event occurs at 3 to 4 months after conception when testosterone triggers development of male external genitals or, in its absence, development of female external genitalia. Testosterone also affects development of the (21) _____ and nervous system. Hormones released during (22) _____ will stimulate the growth of the reproductive system and secondary sex characteristics. These biological events trigger a number of (23) _____ reactions that will further differentiate males and females.

     Evidence from several sources indicates that biological factors do influence the development of males and females. Children who are chromosomally XX but who were exposed to male hormones prenatally are called (24) _____. (***How are these girls behaviorally different from other girls?***) The level of male hormones may also relate to (25) _____ in animals and humans. Social labeling also has an impact on gender development. Evidence suggests that there may be a sensitive or (26) _____ period between 18 months and 3 years of age when gender identity is established. (***Can you explain the evidence that suggests this?***)

     According to Freud's psychoanalytic theory, both biology and environment contribute to gender-role development. Preschool-age children are in the (27) _____ stage of psychosexual development. A boy in this stage experiences a(n) (28) _____ complex and a girl is said to experience a(n) (29) _____ complex. In both cases, the children experience love for their parent of the other sex and as a result of this, experience jealousy and conflict with the same-sex parent. The conflict is resolved through (30) _____ with the same-sex parent. (***What is the psychoanalytic rationale for why boys seem to learn gender stereotypes and gender-typed behaviors faster than girls?***)

     Social learning theorists believe that gender-role development occurs through (31) _____ where children are reinforced for sex-appropriate behaviors and punished for behaviors considered appropriate for members of the other sex. (***How can differential treatment lead to differences in ability?***) According to this view, sex-role development also occurs through (32) _____ where children adopt attitudes and behaviors of same-sex models. (***What are some likely sources of gender-stereotyped behavior that children watch?***)

     Cognitive-developmental theorists argue that gender-role development depends on a child's level of cognitive development. Children must first acquire basic gender (33) _____, or the recognition of being male of female. They must also acquire gender (34) _____, the understanding that gender identity is constant across time, and (35) _____, or knowing that gender is constant across situations. (***What level of cognitive development is needed for these understandings?***) According to this view, once children understand that biological sex is unchanging, they actively socialize themselves by seeking out same-sex models. (***What are criticisms of this view of gender-role development?***)

An information processing model proposed by Martin and Halverson suggests that children acquire (36) _____, which are organized sets of expectations and beliefs about males and females and these beliefs influence the things that children pay attention to and remember. According to this theory, children classify people and things as belonging to a simple in-group or out-group. Children then construct an (37) _____ by collecting more elaborate information about the role of their own sex. (*What evidence supports this perspective?*)

Together, the biosocial, social learning, and cognitive theories help explain how gender-typed behaviors develop. Biological factors guide development, people react to a child's gender, and children actively socialize themselves to act in ways consistent with their understandings of their gender.

THE ADULT
Gender Roles

In adulthood, male and female roles are often similar until marriage and parenthood begin to differentiate the roles. The roles become more similar again during middle age when child care responsibilities decline.

Masculinity, Femininity, and Androgyny

Sandra Bem argues that masculinity and femininity are two separate psychological dimensions. Someone who is (38) _____ has masculine-stereotyped traits as well as feminine-stereotyped traits. Gutmann refers to demands placed on a person by parenthood as the (39) _____. The demands often mean that men emphasize their masculine qualities and women emphasize their feminine qualities. Gutmann proposes that when no longer constrained by the parental imperative, psychologically masculine men adopt more (40) _____ qualities and psychologically feminine women adopt more (41) _____ qualities. A related hypothesis is that a midlife (42) _____ occurs, and adults retain their gender-typed qualities but add qualities associated with the other gender. Gutmann's hypothesis is partially supported. Parenthood does tend to make people more traditionally sex-typed, but they tend to become (43) _____ in the postparental phases of life, rather than replacing sex-typed traits with other-sex traits. Thus, they experience the androgyny shift.

Androgynous people tend to be more flexible in their (44) _____ than traditionally sex-typed persons. However, it is not androgyny per se, but a person's (45) _____ traits that are associated with high self-esteem and good adjustment. And while androgynous parents seem to raise children who are androgynous, some evidence suggests that these children are less competent and less socially responsive and assertive than children of traditionally sex-typed parents. (*What other characteristics are associated with androgyny?*)

SEXUALITY OVER THE LIFE SPAN
Are Infants Sexual Beings?

According to Freud, infants who are in the oral stage of psychosexual development gain pleasure from activities such as sucking and biting. The genitals of infants are sensitive to stimulation and both male and female infants have been observed to engage in masturbation-like activities, although these are not interpreted sexually in the same way that they are for adults.

Childhood Sexuality

Children's understanding of sex and reproduction has been related to their level of (46) _____ development. They often interpret information about sex and reproduction in terms of what they already know (assimilation). According to Freud, preschoolers in the (47) _____ stage are interested in their genitals, and school-aged children are in a (48) _____ in which sexuality is repressed.

Contrary to what Freud believed, sexual interest and experimentation do not decrease during childhood. Children's sexual behaviors are influenced by parental and societal attitudes. In (49) _____ societies, children are typically not allowed to express any sexuality. In (50) _____ societies, there are rules prohibiting sexual behaviors by children but children often violate the rules without punishment. In (51) _____ societies, children are free to express their sexuality and in fact, may be encouraged to explore their sexuality. (**Where does the U.S. fit in this classification?**)

Children who are sexually abused exhibit a variety of problems common to emotionally disturbed individuals, such as anxiety and depression. In particular, lack of self worth and distrust of others affect victims' abilities to build successful relationships. One problem among victims of sexual abuse is their tendency to act out sexually, called (52) _____. A second problems is (53) _____, a clinical disorder involving flashbacks and nightmares about the event.

Adolescent Sexuality

As part of establishing their sexual identity, adolescents must become aware of their sexual (54) _____. Many establish a heterosexual orientation without much thought. Others may experiment with homosexual activities, but do not necessarily end up with an enduring homosexual orientation. (**What factors influence the development of sexual orientation?**)

Sexual morality of adolescents has changed during this century and includes these beliefs:
1) Sex with (55) _____ is acceptable.
2) The (56) _____ is declining but has not disappeared.
3) There is increased confusion about sexual (57) _____ since individuals must now decide for themselves what is right or wrong, rather than adhering to general rules.

Sexual behaviors have also changed during the last century. Adolescents engage in sexual behaviors at earlier ages and more adolescents are having sexual intercourse. Since many sexually active adolescents fail to use (58) _____, there are a number of unplanned pregnancies.

Adult Sexuality

People continue to be sexual beings throughout middle and late adulthood. Frequency of sexual intercourse declines with age for both single and married individuals. In part, this decline results from (59) _____ changes in men and women as they get older. Sexual capacity can also be affected by diseases and use of prescribed drugs, which both increase as a person gets older. Societal attitudes and lack of a (60) _____ also contribute to the decline of sexual activity of older adults.

APPLICATIONS: CHANGING GENDER-ROLE ATTITUDES AND BEHAVIOR

Changing gender-role attitudes and behaviors is possible but not easy. Young children are more receptive to changes than older children but do not always retain changes brought about by short term training.

REVIEW OF KEY TERMS

Below is a list of terms and concepts from this chapter. Use these to complete the following sentence definitions. You might also want to try writing definitions in your own words and then checking your definitions with those in the text.

androgenized females
androgyny
androgyny shift

double standard
Electra complex
expressive role

gender consistency   gender typing
gender identity   identification
gender intensification   instrumental role
gender role   Oedipus complex
gender-role norms   parental imperative
gender-role stereotypes   posttraumatic stress disorder
gender schema   sexual orientation
gender segregation   social-role hypothesis
gender stability

1.   Understanding that gender identity is stable over time is _____.

2.   A behavior pattern or trait that defines how to act as female or male in a particular society is
      called a _____.

3.   The _____ refers to the belief that sexual behaviors that are acceptable for males are
      not acceptable for females.

4.   A _____ is an organized set of beliefs and expectations about males and females that
      influence the type of information that is attended to and remembered.

5.   _____ refer to generalizations about what males and females are like.

6.   _____ is the understanding that gender is constant despite changes in appearance or
      activities.

7.   The process by which children learn their biological sex and acquire the motives, values, and
      behaviors considered appropriate for members of that sex is _____.

8.   The _____ consists of gender-role norms that encourages boys to be dominant,
      independent, assertive, and competitive.

9.   Societal standards about what males and females should be like are contained in
      _____.

10.   The requirements or demands imposed on a person by parenthood are referred to as the
      _____.

11.   _____ is the awareness of one's self as male or female.

12.   The possession of both masculine-stereotyped traits and feminine-stereotyped traits is called
      _____.

13.   Gender-role norms that encourage girls to be kind, nurturant, cooperative, and sensitive to the
      needs of others form the _____.

14.   Females who were exposed prenatally to male hormones and have external genitals that appear
      masculine are labeled _____.

15. Through the process of _____, children internalize the attitudes and behaviors of the same-sex parent.

16. _____ refers to one's preference for sexual partners of the same or other sex.

17. The Freudian term for a boy's feelings of love toward his mother and fear of his father is _____.

18. _____ consists of a cluster of symptoms, including nightmares and flashbacks, associated with an extremely traumatic experience.

19. The concept of _____ refers to the addition of characteristics typically associated with the other sex to traditionally gender-typed characteristics already held by an individual.

20. The Freudian term for a girl's feelings of love toward her father and rivalry with her mother is _____.

21. _____ refers to the separation of people into groups of males and females.

22. In the process of _____, there is an increase in sex differences as a result of pressure to conform to gender roles.

23. According to the _____, differences in the societal roles of men and women help create and maintain gender-role stereotypes.

MULTIPLE CHOICE SELF TEST

For each multiple choice question, read all alternatives and then select the best answer.

1. The process by which children learn their biological sex and acquire the motives, values, and behaviors considered appropriate for the members of that sex is called
   a. gender typing
   b. gender-role norms
   c. gender differences
   d. gender consistency

2. Which one the following is <u>true</u> regarding psychological differences between males and females?
   a. Males and females do not actually differ on any psychological traits or abilities.
   b. Wherever there is a difference between males and females, males outperform females.
   c. There are no differences between males and females throughout childhood, but beginning in adolescence, males outperform females in most areas.
   d. Females tend to outperform males on verbal tasks and males tend to outperform females on tests of mathematical reasoning.

3. Females in our society have historically been encouraged to assume a(n)
   a. gender role
   b. instrumental role
   c. expressive role
   d. androgynous role

4. Most children can correctly label themselves as males or females by age _____ and begin to understand that one's sex does not change around age _____.
   a. 5 years; 11 years
   b. 3 years; 6 years
   c. 18 months; 3 years
   d. 2 years; 3 years

5. Money and Ehrhardt's biosocial theory of gender-role development suggests that
   a. there are real biological differences between boys and girls and these differences influence how people react to the children
   b. biological differences between males and females cause them to behave differently and to have different levels of expertise in areas such as math and verbal skills
   c. biological differences males and females may exist, but these differences have no impact on psychological differences between males and females
   d. biological factors affect males' behavior but not females' behavior

6. A woman who receives male hormones while she is pregnant may deliver a child who is
   a. genetically XY and has external genitals that appear feminine
   b. genetically XX and has external genitals that appear masculine
   c. genetically XX and becomes very masculine appearing following puberty
   d. mentally retarded

7. According to Freud's psychoanalytic explanation, boys resolve their Oedipus complexes and girls resolve their Electra complexes
   a. when they move into the phallic stage of development
   b. out of love for their parents
   c. by identifying with the parent of the other sex
   d. by identifying with the same-sex parent

8. Social learning theorists explain sex-typing as the result of
   a. the child's understanding of gender identity and gender constancy
   b. the child's desire to be like his or her parents
   c. the parents differentially reinforcing behaviors and the child's observation of same-sex models
   d. chromosomal and hormonal differences between males and females

9. According to cognitive-developmental theorists, gender-role development
   a. begins with children's understanding that they are girls or boys
   b. begins with children imitating same-sex models
   c. begins when parents differentially reinforce boys and girls
   d. depends on observational learning

10.   When children realize that their gender is stable over time, they have achieved _____, and when they realize that their gender is stable over situations, they have achieved _____.
    a.   gender stability; gender identity
    b.   gender identity; gender consistency
    c.   gender consistency; gender stability
    d.   gender stability; gender consistency

11.   Gender schemas
    a.   determine a child's behavior in ambiguous situations
    b.   influence the kinds of information that children attend to
    c.   refer to the child's understanding that their gender is stable over time
    d.   reflect the fact that children have difficulty understanding their appropriate gender roles

12.   Which of the following accurately characterizes developmental changes in thinking about gender roles?
    a.   Preschoolers are the most rigid in their thinking about gender roles.
    b.   The period of young adulthood is when people hold the most rigid beliefs about gender roles.
    c.   Children in early elementary school and adolescence hold the most rigid beliefs about gender roles.
    d.   Children in middle childhood hold the most rigid beliefs about gender roles.

13.   Which of the following is true regarding changes in sexual attitudes?
    a.   Regardless of how they may act, most adolescents believe that premarital sex is wrong.
    b.   Most adolescents are quite knowledgeable about sex and clearly understand today's sexual norms.
    c.   The "double standard" for males and females sexual behavior no longer exists.
    d.   Most adolescents believe that sex with affection is OK.

14.   In Sandra Bem's model, an androgynous individual is a person who is
    a.   high in both masculine and feminine traits
    b.   high in masculine traits and low in feminine traits
    c.   low in masculine traits and high in feminine traits
    d.   low in both masculine and feminine traits

15.   With respect to androgyny, research indicates that
    a.   androgynous people are less flexible in their behavior than sex-typed people
    b.   children of androgynous parents are more socially responsible and assertive than children of sex-typed people
    c.   the possession of masculine traits leads to higher self-esteem and good adjustment
    d.   the possession of feminine traits by men leads to better adjustment

REVIEW THE THEORIES OF GENDER-TYPING

For each theory of gender typing listed below, note the contribution that it has made to our understanding of the development of gender typing. Use the description of the theories in the text and Table 11.1 to check your answers.

THEORY	CONTRIBUTION
Biosocial Theory	
Social Learning Theory	
Cognitive-Developmental Theory	
Gender Schema Theory	

APPLICATION QUESTIONS

By answering the following questions, you will strengthen your understanding of the material in this chapter. These questions require higher level thinking skills such as integration and application of concepts. To get you started, there is a sample answer or outline provided for the first question. This illustrates one possibility, but there are other answers you could provide that might be just as good. For the other questions, you can check yourself by referring to the text (a hint is provided), or by asking a peer or your instructor to review your answer.

1. One issue debated by scholars in the field of gender roles is the existence of actual differences between males and females. Are there "real" gender differences? Discuss all sides of this issue and provide evidence to support each position.
   [Sample answer provided]

2. Which theory of gender-role development seems to have the most empirical support? Justify your answer.
   [Hint: Review each section under "Theories of Gender-Role Development," paying particular attention to the *evidence* for each. Also review the subsection on integration of the theories. In your answer, be sure you do more than *describe* each theory; the focus should be on whether or not there is evidence to support or weaken the theory.]

3. Which ideas of Freud seem to be accurate regarding early sexuality and gender-role development, and which ideas of Freud have not been supported?

[Hint: There are references to Freud throughout the sections on sexuality, so review this part of the chapter with Freud's theory and stages of psychosexual development in mind.]

4.   What happens to gender roles and gender differences during adulthood?
        [Hint: Review the section on "The Adult."]

ANSWERS

Chapter Summary and Guided Review (Fill-in the blank)

1.	chromosomes	31.	differential reinforcement
2.	hormones	32.	observational learning
3.	gender roles	33.	identity
4.	norms	34.	stability
5.	stereotypes	35.	consistency
6.	gender typing	36.	gender schemata
7.	expressive	37.	own-sex schema
8.	instrumental	38.	androgynous
9.	verbal	39.	parental imperative
10.	spatial	40.	feminine
11.	mathematical	41.	masculine
12.	aggressive	42.	androgyny shift
13.	stereotypes	43.	androgynous
14.	social role	44.	behavior
15.	gender identity	45.	masculine
16.	stereotypes	46.	cognitive
17.	segregation	47.	phallic
18.	intensification	48.	latency period
19.	biosocial	49.	restrictive
20.	testosterone	50.	semirestrictive
21.	brain	51.	permissive
22.	puberty	52.	sexualized behavior
23.	social	53.	posttraumatic stress disorder
24.	androgenized females	54.	orientation
25.	aggression	55.	affection
26.	critical	56.	double standard
27.	phallic	57.	norms
28.	Oedipus	58.	contraception
29.	Electra	59.	physiological
30.	identification	60.	partner

Review of Key Terms

1.	gender stability	6.	gender consistency
2.	gender role	7.	gender typing
3.	double standard	8.	instrumental role
4.	gender schema	9.	gender-role norms
5.	gender-role stereotypes	10.	parental imperative

11.	gender identity	18.	posttraumatic stress disorder
12.	androgyny	19.	androgyny shift
13.	expressive role	20.	Electra complex
14.	androgenized females	21.	gender segregation
15.	identification	22.	gender intensification
16.	sexual orientation	23.	social-role hypothesis
17.	Oedipus complex		

Multiple Choice Self Test

1.	A	6.	B	11.	B
2.	D	7.	D	12.	C
3.	C	8.	C	13.	D
4.	B	9.	A	14.	A
5.	A	10.	D	15.	C

Application Questions

1.   *Some people would argue that there are no "real" differences between men and women other than their different reproductive systems and genitals. People on this side of the issue insist that there are no meaningful psychological, intellectual, or behavioral differences between men and women. They argue that what may appear to be gender differences are actually the result of socialization differences, not inherent differences. Consequently, they believe that if society treated men and women similarly, they would behave similarly.*

Other people believe that there are some differences between males and females. They cite the four "well-established" sex differences that Maccoby and Jacklin reported in their classic review: Math ability, spatial ability, and aggression (all in favor of males), and verbal ability (in favor of females). Some people believe that these four differences result from socialization. Others, however, believe there is evidence that there are intrinsic differences. For example, differences in aggression show up very early in life and are observed cross-culturally, which suggests there may be a biological or genetic component to sex differences in aggression.

Finally, there are still other who believe that there are additional differences between men and women, including activity level, compliance, cooperativeness, nurturance, and others. Again, some of these people believe these differences result from socialization but others think that men and women are different because of physiological differences.

CHAPTER TWELVE

SOCIAL COGNITION AND MORAL DEVELOPMENT

OVERVIEW

Whether you realize it or not, you use social cognitive skills every day when you think about your own or another person's thoughts, behaviors, motivations, or emotions. This chapter discusses what these skills are, how they change across the life span, factors that can foster these skills, and the importance of these skills to other areas of development.

A large portion of this chapter is devoted to moral development, including the theoretical explanations of moral affect (Freud's psychoanalytic theory), moral reasoning (Kohlberg's and Piaget's cognitive-developmental theories), and moral behavior (social-learning theory). Each theory is evaluated in light of research findings.

Particularly interesting in this chapter are the discussions of how to foster moral maturity and increase social cognitive skills and the correlates of antisocial behavior. The Application sections revisits these topics by discussing ways to combat youth violence.

LEARNING OBJECTIVES

After reading and studying the material in this chapter, you should be able to answer the following questions.

1.   What is social cognition?

2.   What is a theory of mind? How is it assessed? What developmental changes occur in the understanding of a theory of mind?

3.   How does person perception develop? How do role taking skills develop? Why are these skills important?

4.   What is morality? What are the three basic components of morality?

5.   What is Freud's explanation for the development of morality?

6.   How did Kohlberg assess moral reasoning? What are the important characteristics of each level and stage of Kohlberg's theory? What are examples of responses at each stage of reasoning?

7.   How do social learning theorists explain moral behavior?

8.   What do infants understand about morality and prosocial behavior?

9.   What changes in moral reasoning and behavior occur during childhood?

10.   What is Piaget's view of moral reasoning during childhood?

11.   What parenting characteristics contribute to the development of morality?

12.   What changes in moral reasoning occur during adolescence? How is moral development related to antisocial behavior of adolescents? What other factors influence antisocial behavior?

13.   What changes in moral reasoning and behavior occur during adulthood?

14.   How does Kohlberg's theory of moral reasoning fare in light of research findings? In what ways might the theory be biased or incomplete?

CHAPTER SUMMARY AND GUIDED REVIEW

The following summary provides an overview of the main points contained in this chapter of the text. Fill-in the blanks with terms that appropriately complete the sentence. Scattered throughout the summary are questions in parentheses. These are meant to encourage you to think actively as you are reading and connect this summary to the more detailed information provided in the text. You can answer these questions as you are filling in the blanks or you can complete all the blanks, then go back and reread the entire summary, addressing the questions in order to provide more depth of understanding.

SOCIAL COGNITION

Social cognition involves the ability to think about thoughts, emotions, motives, and behaviors of one's self and others.

Developing a Theory of Mind

Using a task called the (1) _____, researchers assess children's understanding that people can have incorrect beliefs and be influenced by these beliefs. This task has been used to determine whether children have a (2) _____, which is the understanding of mental states and the role of mental states on behavior. Research shows that many children with autism lack this understanding, which may limit their abilities to have successful social interactions.

Precursors of a theory of mind can be seen as young as 9 months, when infants and care givers look at the same object together, showing (3) _____. Other research shows that two year olds develop a desire psychology based on what they want. By age four, they develop (4) _____ psychology, which incorporates an understanding of beliefs. (*What factors influence the development of a theory of mind?*)

Person Perception

How do children perceive other people? Young children describe people in terms of (5) _____ traits and behaviors. By age seven or eight, children use psychological traits to describe others, and by eleven or twelve years, they can make social comparisons of people based on psychological characteristics.

Role-Taking Skills

Role-taking skill is the ability to assume another person's perspective. Selman has concluded that role-taking skills develop in stages. Preschool children tend to be (6) _____ and have trouble assuming another person's perspective. With concrete operational thought, children can understand that there are different perspectives even if people have received the same information. With the development of formal operational thought, adolescents can simultaneously consider two different perspectives and how they fit with the perspective of the broader social group. (*What are the implications of good social cognition skills such as role-taking?*)

Social-Cognitive Development in Adulthood

Social cognitive skills of adults are advanced in some ways, but also may show some losses. Elderly adults who continue to use their social cognition skills show no decline in these abilities.

PERSPECTIVES ON MORAL DEVELOPMENT

The ability to distinguish right from wrong, act on this distinction, and experience the accompanying emotion implies morality. Morality includes an emotional or (7) _____, component, a behavioral component, and a (8) _____ component that focuses on how a person reasons and makes decisions about moral dilemmas.

Moral Affect: Psychoanalytic Theory

Freud's psychoanalytic theory focused on moral affects. A child who has done something wrong typically feels some negative emotion such as guilt or shame. Being able to experience another person's feelings, or (9) _____, is another moral affect. Freud believed that morality was not present until the (10) _____ developed during the phallic stage of psychosexual development. At this time, children (11) _____ the moral standards of the same-sex parent. (*Can you describe the specific process through which this occurs?*) The specifics of Freud's theory are not well supported.

Moral Reasoning: Cognitive-Developmental Theory

Cognitive developmental theorists such as Piaget and Kohlberg focused on moral reasoning. Kohlberg developed a theory of moral reasoning that consists of three levels, each with two stages. Progress through these stages follows an (12) _____, or fixed order. The (13) _____ level consists of stage 1, the punishment-and-obedience orientation, where the emphasis is on the (14) _____ of an act, and stage 2, called (15) _____, where an act is judged by whether it satisfies personal needs or results in personal gain. The (16) _____ level consists of stage 3, the "good boy" or "good girl" morality, where actions are right if they please others or are approved by others, and stage 4, the authority and social-order-maintaining morality with its focus on conforming to (17) _____. The last level of moral reasoning is (18) _____ morality, which includes stages 5 and 6. Stage five is the morality of contract, individual rights, and democratically accepted law, and stage six is the morality of individual principles of conscience. (***Can you provide responses that portray these six different stages?***)

Moral Behavior: Social Learning Theory

Social learning theorists focus mainly on moral behaviors. According to this view, moral behavior is learned the same way everything else is learned -- through reinforcement (or punishment) and through (19) _____. A major difference between social learning theory and the other theories of moral development is that social learning theorists view morality as (20) _____ behavior rather than a general trait.

THE INFANT

Infants in our society are often viewed as lacking any sense of morality, or as being (21) _____.

Early Moral Training

Although infants are not held morally responsible for their actions, they are learning lessons about what is right and wrong. Children must learn to experience negative emotions when they do something wrong and to control their impulses to violate rules. (***How can parents help children develop a sense of morality?***) In addition to parent's actions, a child's (22) _____ is an important influence on moral development. The interaction between the child and his/her environment is an example of (23) _____. (***What is an example of this?***)

Prosocial Behavior

Infants display some rudimentary signs of (24) _____ or understanding another person's feelings. They are not yet able to share or help another person or otherwise engage in (25) _____ behaviors until sometime during the second year of life.

THE CHILD
Research on Kohlberg's View

School-aged children typically reason at the (26) _____ level when tested with Kohlberg's moral dilemmas.

Research on Piaget's View

According to Piaget, preschool children are premoral and show little awareness of rules. Elementary school-age children take rules very seriously and believe that consequences are more important than intentions. Older children view rules as agreements between individuals and believe intentions are more important than consequences.

Research on Piaget's theory of moral reasoning indicates that he underestimated young children.

When Piaget's moral reasoning tasks are simplified, even young children can consider a person's (27) _____ when making moral judgments. In addition, young children may not view rules as sacred. Turiel reports that young children distinguish between two kinds of rules in daily life. (28) _____ rules focus on basic rights and privileges of individuals and (29) _____ rules focus on what social consensus deems right or wrong. Even young children understand the difference between these two types of rules and understand that violating a (30) _____ rule is the more serious transgression.

Moral Behavior

Research with children on resistance to temptation indicates that moral behavior is not consistent across (31) _____. (***How have researchers studied resistance to temptation?***) Moral inconsistency due to situation-specific differences supports (32) _____ theory. These theorists recommend that parents foster moral maturity using the same principles that apply to other behaviors: reinforcement and punishment, and observation of moral behavior.

Moral development has been related to parental discipline styles. Disciplining by withholding attention, love, or approval is called (33) _____. (34) _____ is the use of physical power to gain compliance to rules. Explaining to a child why a behavior is wrong and pointing out how it affects other people is (35) _____. The use of (36) _____ is associated with higher levels of moral maturity than use of the other two discipline styles. (***Can you explain why this is true?***) The use of (37) _____ is often associated with immature moral responses, and (38) _____ has been found to have mixed effects. The way children respond to moral training may depend on their (39) _____. (***How might this affect moral training?***)

THE ADOLESCENT
Changes in Moral Reasoning

Most adolescents reason at the (40) _____ level of Kohlberg's model, and they begin to view morality as an important part of their identity.

Antisocial Behavior

Some adolescents engage in antisocial and delinquent behaviors. There is a weak connection between these behaviors and level of moral reasoning. According to Kenneth Dodge, the way that social cues are processed may provide a better explanation of these behaviors. There are five steps in processing information, starting with encoding and then (41) _____ of the information. Clarifying goals, searching for possible responses and evaluating these options are followed by the last step, (42) _____. Aggressive adolescents are likely to have problems with every step of processing information. (***Can you provide some examples of faulty information processing that might lead to aggressive behavior?***)

This model helps us to understand the behavior but does not fully explain why someone processes information in this maladaptive way. Recent research (see Box 12.2) on different types of aggression begins to shed some light on this. Some children show (43) _____ aggression when they become frustrated and lash out in anger. Other children show (44) _____ aggression, which they plan in order to get what they want. (***What differences emerge between these groups of aggressive children?***) Aggression is likely determined by a combination of genetic and environmental influences. According to Gerald Patterson, (45) _____ family environments, where members try to control one another, are associated with antisocial children.

THE ADULT
Moral Development

Some adults move into Kohlberg's (46) _____ level of moral reasoning and moral reasoning does not deteriorate in old age, and indeed it may improve.

Religion and Adult Life

Religiousness develops similarly to morality. Religious activity and beliefs are fairly consistent from middle to old age. Adults who are highly involved in religion tend to be better adjusted than those who are not.

KOHLBERG'S THEORY OF MORAL DEVELOPMENT IN PERSPECTIVE
Support for Kohlberg

There is support for Kohlberg's claim that moral development is stage-like.

Factors that Promote Moral Growth

Cognitive developmental theorists claim that cognitive growth and relevant social experiences contribute to moral development. Research suggests that general cognitive abilities are necessary but not sufficient for moral development. (***Can you specify how different levels of cognitive reasoning are related to different levels of moral reasoning?***) Kohlberg believed that one important social experience was interacting with others, particularly peers, in order to be exposed to different levels of moral reasoning, which could create cognitive (47) _____. This was thought to be necessary in order to advance to higher levels of reasoning. (***What are some other important social experiences that affect moral development?***)

Is the Theory Biased?

Kohlberg has been criticized for several reasons. One important criticism is that his theory is biased in several ways. It may be biased against people from different cultures, people with conservative values, and against women. In some studies, women reason at stage (48) _____ while men reason at stage (49) _____. Carol Gilligan argues that women reason using a morality of (50) _____ and men reason using a morality of (51) _____. (***Can you explain what these perspectives mean?***) Gilligan claims that neither focus is "right;" they are simply different ways to reason, and reflect differences in how boys and girls are traditionally raised in our society. Gilligan's theory is not well supported by research.

Is the Theory Incomplete?

Another criticism of Kohlberg's theory is that it is incomplete because it ignores moral affect and behavior. Kohlberg would predict that moral behavior is related to level of moral reasoning. Overall, however, this relationship is weak.

REVIEW OF KEY TERMS

Below is a list of terms and concepts from this chapter. Match each one with its appropriate definition. You might also want to try writing definitions in your own words and then checking your definitions with those here in the Study Guide or in the text.

amoral	false belief task
belief-desire psychology	induction
coercive family environment	internalization
conventional morality	joint attention
desire psychology	love withdrawal
empathy	moral affect

morality   proactive aggression
morality of care   reactive aggression
morality of justice   prosocial behavior
moral reasoning   role-taking skills
moral rules   social cognition
postconventional morality   social-conventional rules
power assertion   theory of mind
preconventional morality

1. The _____ is used to assess the understanding that people can have incorrect beliefs that influence their behavior.

2. _____ are standards of what behaviors are right or wrong based on rights and privileges of individuals.

3. Kohlberg's fifth and sixth stages are part of the _____ in which judgments are based on broad principles of justice that have validity separate from the views of any particular person or group.

4. _____ is the cognitive process of deciding whether an act is right or wrong.

5. _____ is a type of discipline style based on physical power of the adult over the child.

6. People who consciously decide to act out against others to dominate them exhibit _____.

7. Kohlberg's first two stages of moral reasoning are part of the _____ in which the personal consequences of a person's actions are used as the basis for judgments.

8. Infants show _____ when they look at an object with a caregiver.

9. A moral perspective that emphasizes one's responsibility for the welfare of others is called _____.

10. Thinking about the thoughts, behaviors, motives, and emotions of oneself and others is called _____.

11. People who lash out in anger when frustrated exhibit _____.

12. _____ is a type of discipline style based on explanations that focus on how the misbehavior affects other people.

13. _____ is a set of principles that allow a person to distinguish right from wrong, and act on this distinction.

14. Understanding that people have mental states that influence behavior shows the presence of a _____.

15. Kohlberg's third and fourth stages are part of the _____ in which actions are judged by whether they conform to the rules set forth by others.

16. Experiencing another person's feelings is _____.

17. The ability to take another person's perspective and understand their thoughts and feelings is _____.

18. _____ is the emotional component of morality, consisting of feelings about right and wrong actions.

19. The lack of any sense of morality is referred to as being _____.

20. A discipline style that is based on threatened or actual loss of love or attention is _____.

21. _____ includes an understanding that a person's beliefs do not always accurately reflect reality.

22. _____ is the process of acquiring the standards of other people as your own.

23. _____ includes positive social acts that show a concern for the welfare of others.

24. _____ are standards for defining what behaviors are right or wrong based on social consensus.

25. A moral perspective that emphasizes the laws defining individual rights is _____.

26. Family interactions that are characterized by power struggles where members try to control each other exist in _____.

27. According to _____, young children understand what they want and often use wants to explain behavior.

MULTIPLE CHOICE SELF TEST

For each multiple choice question, read all alternatives and then select the best answer.

1. Having a theory of mind shows an understanding that
    a. people's behavior is guided by a set of internalized set of rules about right and wrong
    b. more than one person is looking at an object at a particular time
    c. people have mental states that influence their behavior
    d. other people experience different emotions

2. Children who are popular and have close friends
    a. reason at the "good boy" "good girl" stage of moral reasoning
    b. tend to use more reactive aggression than proactive aggression
    c. are more likely to have an intuitive theory of emotions
    d. tend to have more advanced role-taking skills than other children

3.	Social cognitive skills
	a.	reach a peak as adolescents finish their formal schooling and then slowly decline
	b.	remain high in socially active older adults
	c.	relate specifically to a person's educational level
	d.	decline from young to older adulthood for most adults

4.	According to Freud's psychoanalytic theory
	a.	children reach moral maturity around age 6 or 7 when they resolve their Oedipal (or Electra) conflicts
	b.	girls are more morally mature than boys since they have less to fear during the phallic stage of development
	c.	children reach moral maturity in adolescence when they enter the genital stage of development
	d.	the reasons behind an act are more important than how one feels about a moral action

5.	Research on Freud's explanation of morality shows that all of the following are PROBLEMS with the explanation EXCEPT:
	a.	males do not have stronger superegos than females
	b.	children do not achieve moral maturity by resolving the conflicts of the phallic stage
	c.	children do not develop greater moral maturity by interacting with cold, punitive parents
	d.	children do not experience feelings in conjunction with moral transgressions

6.	A child says that it is wrong to cheat because he or she might get caught would be in Kohlberg's _____ stage.
	a.	punishment-and-obedience orientation (stage 1)
	b.	instrumental hedonism (stage 2)
	c.	"good boy" or "good girl" morality (stage 3)
	d.	authority and social-order-maintaining morality (stage 4)

7.	A teenager who begins smoking because all his friends are doing it, is probably in Kohlberg's _____ stage.
	a.	instrumental hedonism (stage 2)
	b.	"good boy" or "good girl" morality (stage 3)
	c.	authority and social-order-maintaining morality (stage 4)
	d.	morality of contract, individual rights, and democratically accepted law (stage 5)

8.	Social learning theorists argue that morality is
	a.	a generalized trait inherent to the person and subject to little change
	b.	a situation-specific trait that is subject to change
	c.	an emotional reaction and cannot be directly observed
	d.	established in early childhood and changes little after this

9.	Piaget argued that elementary school children
	a.	are largely unaware of moral rules and so do not always act appropriately
	b.	base decisions on both consequences of an action and intentions of the actor
	c.	believe that rules can be changed at any time
	d.	believe that the consequences of an action are more important than intentions of the actor

10. Standards of what behaviors are right or wrong based on rights and privileges of individuals are termed
    a. postconventional rules
    b. social-conventional rules
    c. moral rules
    d. altruistic rules

11. Recent studies of Kohlberg's and Piaget's theories of moral reasoning suggest that
    a. there is no relationship between level of cognitive development and moral reasoning
    b. they underestimated children's moral reasoning capabilities
    c. they overestimated children's moral reasoning capabilities
    d. they focused too much attention on children's actions in a moral situation

12. Parents who discipline their children by making them anxious about whether they will receive affection or approval are using
    a. love withdrawal
    b. power assertion
    c. emotional assertion
    d. induction

13. Parents who use an inductive style of discipline
    a. indoctrinate their child with their own values and beliefs
    b. withhold attention until their child complies with rules
    c. use their power to get their child to comply with rules
    d. explain to their child why the behavior is wrong and emphasize how it affects other people

14. Moral maturity can be fostered by
    a. using an inductive style of discipline
    b. using love-withdrawal as the major disciplinary method
    c. using power assertion as the major disciplinary method
    d. harsh discipline that leaves the child in no doubt about whether a behavior is acceptable or not

15. Carol Gilligan claims that men and women score at different levels on Kohlberg's moral dilemmas because
    a. males operate on the basis of a morality of justice and women do not
    b. Freud was right--females are less morally mature
    c. males are more concerned about the needs of others
    d. males reason about real life dilemmas while women reason about hypothetical moral issues

REVIEW KOHLBERG'S SIX STAGES OF MORAL REASONING

For this exercise, indicate how a person in each of Kohlberg's six stages would respond to the following Kohlberg dilemma. Use Box 12.1 in the text to check your answers.

Once there was man named Henry, who lived in a small town. Early one morning Henry and his wife were driving to town along a winding country road. It was still very early in the morning, and the sun was just beginning to rise. A very heavy fog still covered the road. It was difficult for Henry to see where he was driving. Suddenly, there was a sharp curve in the road. Henry lost control of the car. Henry was not hurt, but his wife was lying unconscious on the floor of the front seat. Henry did not know how badly she was hurt, but worried because it might be hours before another car came along the isolated road. Henry's car was completely smashed, and there were no other cars passing by on the road. There were no houses in sight. But Henry did see a small farm truck with keys locked in it. So he broke the truck's window, put his wife into the truck, and drove her to the hospital. Should Henry have stolen the truck?

MORAL STAGE	EXPLANATION
Stage 1: Punishment & obedience orientation	
Stage 2: Instrumental hedonism	
Stage 3: "Good boy" or "good girl" morality	
Stage 4: Authority & social-order-maintaining morality	
Stage 5: Morality of contract, individual rights, and democratically accepted law	
Stage 6: Morality of individual principles of conscience	

APPLICATION QUESTIONS

By answering the following questions, you will strengthen your understanding of the material in this chapter. These questions require higher level thinking skills such as integration and application of concepts. To get you started, there is a sample answer or outline provided for the first question. This illustrates one possibility, but there are other answers you could provide that might be just as good. For the other questions, you can check yourself by referring to the text (a hint is provided), or by asking a peer or your instructor to review your answer.

1. What is it about an induction approach to discipline that leads to greater moral maturity in comparison to children raised with power assertion or love withdrawal?
    [Sample answer provided]

2.	On Halloween night, several of your friends try to talk you into going out with them to pull some pranks in the neighborhood (e.g., soaping the neighbor's windows, scaring young children, and knocking over gravestones). You are considering it. What preconventional, conventional, and postconventional answers might you give (either to join in or to abstain)?
	[Hint: Review the section in the text on Kohlberg's theory and Box 12.1, which gives sample answers for each stage of moral reasoning.]

3.	What can parents do to increase a child's social cognitive skills and foster moral maturity?
	[Hint: There is information on this issue in several places throughout the chapter, including within the discussion of "Theory of mind," "Role-taking skills," "Early moral training," and "How does one raise moral children?" In addition, the Application on "Combating youth violence" provides useful information.]

ANSWERS

Chapter Summary and Guided Review (Fill-in the blank)

1.	false belief task	27.	intentions
2.	theory of mind	28.	moral
3.	joint attention	29.	social-conventional
4.	belief-desire	30.	moral
5.	physical	31.	situations
6.	egocentric	32.	social learning
7.	affective	33.	love withdrawal
8.	cognitive	34.	power assertion
9.	empathy	35.	induction
10.	superego	36.	induction
11.	internalize	37.	power assertion
12.	invariant	38.	love withdrawal
13.	preconventional	39.	temperaments
14.	consequences	40.	conventional
15.	instrumental hedonism	41.	interpretation
16.	conventional	42.	enactment
17.	laws or rules	43.	reactive
18.	postconventional	44.	proactive
19.	observation	45.	coercive
20.	situation-specific	46.	postconventional
21.	amoral	47.	disequilibrium
22.	temperament	48.	three
23.	goodness of fit	49.	four
24.	empathy	50.	care
25.	prosocial	51.	justice
26.	preconventional		

Review of Key Terms

1.	false belief task	3.	postconventional morality
2.	moral rules	4.	moral reasoning

5. power assertion
6. proactive aggression
7. preconventional morality
8. joint attention
9. morality of care
10. social cognition
11. reactive aggression
12. induction
13. morality
14. theory of mind
15. conventional morality

16. empathy
17. role taking skills
18. moral affect
19. amoral
20. love withdrawal
21. belief-desire psychology
22. internalization
23. prosocial behavior
24. social-conventional rules
25. morality of justice
26. coercive family environments

Multiple Choice Self Test

1.	C	6.	A	11.	B		
2.	D	7.	B	12.	A		
3.	B	8.	B	13.	D		
4.	A	9.	D	14.	A		
5.	D	10.	C	15.	A		

Application Questions

1. *Induction encourages children to think about how their actions affect other people. This gets them away from thinking egocentrically and focusing solely on how things benefit or harm themselves. This also fosters empathy. By pointing out why a child's behavior was wrong, parents can communicate standards of behavior that children can incorporate into their future actions. All these things help advance morality, particularly in children with temperaments that are high in emotionality and low in impulsivity.*

CHAPTER THIRTEEN

ATTACHMENT AND SOCIAL RELATIONSHIPS

OVERVIEW

Relationships with others have a tremendous influence on our lives. As noted in the text, close relationships provide learning opportunities that affect all areas of development. They also provide social support that helps us celebrate positive events and protects us from negative events. This chapter discusses the first major relationship--the one that develops between infants and their caregivers--and how the quality of this relationship influences later development.

The chapter also covers peer relations and friendships, including how they evolve and change over the life span and factors that contribute to the quality of social relationships (for instance, why are some children more popular than others?). For children, play is particularly important because it provides opportunities to interact with others and learn skills for successful social relationships. In particular, pretend play is associated with better performance on some tests of cognitive development, language, and creativity.

The section on adolescents provides an interesting look at attachment relationships between adolescents and their parents. It also covers the transition from platonic, largely same-sex social interactions to romantic, opposite-sex interactions. The discussion of romantic relationships is continued in the section on adults, with an examination of factors that contribute to mate selection. Finally, the chapter ends by exploring ways that socially isolated and lonely people might develop more rewarding relationships.

LEARNING OBJECTIVES

After reading and studying the material in this chapter, you should be able to answer the following questions.

1.   How do relationships with others contribute to development?

2.   How does Bowlby's attachment theory explain attachment?

3.   In what ways are infants emotional beings? How are emotions socialized and regulated?

4.   What factors contribute to a caregiver's attachment to an infant?

5.   How do infants become attached to a caregiver? What are some observable signs of infant attachment?

6.   How is quality of attachment assessed? What are the types of attachment relationships between infants and caregivers? How do these relate to later development?

7.   What infant and caregiver factors determine the quality of early attachments between infant and caregiver?

8.   What features characterize peer relations and friendships at different points of the life span?

9.   What different types of play evolve during the first few years of life? What are the developmental benefits of play?

10.   What factors contribute to peer acceptance and popularity, or to peer rejection, during childhood?

11.   How do relationships with peers and parents change during adolescence? How do peers and parents influence adolescents' lives?

12.   How do social networks and friendships change during adulthood?

13.   What factors contribute to mate selection? How does type of early attachment style relate to type of romantic relationship?

14.   How can socially isolated and lonely people develop more rewarding relationships?

CHAPTER SUMMARY AND GUIDED REVIEW

The following summary provides an overview of the main points contained in this chapter of the text. Fill-in the blanks with terms that appropriately complete the sentence. Scattered throughout the summary are questions in parentheses. These are meant to encourage you to think actively as you are reading and connect this summary to the more detailed information provided in the text. You can answer these questions as you are filling in the blanks or you can complete all the blanks, then go back and reread the entire summary, addressing the questions in order to provide more depth of understanding.

PERSPECTIVES ON RELATIONSHIPS
What Can We Gain from Relationships?

Social relationships are important because they provide us with learning experiences and with (1) _____, or emotional and practical help that provides strength and helps protect us from stress. People who provide support are said to be part of a (2) _____ that changes across the life span.

Which Relationships are Most Critical?

Some developmentalists believe that the relationship between parent and infant is the most important and may set the stage for all other social relationships. John Bowlby developed an influential theory of parent-child attachment. According to Bowlby, attachment is a strong affection that binds one person to another. Infants express attachment by trying to maintain (3) _____ to the figure of their attachment and by showing a preference for this person. Bowlby claims that infants are biologically predisposed to form attachments. Some species experience (4) _____, an innate form of learning where the young will follow and become attached to the first moving object they encounter during a (5) _____ early in life. Bowlby believes that early attachments between parent and infant affect later development because infants develop (6) _____ models, or representations, of what relationships should be like.

Relationships with members of one's social group, or (7) _____, are also important and are quite different from relationships with parents. One theorist placed special emphasis on the significance of (8) _____, or close friendships with peers of the same sex that emerge at around 9-12 years of age.

THE INFANT

Infants are social creatures right from the start, although the nature of social relationships changes substantially throughout infancy. Attachments are emotional connections.

Early Emotional Development

Research confirms that infants show a wide range of emotions, which emerge in a predictable order during the first two years. The earliest emotions may be (9)_____ predisposed, but then environment and culture begin to influence emotional expressions. For example, infants in our culture learn that (10) _____ emotions are more welcomed than (11)_____ ones. Infants also monitor the emotional reactions of other people in ambiguous situations to regulate their own reactions, a process called (12) _____. To manage their own emotions, infants must develop strategies for (13) _____, the process of initiating, maintaining, and altering emotional responses. (*What are some of these early strategies?*)

The First Relationship

Just as infants become attached to caregivers, caregivers become attached to their infants. Infants have a number of features that seem to facilitate the development of attachment. (***What are some*** *of these features?*) Infants and caregivers learn to take turns responding to each other's leads in (14) _____ routines or interactions.

Sometimes a close relationship does <u>not</u> develop between infants and caregivers. This may result because some babies are more difficult to love, some adults have trouble responding to infants, and the broader social context may not be conducive to developing a healthy relationship.

Infants progress through several phases as they develop a relationship with their caregivers. In the first phase, called (15) _____ responsiveness, infants are responsive to social stimuli but show no preference for one person over another. In the second phase, (16) _____ responsiveness, infants begin to show preferences for familiar companions. In the third phase, active (17) _____, or true attachment, infants will actively pursue the object of their attachment. The final phase represents a more goal-corrected (18) _____ between child and attachment figure.

One sign that an attachment has formed is (19) _____, which occurs when infants are separated from the object of their attachment. Infants may also show (20) _____, or a wary response to the approach of an unfamiliar person. (***What factors can affect this response?***) Once infants have formed an attachment, they often use that attachment figure as a (21)_____ for exploration. Thus, attachment facilitates exploratory behavior.

Types of Attachment

The (22)_____ test is a procedure for measuring the quality of an infant's attachment by observing the infant's reaction to a series of mildly stressful events. Infants who are (23) _____ attached show distress when separated from their caregiver, joy when reunited, and use of caregiver as a secure base. Infants characterized by (24) _____ attachment show distress when separated from their caregiver, but are ambivalent about being reunited, and do not really use the caregiver as a secure base. Infants characterized by (25)_____ attachment show little distress at separation from caregiver, avoid the caregiver when reunited, and do not use the caregiver as a secure base. Infants who have been abused often show a fourth pattern of attachment called (26) _____, which is a combination of elements from the resistant and avoidant styles of attachment.

What factors influence the quality of early attachment? Freud claimed that feeding is critical for the development of attachment because of the oral pleasure it provides. However, Harlow's research with monkeys does not support this. Harlow used the term (27) _____ to describe the pleasurable sensations provided by clinging to something soft and warm. Research indicates that the availability of contact comfort contributes more to attachment than feeding. Research shows that infants develop secure attachments to caregivers who are generally responsive to their needs. (***Which theories are supported by these findings? Explain how they are supported***.) Inconsistent parenting is associated with (28)_____ attachment and inappropriate amounts (too much or too little) stimulation are associated with (29) _____ attachment. In addition to the way parents interact with their infants, quality of attachment is influenced by the infant's (30) _____. Secure attachment can occur with any temperament style as long as there is a good fit with the caregiver's behavior.

Early Attachment and Later Development

Research with infants who have been raised in deprived environments shows that social isolation early in life has an adverse effect on development and the negative effects persist into childhood and adolescence. Normal development seems to require sustained interactions with responsive caregivers. Whether an infant has a secure or insecure attachment impacts on later development. (***What are the outcomes for children who are securely or insecurely attached as infants?***)

Research shows that children who had secure attachments as infants process information differently than children who had insecure attachments. This supports Bowlby's idea that infants form

(31) _____ of attachment relationships. Research also shows that quality of attachment can change over time, so an insecure attachment can become a secure one if interactions with others become more positive.

First Peer Relations

Infants are interested in other infants and begin to interact socially with them around six months of age through smiles, vocalizations, and gestures. Some researchers have suggested that infants progress through three stages of sociability. In the first stage, (32) _____, two infants are engaged together as they play with the same toy, but their focus is on the toy, not on each other. In the second stage, (33) _____, infants are more responsive to the behavior of their play partner and in the third stage, (34) _____, interactions between infants are more clearly social. By the end of their second year, infants are able to distinguish between infants as well as adults and act more sociable in the presence of familiar infants.

THE CHILD
Parent/Child Attachments

Children's attachments to their parents change throughout childhood. Interactions become more like a (35) _____ partnership where children are able to take the goals and plans of another person into consideration and act on the basis of this information.

Peer Networks

Children increasingly spend more time with their peers and in these interactions, children spend more and more time with same-sex peers.

Play

Children between the ages of 2 and 5 play quite a bit, which provides opportunities to interact with others sharpens their social skills. Their play becomes more (36)_____ and more imaginative. According to Parten's scale for classifying children's play, children who are engaged in no particular activity are in the category of (37)_____ play. Children who play alone are engaged in (38)_____ play. (39)_____ play involves watching others as they play and (40)_____ play is when two children play next to each other but not with each other. In (41)_____ play, children interact with one another, but only in (42) _____ play are children really united toward a common goal.

Children increasingly engage in more associative and cooperative play, which are the most social of these play categories. Play of preschool-aged children also becomes more imaginative. They engage in (43) _____ play when they use one thing to symbolize something else. They increasingly engage in (44) _____ play, combining their capacity for imaginary play with their social play.

Elementary school children engage in less symbolic play and more in organized games with (45) _____. According to Piaget, children must be in the (46) _____ stage of cognitive development to play games with rules.

Play is important for a number of reasons. It contributes to cognitive and social development because children get an opportunity to role play, cooperate with others, and resolve conflicts. (47) _____ development is enhanced through play because children can express feelings that they might otherwise keep to themselves.

Peer Acceptance and Popularity

Peer acceptance is often studied through (48) _____ techniques where likes and dislikes among the members of a group are examined, and children can be classified into four district categories of social status. (*What are these four categories?*) Several factors influence popularity, including some personal characteristics that the child has little control of (e.g. physical appearance, and names.) A child's competencies are also important. (*Can you describe specific factors that have been found to be related to whether a child is popular or rejected?*)

Friendships

For preschool-age children, friendships are based largely on (49) _____ activity. School-age children are more likely to have friendships based on (50) _____ where each partner acts with respect and kindness towards the other. Friends are also more likely to be (51) _____ similar to one another.

Contributions of Peers to Development

Peers may be as important to development as parents. Peer interactions contribute to development of social skills and behaviors, and to emotional development.

THE ADOLESCENT

Adolescents spend even more time with peers than children do, and the quality of peer interactions changes.

Attachments to Parents

Adolescents remain attached to their parents and may experience anxiety when separated. Those who are securely attached to their parents show better adjustment to transitions such as going to college. (*What are other benefits of a secure attachment between adolescents and parents?*)

Friendships

Friendships during adolescence focus on mutual (52) _____ and (53) _____ between the partners. Adolescents tend to choose friends who are similar in (54) _____ traits. (*How do males and females differ in their friendships during adolescence?*)

Changing Social Networks

In late childhood, children are often members of same-sex (55) _____ and interact little with the other sex. Collections of several cliques constitute a (56) _____, which serves mainly as a vehicle for structured social activities. After interacting with other-sex peers in a group setting, adolescents often begin to form couples and the existence of crowds begins to dissolve. Adolescents begin to move from same-sex peer groups to dating relationships. In our society, first dates typically occur around the age of fourteen and are usually informal arrangements.

Parent and Peer Influence

Researchers have used (57) _____, or the tendency to yield to the opinions of another person, to study parent and peer influence on adolescents. Conformity to adults tends to decrease with age. Conformity to peers to engage in antisocial acts increases with age, levels off, and then decreases by the end of high school. Despite the influence of peers during adolescence, parents and peers are not typically in conflict since adolescents consult peers and parents on different issues, not the same issues.

THE ADULT
Social Networks

Friendships continue to be important during adulthood, although the nature of the social network changes somewhat over time. Young adults spend a great deal of time interacting with members of the other sex. They also have more friends than middle-aged or older adults. The social network of most adults seems to shrink as they marry and as they get older. The (58) _____ hypothesis suggests that we narrow our social network to include people who are most important to us and this may result in an increase in the (59) _____ of the relationship.

Romantic Relationships

Udry has suggested that mate selection involves sifting through all potential partners and narrowing down the selections until one partner remains, usually someone who shares many similarities.

There may be some similarities between infants who are attached to a parent and adults who are in love with a romantic partner. As infants, we construct working models for attachment relationships that influence our adult relationships. Adults with a (60) _____ working model of attachment feel good about themselves and others and feel comfortable entering into relationships. Adults with a (61) _____ working model feel positive about others but not about themselves. They desperately want a relationship but fear abandonment. Adults with a (62) _____ working model feel positive about themselves but not about others. They deny any need for relationships and are very self-reliant. Adults with a (63) _____ working model of attachment hold negative views of themselves and others, and while they express a need for relationships, they also have a fear of closeness. (***Can you describe the implications of these attachment styles for adults?***)

Adult Friendships

Friendships continue to be important to adults. Men and women continue to show different styles of interacting with friends. (***What are these differences?***) Adults especially value friendships that have lasted many years, even if the friends live geographically distant from one another. Adults typically perceive friendships as most satisfying when they are (64) _____ or balanced.

Adult Relationships and Adult Development

Just as attachment is critical for normal infant and child development, friendships are important for normal adult development. However, it is the (65) _____ of friendships that is important, not the quantity of friendships. It seems important that adults have a (66) _____ or person to whom they are particularly close and to whom they express their feelings and thoughts.

APPLICATIONS: BUILDING GOOD RELATIONSHIPS

Some children and adults are socially isolated or lonely. These individuals often lack social cognition skills that can be improved through a variety of techniques to help develop better social relationships. (***What are some of the methods that can help socially isolated individuals?***)

REVIEW OF KEY TERMS

Below is a list of terms and concepts from this chapter. Use these to complete the following sentence definitions. You might also want to try writing definitions in your own words and then checking your definitions with those in the text.

attachment	contact comfort
attachment theory	crowd
avoidant attachment	disorganized/disoriented attachment
chumship	emotion regulation
clique	equity
confidant	imprinting
conformity	internal working model

peer
pretend play
resistant attachment
secure attachment
secure base
separation anxiety
social convoy
social pretend play

social referencing
social support
socioemotional selectivity hypothesis
sociometric techniques
stranger anxiety
Strange Situation test
synchronized routines

1. _____ is an innate form of learning in which the young of a species will follow and become attached to a moving object (usually the mother) during a critical period early in life.

2. A caregiver-infant relationship characterized by distress at separation, ambivalence at being reunited, and little use of caregiver as a secure base is called a(n) _____.

3. When separated from a caregiver to whom they are attached, many infants show wariness or fear called _____.

4. A _____ is a small, same-sex friendship group.

5. _____ is the sense that there is a balance of contributions and benefits in relationships between spouses, friends, and other intimates.

6. A close friendship with peers of the same age that emerges at about age 9 to 12 is a _____.

7. A collection of several heterosexual cliques constitutes a _____.

8. Harlow used the term _____ for the pleasure derived from clinging to something soft and warm.

9. A caregiver-infant relationship characterized by little distress at separation, avoidance of caregiver when reunited, and little exploration is a(n) _____.

10. A _____ is a member of one's social group and is usually of similar age and behavioral functioning.

11. A _____ is someone to whom an individual feels an especially close attachment and with whom thoughts and feelings can be shared.

12. The _____ consists of a series of mildly stressful events designed to measure the quality of an infant's attachment to a caregiver.

13. Infants may exhibit wariness or _____ when approached by an unfamiliar person.

14. _____ attempts to explain the bond that develops between parent and child as well as the emotional ties between other people.

15. The emotional and practical assistance that helps protect individuals from stress is
    _____.

16. _____ is the tendency to change or develop opinions to go along with those of
    another person or group.

17. _____ are the integrated interactions between partners who take turns responding to
    each other's leads.

18. Infants must learn strategies for _____ in order to successfully initiate, maintain, and
    alter their emotional responses.

19. An attachment figure who serves as a safe place from which an infant can explore the
    environment is considered to be a _____.

20. _____ is a strong affectionate tie that binds a person to an intimate companion.

21. A caregiver-infant relationship characterized by distress at separation, joy at being reunited, and
    use of caregiver as a secure base indicates the presence of a _____.

22. Using one thing to represent something else in a playful context is _____.

23. _____ are methods of studying social groups by determining likes and dislikes
    among the members of the group.

24. The changing composition of one's social support system over the life span is reflected in one's
    _____.

25. A combination of resistant and avoidant styles of attachment in which infants are confused about
    whether to approach or avoid a parent is a _____.

26. According to the _____, we narrow our social contact to the people who are most
    important to us.

27. A(n) _____ is a cognitive representation about social interactions, which shapes
    expectations for future relationships.

28. Social play and symbolic play are combined in _____.

29. Through the process of _____, infants monitor the emotional reactions of others and
    use this information to guide their own behavior.

For each multiple choice question, read all alternatives and then select the best answer.

1. Infants show attachment through which of the following behaviors?
   a. showing a preference for one person over another
   b. trying to maintain proximity to a person
   c. showing distress when a person leaves
   d. all of the above

2. According to Bowlby's attachment theory:
   a. infants must develop an attachment during a critical period early in life or they will not form later attachments
   b. infants become attached to the caregiver who feeds them
   c. infants are biologically predisposed to form attachments
   d. through reinforcement, infants learn to form attachments

3. In the discriminating social responsiveness phase of developing attachment, infants
   a. respond to many different social stimuli such as voices and faces
   b. respond differently depending on the social situation
   c. show preferences for familiar companions
   d. show clear attachment by following the object of their attachment and protesting when this person leaves

4. Stranger anxiety would be greatest in which of the following situations?
   a. Seated on mother's lap at the doctor's office while mom warmly greets the doctor.
   b. Seated on mother's lap at home while mom warmly greets the next door neighbor.
   c. Seated on mother's lap at home while mom neutrally greets a salesperson.
   d. Seated across from mother at the doctor's office while mom neutrally greets the doctor.

5. According to Freud, infants become attached to their mothers because
   a. mothers become associated with pleasurable sensations
   b. mothers are generally responsive to their needs
   c. they are innately predisposed to form attachments
   d. mothers provide oral pleasure

6. Which of the following describes infants who have resistant attachment?
   a. Infants use their mother as a secure base, they are upset when she leaves them, and welcome her when she returns.
   b. Infants are upset when their mother leaves them and are ambivalent when she returns.
   c. Infants are not really distressed when their mother leaves them and do not welcome her back when she returns.
   d. Infants are not really distressed when their mother leaves them and express joy when reunited with mother.

7. With respect to the relationship between security of attachment during infancy and social competence during adulthood, research suggests that
   a. quality of infant attachment does not predict adult social competence as well as peer relations during adolescence do
   b. quality of infant attachment has no relation to social competence during adulthood
   c. quality of infant attachment to parents is the most important predictor of adult social competence
   d. individuals who were securely attached as infants always have positive social relationships

8. The finding that infant monkeys in Harlow's research preferred the cloth surrogate over the wire surrogate regardless of which one provided food
   a. supports Erikson's claim that general responsiveness is important to development of attachment
   b. shows that there is an innate predisposition to form attachments
   c. shows that Freud's emphasis on feeding behavior cannot fully explain development of attachment
   d. supports learning theory explanations of attachment since infants become attached to the mother who reinforced them with food

9. Social referencing refers to an infant's ability to
   a. recognize familiar companion
   b. compare self to others
   c. use other people's reactions to guide their own behavior
   d. imitate other people's behavior

10. Effects of early social deprivation in human infants
   a. cannot be overcome
   b. can be overcome if the infants are placed with affectionate and responsive caregivers
   c. can be overcome if the infants are exposed to multiple caregivers
   d. are usually not significant

11. The capacity for pretend play emerges
   a. at birth
   b. around 6-7 months of age
   c. around 1 year
   d. around 3 years

12. Children who do not actually participate in play with others but watch others play are engaged in
   _____ play.
   a. solitary   c. parallel
   b. unoccupied   d. onlooker

13. Pretend play
   a. can be used to assess children's level of intellectual functioning
   b. can provide children the opportunity to work through problems
   c. shows the same pattern in all children
   d. increases when children enter elementary school

14. With respect to conformity to pressure during adolescence
    a. there is no difference between conformity to pressure from adults and pressure from peers
    b. conformity to peer pressure for antisocial acts increases, peaks around ninth grade, and then decreases
    c. adolescents are more likely to conform to peer pressure for prosocial acts than antisocial acts
    d. adolescents are more likely to conform to parental pressure than peer pressure

15. Steve, a 32-year-old, is fiercely self-sufficient and refuses to accept help from others. He claims that he has no time for relationships and when he does date, he feels that his partner wants more out of the relationship than he does. Steve's internal working model of attachment is BEST characterized as:
    a. secure
    b. preoccupied
    c. dismissing
    d. fearful

PEOPLE AND THEIR IDEAS

We have reviewed lots of ideas and concepts from this chapter. Now consider the people who contributed many of these ideas. Use the matching exercise below to review the contributions of some of the more influential people discussed in this chapter. Write the appropriate letter next to the person's name.

1. Mary Ainsworth   _____
2. John Bowlby   _____
3. Harry Harlow   _____
4. Konrad Lorenz   _____

a. Developed a theory of attachment that combined elements of ethological and psychoanalytic theories.
b. Conducted research with goslings that demonstrated the process of imprinting during a critical period of development.
c. Conducted research with monkeys demonstrating that contact comfort was more important than feeding practices in the development of attachment.
d. Created an assessment protocol that allows researchers to determine the quality of young children's attachment to their caregiver.

APPLICATION QUESTIONS

By answering the following questions, you will strengthen your understanding of the material in this chapter. These questions require higher level thinking skills such as integration and application of concepts. To get you started, there is a sample answer or outline provided for the first question. This illustrates one possibility, but there are other answers you could provide that might be just as good. For the other questions, you can check yourself by referring to the text (a hint is provided), or by asking a peer or your instructor to review your answer.

1. What are the likely outcomes for children who, as infants, were insecurely attached to their caregiver? What factors influence the outcome for these children?
   [Sample answer provided.]

2. What aspects of children's development are fostered by engaging in pretend play?
   [Hint: Review the section in the text on "What good is play?"]

3. What factors influence whether a child is popular or rejected in peer relationships?
   [Hint: Review the section in the text on "Peer acceptance and popularity?"]

ANSWERS

Chapter Summary and Guided Review (Fill-in the blank)

1.	social support	34.	complementary interactive
2.	social convoy	35.	goal-corrected
3.	proximity	36.	social
4.	imprinting	37.	unoccupied
5.	critical period	38.	solitary
6.	internal working	39.	onlooker
7.	peers	40.	parallel
8.	chumships	41.	associative
9.	biologically	42.	cooperative
10.	positive	43.	pretend
11.	negative	44.	social pretend
12.	social referencing	45.	rules
13.	emotion regulation	46.	concrete operations
14.	synchronized	47.	emotional
15.	undiscriminating social	48.	sociometric
16.	discriminating social	49.	common
17.	proximity seeking	50.	mutual loyalty
18.	partnership	51.	psychologically
19.	separation anxiety	52.	intimacy
20.	stranger anxiety	53.	self-disclosure
21.	secure base	54.	psychological
22.	Strange Situation	55.	cliques
23.	securely	56.	crowd
24.	resistant	57.	conformity
25.	avoidant	58.	socioemotional selectivity
26.	disorganized/disoriented	59.	quality
27.	contact comfort	60.	secure
28.	resistant	61.	preoccupied
29.	avoidant	62.	dismissing
30.	temperament	63.	fearful
31.	internal working models	64.	equitable
32.	object-centered	65.	quality
33.	simple interactive	66.	confidant

Review of Key Terms

1. imprinting
2. resistant attachment
3. separation anxiety
4. clique
5. equity
6. chumship
7. crowd
8. contact comfort
9. avoidant attachment
10. peer
11. confidant
12. Strange Situation test
13. stranger anxiety
14. attachment theory
15. social support

16. conformity
17. synchronized routines
18. emotion regulation
19. secure base
20. attachment
21. secure attachment
22. pretend play
23. sociometric techniques
24. social convoy
25. disorganized/disoriented attachment
26. socioemotional selectivity hypothesis
27. internal working model
28. social pretend play
29. social referencing

Multiple Choice Self Test

1.	D	6.	B	11.	C		
2.	C	7.	A	12.	D		
3.	C	8.	C	13.	B		
4.	D	9.	C	14.	B		
5.	D	10.	B	15.	C		

People and Their Ideas

1. D
2. A
3. C
4. B

Application Questions

1.   *Infants with insecure attachments tend to have parents who are inconsistent with their caregiving or provide inappropriate amounts (too much or too little) of caregiving. Characteristics of the infant also influence whether a secure or insecure attachment develops between parent and child. In situations where there is a poor fit between the infant's temperament and the parent's caregiving style, an insecure attachment may develop and have long lasting effects. Children who had been insecurely attached as infants tend to be less curious and less likely to pursue their goals than children who had been securely attached. They also tend to be socially withdrawn and less likely to draw other children into play. This carries through to adolescence, with insecure children less adjusted in terms of both intellectual and social skills. These differences may relate to how children process information. Children who have formed insecure attachments develop internal working models that lead them to have negative expectations of interactions with others. In contrast, securely attached children tend to remember positive events and have more positive expectations of interactions.*

CHAPTER FOURTEEN

THE FAMILY

OVERVIEW

We all live in some sort of family, whether it is our family of origin with our mother and/or father and siblings, or in a family with our spouse and possibly our own children. Or we might be a member of a gay or lesbian family or a single adult who thinks of friends as family. What effects do these family systems have on our development? This chapter focuses on this question, looking at both traditional and nontraditional types of families. At the beginning of the chapter, it is noted that traditional families of a working father and a stay-at-home mother are no longer typical. Cultural changes of the 20th century have led to many different family configurations.

Have you ever wondered what life is like for parents after their children are grown and leave home? Or perhaps you are curious about whether siblings, amid the rivalry and fighting, have any positive influences on one another? Do fathers interact any differently with their babies than do mothers? Are adolescents and their parents consistently battling it out with one another? These are the sorts of questions that this chapter on the family addresses. In reading the research about family systems across the life span, you may gain some insight into processes within your own family.

LEARNING OBJECTIVES

After reading and studying the material in this chapter, you should be able to answer the following questions.

1. How is the family viewed by the family systems theory?

2. How do individual family systems change? How have families in general changed during the 20th century?

3. How is the father/infant relationship similar to and different from the mother/infant relationship?

4. How do parents indirectly affect their children?

5.   What are two basic dimensions of parenting? What patterns of child rearing emerge from these dimensions? How do these parenting styles affect children's development?

6.   How do social class, culture, and ethnic variations affect parenting style?

7.   What effects do children have on their parents?

8.   What features characterize sibling relationships across the life span? How do siblings contribute to development?

9.   What are relationships like between adolescents and their parents?

10.   How does marriage and parenthood affect adults? What changes occur in the family as the children mature and leave home?

11.   What sorts of roles do grandparents establish with their grandchildren?

12.   How do various family relationships change during adulthood?

13.   What sorts of diversity exist in today's families? What is the life satisfaction of people in these different types of families?

14.   How does divorce affect family relationships?

15.   How can spouse abuse and child abuse be reduced?

The following summary provides an overview of the main points contained in this chapter of the text. Fill-in the blanks with terms that appropriately complete the sentence. Scattered throughout the summary are questions in parentheses. These are meant to encourage you to think actively as you are reading and connect this summary to the more detailed information provided in the text. You can answer these questions as you are filling in the blanks or you can complete all the blanks, then go back and reread the entire summary, addressing the questions in order to provide more depth of understanding.

UNDERSTANDING THE FAMILY

The Family as a System

According to family systems theory, the family is a social system, meaning that it is a whole unit consisting of interrelated parts. The (1) _____ family consists of a mother, father, and at least one child. In a(n) (2) _____ family, parents and their children live with other relatives.

The Family as a System within Other Systems

Families exist within a larger social system and cultural context influences the experiences within families.

The Family as a Changing System

Family membership changes over time and the relationships within families also develop and change over time. One family development theory uses the concept of a family (3) _____ to characterize the sequence of changes in family membership and relationships that occur over time.

A Changing Family System in a Changing World

The changing family exists within a changing world and several social changes of the 20th century have significantly affected the family. Our society has a greater number of single adults and more adults are delaying marriage and childbearing than in the past. More women are participating in the labor force and our society has seen a rise in the divorce rate and in the number of children living in poverty. There are more single-parent families and more (4) _____ families as divorced adults remarry. For a variety of reasons, adults today spend more years without children than in past generations, and increased longevity contributes to longer relationships with parents, grandparents, and even great-grandparents. These multigenerational (four or more) families are referred to as (5) _____ families.

THE INFANT

The Mother/Infant Relationship

Mothers are traditionally the primary caregivers for infants, and mothers and infants typically develop an attachment to one another. The mother-infant relationship is (6)_____, meaning that mothers can affect the development of their infants and infants can affect the behavior of their mothers.

The Father/Infant Relationship

Fathers are equally capable of parenting, however they differ from mothers in both the quantity and quality of the parenting that they actually provide. Mothers spend more time with children than fathers do, and mothers' interactions with their children tend to be related to providing care while fathers' interactions are more likely to be (7)_____ oriented. Fathers are likely to treat boys and girls more differently than do mothers and contribute to the gender-role development of both sons and daughters. Boys and girls both benefit from having fathers who are involved in their development.

The Family

<u>Mothers, Fathers, and Infants: The System at Work</u>

In addition to these effects, parents have many (8)_____ effects on their children through their ability to influence their spouses. (***Can you provide several examples of this type of effect?***) Children benefit from a three-person system in which parents support each other, allowing each to be good parents.

THE CHILD
<u>Dimensions of Child Rearing</u>

Good parenting is defined by the specific culture or subculture in which families live. One dimension of parenting, called (9) _____, describes how affectionate and sensitive parents are toward their child. A second dimension of parenting, (10)_____, describes the degree of autonomy that parents allow their children. Four basic patterns of child rearing emerge from crossing these two dimensions. A(n) (11) _____ parenting style is a very restrictive style where parents impose many rules without explaining their importance, and often use physical means to gain compliance to the rules. A(n) (12) _____ parenting style is one where children are allowed a fair amount of freedom, but rules are clearly stated, explained, and enforced. A(n) (13) _____ parenting style is a lax style of parenting where few rules are imposed on children and children are encouraged to express their feelings and impulses. Finally, (14) _____ parenting occurs when parents are uninvolved in their children's upbringing. (***What are the characteristics of children raised with each of these styles? Which of these styles of parenting seems to have the "best" outcome in our society?***)

Parenting styles are related to socioeconomic factors. (***Can you describe differences in parenting or goals associated with social class?***) Differences might result because of stresses associated with economic problems, or because of differences in skills useful or necessary to parents in blue-collar versus white-collar jobs. Culture and ethnic variations also lead to differences in parenting styles.

According to a (15) _____, parenting style is also influenced by the child. That is, children can influence their parents. A child's age, competence level, and (16) _____ can all elicit a particular style of parenting and a compatible discipline method from the parent. Boys with (17) _____ seem to elicit "bad parenting" from all mothers.

<u>Sibling Relationships</u>

A second child in the family often creates (18) _____, or feelings of competition, jealousy, and resentment between siblings. Many sibling relationships are also characterized by ambivalence. While sibling relationships can involve negative conflicts, siblings also have many positive effects on one another. For example, siblings provide (19) _____ for one another. Older siblings often provide (20) _____ services for younger siblings and serve as (21) _____ for new behaviors.

THE ADOLESCENT
<u>Parent/Child Closeness</u>

Some people believe that adolescence is a particularly stressful period for parent-child relationships. Most teenagers, however, view their relationship with their parents as positive and close.

<u>Renegotiating the Relationship</u>

A major task of adolescence is to achieve (22) _____, or the ability to function independently. This creates some conflict with parents until adolescents and parents renegotiate the power and rules between them. While adolescents work to achieve autonomy, they also try to maintain a close attachment with their parents. (***How can parents help adolescents successfully achieve autonomy?***)

THE ADULT

Establishing the Marriage

Most adults in our society marry and typically marry for love. Marriage is a major adjustment for both partners, and some deterioration in the relationship occurs during the first year.

New Parenthood

Many couples have children within a few years of getting married and this is another major life transition with both positive and negative changes. Marital satisfaction tends to (23) _____ from before to after the birth of a child and this change is more pronounced for women than men. Some babies are more difficult than others, which increases stress, and some adults are less equipped to deal with the stress of parenthood. A lack of resources, including spousal support, can also increase stress of parenthood.

The Child-Rearing Family

Having a second child is another stressful event for the family and marital satisfaction typically remains somewhat depressed with the addition of more children to the family. Despite these declines, marital satisfaction is generally high overall.

The Empty Nest

As children reach maturity and leave their parent's home, the family system changes once again. "Empty nest" is used to describe the family structure after all children have left the home. Marital satisfaction tends to (24) _____ following the departure of children. (*Why do parents react this way to their children leaving home?*)

Grandparenthood

Many adults become grandparents in middle-age and do not fit the stereotyped image of white-haired elderly grandparents. Researchers have identified three major styles of grandparenting. (25) _____ grandparents are largely symbolic figures who do not interact a great deal with grandchildren. (26) _____ grandparents frequently see their grandchildren and enjoy sharing activities with them. Grandparents who are (27) _____ assume a parent like role and provide some degree of child care for their grandchildren. Relationships between grandchildren and their (28) _____ grandmothers tend to be the closest.

Changing Family Relationships

As noted above, marital satisfaction appears to decline when children enter the family and increases when children leave the family. Women tend to be more affected by changes in the family structure than men. Many factors other than stage of family life cycle determine marital satisfaction. (*What are some of these factors?*)

Sibling relationships also change across the life span. Adult siblings typically keep in touch with each other, but the relationship is less intense than when siblings were young, and adult siblings rarely discuss intimate problems with each other. Nevertheless, siblings often report feeling close to one another, particularly as they get older. The sibling relationship can change in response to specific events, such as geographical moves, divorces, loss of a spouse, or illness.

Parents and children develop new relationships as the children become adults and leave home. The relationships are often more (29) _____, with recognition that each is an individual and has roles other than parent or child. Middle-aged adults continue to feel close to their parents. Many families are part of a (30) _____ family where they live in separate households but have close and frequent interaction with other relatives. The relationships among different generations tend to be (31) _____, which means that each contributes something to the relationship and gets something back in return. In most cases, there is no (32) _____ in which parents become dependent on their children and their middle-age children take on the caregiving role. Middle-aged adults may also experience (33) _____ because of the demands from both their children and their parents. This can lead to (34) _____ as their personal resources become stretched by providing care for aging parents who may have impairments.

DIVERSITY IN FAMILY LIFE
Adult lifestyles in our culture have become quite diverse. Many adults delay marriage, remain single, or become single through divorce or death of a spouse.

Singles
There are an increasing number of adults who never marry. Living with a romantic partner without being married, or (35) _____, is more common than it used to be. Some couples use living together as a test of compatibility before marrying. However, couples who live together before marrying actually seem to be more dissatisfied with the marriage and more likely to (36) _____ than couples who marry without first living together. Adults who never marry have a somewhat lower overall sense of happiness than married adults, but they are not as unhappy as (37) _____ single adults.

Childless Married Couples
More couples are choosing not to have children than in the past, although for many couples, childlessness is not a choice, but a result of infertility. Childless couples tend to have somewhat higher marital satisfaction than couples with children during the child-rearing years. Following the child-rearing years, couples with and without children are similar in their levels of marital satisfaction. As older adults, individuals who have lost their spouse and never had children may experience a lack of (38) _____.

Gay and Lesbian Families
Overall, gay and lesbian couples are more similar to heterosexual couples than they are different. The division of labor between these couples tends to be more (39) _____ than that of married couples.

Families Experiencing Divorce
Many marriages today will end in divorce, making divorce a typical part of the family life cycle. Divorce is a series of experiences, not a single event that has finite beginning and end points. It is unclear what processes cause divorce, but there are several factors that seem to place some couples at a greater risk for divorce than other couples. (***What are some factors that increase the likelihood of divorce?***) Families experiencing a divorce typically go through a (40) _____ period during which there is much disruption. The stress of a divorce places individuals at greater risk for depression, physical problems, and even death. Adults experiencing divorce often have problems parenting. Custodial mothers tend to become less accepting and responsive, as well as less consistent in their discipline. While custodial mothers often use a more restrictive style of parenting, noncustodial fathers tend to be (41) _____. Most of the problems between parents and children dissipate in the two years following a divorce, but the divorce continues to affect both children and adults.

Remarriage and Reconstituted Families
Most divorced parents remarry within five years after a divorce, often creating reconstituted families. While boys seem to suffer more than girls when parents divorce, they apparently benefit more than girls when their custodial mothers remarry. (***What are some possible reasons for this finding?***)

APPLICATIONS: CONFRONTING THE PROBLEM OF FAMILY VIOLENCE

Unfortunately, some families experience violence in the forms of child abuse, spouse abuse, and elder abuse. Many child abusers were abused or neglected themselves as children. They may also be intolerant of normal behaviors of young children. Some children may have characteristics that make them more likely targets of abuse than other children. In addition to parent and child characteristics, the surrounding social climate and lack of social (42) _____ may contribute to the likelihood of abuse in the family. Child abuse negatively impacts on its victims in a number of ways. (***Can you describe some developmental consequences of abuse?***) By identifying families that are high-risk candidates for family violence, it may be possible to provide the support necessary to prevent abuse from occurring.

REVIEW OF KEY TERMS

Below is a list of terms and concepts from this chapter. Use these to complete the following sentence definitions. You might also want to try writing definitions in your own words and then checking your definitions with those in the text.

acceptance/responsiveness	family systems theory
authoritarian parenting	indirect effects
authoritative parenting	latchkey children
autonomy	middle generation squeeze
beanpole family	modified extended family
caregiver burden	neglectful parenting
child effects model	nuclear family
cohabitation	parent effects model
demandingness/control	permissive parenting
empty nest	reconstituted family
extended family household	role reversal
family development theory	sibling rivalry
family life cycle	transactional model

1.   A family that consist of parent, stepparent, and at least one child from a previous marriage is called a _____.

2.   A flexible parenting style in which parents set clear rules and provide explanations for rules but allow children some freedom and input is _____.

3.   According to the _____, children influence their parents.

4.   A _____ consists of a mother, father, and at least one child.

5.   In a _____, nuclear families live in separate households but have close ties and frequent interaction with other relatives.

6.   _____ refers to the feelings of competition, jealousy, and resentment that can develop between siblings.

7. When single adults live with a romantic partner without being married, they are in an arrangement called _____.

8. A dimension of parenting that describes the degree of autonomy that parents allow their children is referred to as _____.

9. In a(n) _____, a family unit lives with other relatives.

10. A critical task of adolescence is achieving _____, in which adolescents must develop independence in various realms.

11. The _____ consists of the sequence of changes in family composition, roles, and relationships that occur from the time people marry to the time they die.

12. _____ is a restrictive parenting style in which parents impose many rules and use power tactics to ensure obedience to these rules.

13. According to a _____, parents and children influence one another reciprocally.

14. After children are grown and leave home, parents may experience the _____ syndrome.

15. A dimension of parenting that describes how affectionate and responsive parents are toward their child is called _____.

16. Middle-aged adults who experience demands from both younger and older generations may experience the _____.

17. _____ is a parenting style in which adults make relatively few demands, encourage children to express their feelings, and rarely exert control over their behavior.

18. The effects that parents have on their children through their influence on their spouse's behavior are _____.

19. _____ occurs in situations where aging parents become dependent on their children and the children become caregivers for their parents.

20. Children who take care of themselves after school until their parents come home are referred to as _____

21. _____ is a style of parenting in which parents are uninvolved in their children's upbringing.

22. The _____ is one where there are four or more generations, usually small, all living at one time.

23. According to _____, the family is whole unit, with interrelated parts that influence each other.

24. According to a _____, parents are assumed to influence their children, but not vice versa.

25. Middle-aged adults who must care for a parent with an impairment may experience _____ as they try to incorporate this with their other family responsibilities.

26. According to _____, the family is viewed as a developing organism.

MULTIPLE CHOICE SELF TEST

For each multiple choice question, read all alternatives and then select the best answer.

1. The family life cycle
   a. refers to the sequence of changes in family membership and roles between marriage and death
   b. refers to family units that consist of a parent, a stepparent and at least one child
   c. refers to the changes that have occurred in the family system during the 20th century
   d. undergoes dramatic changes every 10 years

2. A family unit consisting of a mother, father, and at least one child is called a _____ family.
   a. reconstituted
   b. extended
   c. nuclear
   d. beanpole

3. Compared to mothers, fathers in general
   a. spend as much time with their children
   b. spend less time with their children
   c. treat boys and girls more similarly
   d. serve as disciplinarian in the family

4. Which type of parenting style places few demands on children and allows them to express their desires freely?
   a. permissive
   b. authoritative
   c. authoritarian
   d. neglectful

5. In which style of parenting do parents value obedience for its own sake and impose many rules that are typically not fully explained to children?
   a. permissive
   b. authoritative
   c. authoritarian
   d. neglectful

6. Children of parents who use a(n) _____ style of parenting are typically more self-reliant and achievement oriented than children raised with other styles of parenting
   a. permissive
   b. authoritative
   c. authoritarian
   d. neglectful

7. Feelings of rivalry or jealousy following the birth of a new sibling
   a. are strongest if parents maintain the same regular schedule they had for the first-born before the arrival of the new baby
   b. can be minimized if the first-born had already established a good relationship with parents
   c. can be minimized if the parents lavish the first child with attention
   d. are always worse if the first-born is a boy

8. With respect to adolescent-parent relationships, research indicates:
   a. there is a huge gap between generations in their values and attitudes
   b. adolescents generally report being unhappy with the relationship
   c. boys are much more dissatisfied with the relationship than girls
   d. adolescents are strongly influenced by their parents on important issues

9. The relationship between adult siblings
   a. disintegrates once the siblings leave school
   b. remains close although less intense than during childhood
   c. involves a great deal of sharing and discussing feelings
   d. continues to be as intense as during childhood

10. Which of the following is true regarding marital satisfaction?
    a. Marital satisfaction is highest following the birth of a child.
    b. Because of the adjustments that must be made, marital satisfaction is lowest right after marriage
    c. Marital satisfaction declines following the birth of a child
    d. Marital satisfaction declines across middle and older adulthood

11. Cohabiting couples who later marry
    a. are more dissatisfied with their marriages than couples who had not lived together before marrying
    b. are more satisfied with their marriages than couples who had not lived together before marrying
    c. are less likely to divorce than couples who had not lived together before marrying
    d. are basically no different from couples who had not lived together before marrying

12. Adults who never marry
    a. typically have some psychological problem
    b. are lonely and maladjusted
    c. are much happier and better adjusted than married adults
    d. are somewhat less happy than married adults

13. Evidence indicates that following a divorce
    a. both boys and girls settle quickly into a new lifestyle with few adjustment problems
    b. boys take longer to adjust than girls and exhibit more behavior problems
    c. girls take longer to adjust than boys and exhibit more depression
    d. neither boys or girls adjust to the new lifestyle within several years of the divorce

14. Reconstituted families where children in a mother-headed family acquire a stepfather
    a. seem to benefit boys more than girls
    b. seem to benefit girls more than boys
    c. seem to benefit boys and girls equally
    d. do not benefit any of the children, just the adults

15. Child abuse is <u>less</u> likely in families where
    a. the parents had been abused themselves and so they know the negative impact that abuse can have
    b. there are multiple sources of stress
    c. there is a strong support network available to parents
    d. parents have difficulty "reading" their child's signals

APPLICATION QUESTIONS

By answering the following questions, you will strengthen your understanding of the material in this chapter. These questions require higher level thinking skills such as integration and application of concepts. To get you started, there is a sample answer or outline provided for the first question. This illustrates one possibility, but there are other answers you could provide that might be just as good. For the other questions, you can check yourself by referring to the text (a hint is provided), or by asking a peer or your instructor to review your answer.

1. What type of parenting dimensions and parent control have the best outcome for children? What makes these parenting styles effective?
   [Sample answer provided.]

2. What are potential advantages and disadvantages for children whose parents divorce?
   [Hint: Review the sections in the text on "Families experiencing divorce" and "Remarriage and reconstituted families."]

3. What affects can children have on their parents across the life span?
   [Hint: There is a little information on this topic scattered throughout the chapter, including the subsection on "Child effects on parents" and the section on "The child-rearing family."]

4. What are potential advantages and disadvantages for individuals who marry, individuals who remain single, couples who have children, and those who do not have children?
   [Hint: Review the section in the text on "Diversity in Family Life."]

Chapter Summary and Guided Review (Fill-in the blank)

1.	nuclear	22.	autonomy
2.	extended	23.	decline
3.	life cycle	24.	increase
4.	reconstituted	25.	remote
5.	beanpole	26.	companionate
6.	reciprocal	27.	involved
7.	play	28.	maternal
8.	indirect	29.	mutual
9.	acceptance/responsiveness	30.	modified extended
10.	demandingness/control	31.	equitable
11.	authoritarian	32.	role reversal
12.	authoritative	33.	middle generation squeeze
13.	permissive	34.	caregiver burden
14.	neglectful	35.	cohabitation
15.	child effects model	36.	divorce
16.	personality	37.	divorced
17.	conduct disorders	38.	social support
18.	sibling rivalry	39.	egalitarian
19.	emotional support	40.	crisis
20.	caretaking	41.	overpermissive
21.	teachers	42.	support

Review of Key Terms

1.	reconstituted family	14.	empty nest
2.	authoritative parenting	15.	acceptance/responsiveness
3.	child effects model	16.	middle generation squeeze
4.	nuclear family	17.	permissive parenting
5.	modified extended family	18.	indirect effects
6.	sibling rivalry	19.	role reversal
7.	cohabitation	20.	latchkey children
8.	demandingness/control	21.	neglectful parenting
9.	extended family household	22.	beanpole family
10.	autonomy	23.	family systems theory
11.	family life cycle	24.	parent effects model
12.	authoritarian parenting	25.	caregiver burden
13.	transactional model	26.	family development theory

Multiple Choice Self Test

1.	A	6.	B	11.	A
2.	C	7.	B	12.	D
3.	B	8.	D	13.	B
4.	A	9.	B	14.	A
5.	C	10.	C	15.	C

1.   *Parents who are warm and responsive foster more positive qualities in their children than parents who are insensitive and rejecting. These positive qualities include secure attachments to parents, high self-esteem, and competence in academic and social settings. It is also important for parents to have some degree of control with respect to decision making. Parents who set no rules (permissive parenting) have children who are impulsive, aggressive, low in self-control, and not very achievement oriented. On the other hand, parents who are overly controlling also tend to have children who exhibit some behavior difficulties. For example, authoritarian parents who set many rules without giving good explanations for why these rules are important and expect strict compliance to them, often have children who are moody, easily annoyed, and not very pleasant. The best child outcomes are seen when parents use authoritative styles of child rearing. Authoritative parents set rules but clearly explain why they are important, they are consistent in their enforcement of rules, and they allow their children to be involved in family decision making. Children raised in authoritative homes tend to be pleasant, self-reliant, cooperative, and achievement-oriented. These traits continue to be evident into adolescence.*

    Children raised in authoritative homes have learned the value of limits and have learned to control their own behavior. Children whose parents are overly permissive never have to learn self-control at home, which follows them into other settings. Similarly, when parents are very restrictive and demanding, they do all the controlling and do not give children the opportunity to learn to control their own behavior.

    Finally, the worst child outcomes result when parents are neglectful; they are simply not involved in their children's lives and signal to their children that they don't really care. These children tend to be resentful, hostile, and prone to getting into trouble as a way of lashing out at uncaring adults.

CHAPTER FIFTEEN

ACHIEVEMENTS

OVERVIEW

What are the major achievements of infancy, childhood, adolescence, and adulthood? What factors contribute to our achievements? This chapter addresses these questions by looking at achievement motivation across the life span. It emphasizes that life outcomes often depend on the goodness of fit between a person and his/her environment.

Even infants show evidence of motivation when they try to control their environments. They sharpen their effectance, or mastery, motivation through play. By childhood, there are clear differences in levels of achievement motivation and you will learn about some of the factors that contribute to these differences. You will also learn which factors contribute to effective schools, and which ones seem to have no effect on the quality of schools. Among adolescents, research reveals the discouraging finding that achievement motivation often declines as children move from elementary school to middle school and to high school. The text discusses a number of factors that may account for this decline. Finally, this chapter covers the work choices of adolescents and how work affects high school students and adults. Daniel Levinson's theory is used to conceptualize the family and work roles that define who we are as adults.

LEARNING OBJECTIVES

After reading and studying the material in this chapter, you should be able to answer the following questions.

1.   What is the need for achievement? What factors influence achievement motivation? How do attributions affect achievement?

2.   What factors influence mastery motivation of infants? How is this related to later achievement?

3.   How does play promote mastery motivation?

4.   What factors contribute to differences in levels of achievement motivation during childhood?

5.   How does school affect children? What factors characterize effective schools?

6.   What changes in achievement motivation occur during adolescence? What factors contribute to these changes?

7.   How do adolescents make vocational choices? How does work affect adolescence?

8.   How does achievement motivation change during adulthood?

9.   How do career paths change during adulthood? How does Levinson's theory conceptualize family and work roles?

10.   How does work affect women's lives?

11.   How are older adults influenced by retirement?

12.   How can the quality of education be improved?

CHAPTER SUMMARY AND GUIDED REVIEW

The following summary provides an overview of the main points contained in this chapter of the text. Fill-in the blanks with terms that appropriately complete the sentence. Scattered throughout the summary are questions in parentheses. These are meant to encourage you to think actively as you are reading and connect this summary to the more detailed information provided in the text. You can answer these questions as you are filling in the blanks or you can complete all the blanks, then go back and reread the entire summary, addressing the questions in order to provide more depth of understanding.

ACHIEVEMENT MOTIVATION
Need for Achievement
        The need for achievement is a motive to compete and succeed whenever one's behavior is being evaluated against a standard. To assess need for achievement in children and adults, researchers often use a technique where subjects compose stories about a picture. (***What assumption is made about these stories?***) Children who score high in need for achievement tend to earn better grades than children who score low, and adults who score high also tend to be successful.

The Value Placed on Achievement

Several factors influence achievement motivation, including the value placed on success in a particular situation.

Expectancies of Success

Our need for achievement is also influenced by our perceived competence in an area and our expectancy of success.

Attributions for Success and Failure

Another influence on need for achievement is how we attribute or explain our successes and failures. Some research has characterized attributions along a dimension called (1)_____. Individuals who believe they are personally responsible for their successes and failures are said to have an (2) _____ locus of control, while those who believe that outcomes depend on factors such as luck and fate have an (3)_____ locus of control. (**Can you give examples of both of these attribution styles?**) Children with internal locus of control tend to earn higher grades than children with external locus of control. Another factor that affects attributions is (4)_____, or the degree to which a cause is changeable. For example, effort would be an unstable cause because this can change depending on how much one works or studies a task. (**Why is it useful to consider stability along with locus of causality?**)

THE INFANT
Early Origins of Achievement Motivation

Infants are thought to have (5) _____ motivation, or the desire to successfully control their environment. Effectance, or mastery, motivation is influenced by the presence of appropriate sensory stimulation, an environment that is (6) _____, and a secure relationship with a caregiver. (**Can you describe how these factors influence effectance motivation?**)

Mastery through Play

Mastery motivation can be seen in early play. Infants first play with their own bodies and learn that certain actions lead to particular outcomes. Next, infants become interested in toys, and by one year of age, they are experimenting with new actions. They engage in (7) _____ play when they use objects for their typical purposes. Pretend play also emerges with the acquisition of the (8) _____, and becomes more mature between ages one and two.

THE CHILD

Young children have developed internal standards of performance and can begin to appraise their performances.

Mastery-Oriented and Helpless Achievement Styles

High achievers tend to attribute their successes to (9)_____ and stable factors, and attribute their failures to (10)_____ factors, or to internal factors that they can change. Students with this pattern of attributions have a (11) _____, which means they thrive on challenges and will keep working on a problem because they believe their work will eventually pay off. Low achievers often attribute their failures to internal and stable causes, which may cause them to develop (12) _____ orientation, or the belief that one cannot control the consequences of certain situations and so fail to act in these situations.

Young children are less likely to develop learned helplessness than older children. Younger children adopt an (13) _____ view of ability because they believe that ability is something that can change. This leads them to adopt (14) _____ in achievement situations so that they

can learn new things and improve their abilities. Older children tend to develop an
(15) _____ view of ability, believing that it is a fixed trait that cannot be changed. This
leads them to adopt (16) _____ to demonstrate what ability they have, but not really to
improve it. Students who maintain a(n) (17) _____ view of ability tend to do better in
school. (*What can parents do to foster their child's achievement and mastery orientation?*)

Schooling and School Achievement

By the age of 6, children spend a significant portion of their time at school. Many children
attend preschool prior to entering kindergarten and first grade. Children in high-quality preschools are
often ahead of children who do not attend preschool in (18) _____ skills, but are no
different in terms of intellectual skills. However, children who come from disadvantaged homes often
benefit (19) _____ from having this experience.

Elementary and secondary schools help develop children's basic knowledge and academic skills.
Schools also expose children to an (20) _____ that socializes them in ways that will help
them be productive citizens.

Some elementary and secondary schools are more effective than others. Factors that do not
contribute to effective schooling include the amount of monetary support that a school receives, the
average size of classes (within a range of 20 to 40 students), and grouping according to ability, a
technique called (21) _____. Factors that do contribute to the effectiveness of a school
include a strong emphasis on (22) _____, well-managed classrooms (both in terms of
classroom activities and discipline problems), and teachers who can work with other teachers. In
addition, student characteristics interact with school factors to affect student outcome, something called
(23) _____. (*Can you explain how ability level interacts with program characteristics?*)

Following the 1954 *Brown v. Board of Education* case, schools were ordered to
(24) _____ so that black and white students were educated in the same schools.
Unfortunately, school integration has not had large effects on children's racial attitudes. Prejudice
among black and white students toward each other decreased somewhat, but not as much as hoped.
Children with disabilities have also been integrated into the regular classroom through the process of
(25) _____. The results of this have been mixed--Sometimes the outcome is positive and
other times, the effects are nonexistent. Use of (26) _____ methods have been successful.
With these types of techniques, students of different races or ability levels are assigned to teams and are
rewarded for team, not individual, performance.

THE ADOLESCENT

Achievement motivation patterns change over the course of childhood and adolescence.
Research suggests that children valued academic achievement more as they progress through school, but
their expectations for (27) _____ drop, and they become more focused on
(28) _____ rewards such as grades and less concerned about the intrinsic satisfaction
associated with achieving greater competence. This trend may occur because of
(29) _____ growth as egocentric thinking decreases. Negative
(30) _____ that children receive at school for their failures may also contribute to this
trend. In addition, peer pressure and changes related to puberty may also influence the achievement
motivation. Finally, declines in achievement motivation are more likely when there is a poor fit between
the adolescent and their school situation.

Making Vocational Choices

According to one theory, adolescents progress through three stages in making a vocational
choice. The first is the (31) _____ stage, in which children base their vocational choices on
wishes or whatever strikes their fancy. As adolescents, they move to the (32) _____ stage in

which they consider their interests as well as their capacities and values. After this, adolescents move into a (33) _____ stage where they narrow down their vocational choice by also considering actual opportunities. Thus, vocational choice is an attempt to find the best fit between one's self and an occupation. Sometimes, societal factors, such as gender norms, influence vocational choice.

Working after School

Many adolescents work during their high school years. Most of the research on working students suggests that there are more negative consequences than positive outcomes. (***What are the outcomes for adolescents who work? What factors can make the work experience for high school students a positive one?***)

Pathways to Adulthood

As they enter adolescence, the educational paths of many individuals are already determined. Intelligence, school aptitude, and achievement motivation are reasonably stable and influence whether an individual gets good grades. Grades, in turn, influence whether an individual graduates from high school and college, and level of education affects the sorts of occupations a person can hold.

THE ADULT
Achievement Motivation

Overall, level of achievement motivation remains fairly stable from childhood and adolescence to adulthood. Research with adults shows some changes in need for achievement, but younger and older men are more similar than different on this quality. Achievement motivation of women declines, at least as it pertains to (34) _____ motivation. Changes in motives during adulthood are influenced more by work and family contexts than by age.

Levinson's Conception of Adult Development

Levinson proposed a theory of adult development that revolves around a person's (35) _____, or overall pattern of a person's priorities and relationships with other people and with society. According to this theory, family and work roles are central to a person's life structure. Life structures are constructed, then questioned, and altered.

Career Paths during Adulthood

According to Levinson's theory, young adults are exploring various career options and launching careers. Middle-aged adults may face a (36) _____ and question their entire life structure. Women seem to go through the same stages of development as men, and may be particularly susceptible to midlife crises because of their dreams for both careers and families. (***What is the support for Levinson's theory and where is the theory weak?***)

Older adults are typically more satisfied with their work than younger adults, and they are as productive as younger workers. Older workers may use a strategy of (37) _____ to cope with changes related to aging. This means that they focus on the most important skills, practice these skills to keep them in good shape, and find ways to get around other skills that may not be as sharp.

Women, Work, and the Family

There are still differences between the employment patterns of men and women. Traditional gender roles continue to operate in the workplace and may make it difficult for women to receive support for their work. Some women face (38) _____ when they are paid less for their work than men are or when they are not promoted as high as men with equal evaluations. Women may experience (39) _____ because of the demands of both work and family. Related to this, women may also experience (40) _____ because of too much to do in too little time. There can be

(41) _____ _____ effects when events at work affect home life, or when things at home carry over to the workplace. Mothers who work can serve as positive role models for their daughters. Sons, though, may be disadvantaged if their mothers work and do not remain close and involved with them at home.

Work and Adult Development

Work is important to adult development, just as play is important to child development. The (42) _____ of a job, or extent to which the job provides opportunities for using one's mind and making independent decisions, is related to intellectual flexibility.

Retirement

Older adults typically retire sometime in their 60's. One researcher has proposed that adjustment to retirement progresses through four phases. In the first, the (43) _____ phase, adults begin to plan for their upcoming retirement. In the (44) _____ phase, they embrace retirement and enjoy the freedom it provides. In the (45) _____ phase, the novelty of retirement wears off, which may lead to the (46) _____ phase, where adults restructure their lifestyle. In general, retirement does not have negative effects on adult development, although it may reduce the person's income. (***What factors contribute to successful adjustment to retirement?***)

Successful Aging

The text presents two general theories about successful aging. One is the (47) _____ theory that suggests that adults will be satisfied with their lives if they can continue to maintain their preexisting activity levels. The other theory of aging holds that successful aging requires (48) _____ of the aging individual from society and vice versa. (***Does one of these theories more accurately portray successful aging? Why?***)

APPLICATIONS: IMPROVING THE QUALITY OF EDUCATION

Cross-cultural research suggests several things that North American educational programs might do differently to improve education. These include more time in school devoted to academics, more homework assignments, greater parental involvement, peers who value academic achievement and have high standards, and a belief that hard work (effort) will result in better learning.

REVIEW OF KEY TERMS

Below is a list of terms and concepts from this chapter. Use these to complete the following sentence definitions. You might also want to try writing definitions in your own words and then checking your definitions with those in the text.

ability tracking
activity theory
aptitude-treatment interaction (ATI)
attribution theory
cooperative learning methods
disengagement theory
effectance motivation
entity view of ability
functional play
inclusion

incremental view of ability
informal curriculum
learned helplessness orientation
learning goal
life structure
locus of control
mastery orientation
mentor
midlife crisis
need for achievement (n Ach)

performance goal   selective optimization with compensation

role conflict   spillover

role overload   substantive complexity

1. The _____ is a learned motive to do well whenever one's behavior is compared to other's behavior or measured against a standard of excellence.

2. According to the concept of _____, events at work can influence home life and events at home can carry over to the work place.

3. Some schools use _____ in which students are grouped and taught according to their competence level.

4. Schools expose children to a(n) _____ that provides information about how to fit into the culture.

5. Children who adopt a _____ in achievement settings try to learn new things to improve their abilities.

6. The concept of _____ conveys the idea that the overall pattern of a person's life reflects their priorities and relationships with other people and with society.

7. According to _____, we create explanations for our behaviors, which influence our future expectations of success and motivation to succeed.

8. _____ refers to the extent to which a job provides opportunities for workers to use their minds and make independent judgements.

9. Adults experience a _____ when the question their life structure and raise concerns about the direction of their lives.

10. The feeling of having too much to do, or too many roles to fulfill in the available time is _____

11. The motive to successfully interact with one's environment is called _____.

12. The process of _____ is intended to fully integrate students with disabilities into the regular classroom.

13. Children who adopt a _____ in achievement settings try to prove their ability rather than improving it.

14. A _____ is someone who serves as a guide or advisor to another person.

15. A(n) _____ involves the belief that ability is a fixed trait that cannot be changed with effort.

16. Infants engage in _____ when they play with objects in realistic ways, such as using a spoon to feed a doll.

17. According to _____, aging adults will find their lives satisfying to the extent that they are able to maintain their existing levels of activity.

18. A dimension of personality called _____ concerns the degree to which people view themselves personally responsible for what happens to them.

19. _____ involve working together in teams to produce a group effort rather than competing individually.

20. _____ refers to the feeling of being pulled in different directions by competing demands of different positions.

21. A strategy called _____ involves focusing on important skills, practicing these skills, and finding ways to get around the need for other skills.

22. _____ refers to the notion that student characteristics and school environment interact to affect student outcome.

23. A(n) _____ involves the belief that ability can be changed (improved) with hard work.

24. An attribution style called _____ credits successes to internal and stable causes and failures to internal causes that can be changed.

25. According to _____, successful aging involves a mutual withdrawal of the aging person from society and society from the aging individual.

26. Individuals with an attribution style with a _____ believe that they cannot control the consequences of certain situations and as a result, they give up trying to succeed in these situations.

MULTIPLE CHOICE SELF TEST

For each multiple choice question, read all alternatives and then select the best answer.

1. A child with an internal locus of control might say which of the following?
   a.   I did well on that test because it was easy.
   b.   I did well on that test because the teacher likes me.
   c.   I did well on that test because I knew the material.
   d.   I did well on that test because I wanted to earn the money Dad promised me for getting an "A."

2.   Children who score high in need for achievement
    a.   have parents who use an authoritarian style of parenting
    b.   have parents who praise success with external rewards and punish failures
    c.   get the same grades as other children but feel happier about them
    d.   tend to get better grades than children who score low on need for achievement

3.   Research on attributions indicates that
    a.   high achievers tend to attribute their successes to internal and stable causes
    b.   high achievers tend to attribute their failures to internal and stable causes
    c.   low achievers tend to attribute everything to external causes
    d.   high achievers tend to give up once they fail a task

4.   Research indicates that
    a.   infants do not have sense of motivation
    b.   from a very early age, infants are motivated to control their environments
    c.   infants can develop effectance motivation if they are externally rewarded for all their efforts
    d.   infants who are insecurely attached to their parents will not develop any mastery motivation

5.   Children with a learned helplessness attributional style
    a.   have high expectations for success and get upset when they cannot achieve these high standards
    b.   work hard to achieve only small gains in performance
    c.   have low expectations for success and give up easily
    d.   believe that external factors are responsible for their failures

6.   Young children are often more confident than older children about their chances for success because younger children:
    a.   adopt an incremental view of ability
    b.   adopt an entity view of ability
    c.   are given easier tasks than older children
    d.   attribute outcomes to external factors while older children attribute outcomes to internal factors

7.   Which of the following strategies would likely lead to the greatest success?
    a.   Viewing failures as evidence that ability is lacking.
    b.   Viewing success as a result of luck or fate.
    c.   Viewing ability as something that can change.
    d.   Viewing ability as a fixed characteristic that cannot change.

8.   One factor that contributes significantly to school effectiveness is
    a.   a comfortable setting where the emphasis is on academics
    b.   average class size
    c.   level of monetary support that the school receives
    d.   strict guidelines and adherence to rules

9. Achievement motivation declines during adolescence for all of the following reasons EXCEPT:
   a. cognitive advances that allow adolescents to understand their strengths and weaknesses
   b. pressure from peers to be popular or athletic
   c. increasingly receiving positive feedback based on quality of their accomplishments rather than effort
   d. having teachers who use cooperative learning styles

10. Vocational choices
   a. are stable across an individual's life span
   b. become increasingly realistic across adolescence
   c. are usually not related to one's ability
   d. are influenced very little by environmental opportunities

11. Research on adolescents and work indicates that
   a. working while in high school is beneficial for most adolescents
   b. there are more potential disadvantages than advantages to working while in high school
   c. work contributes to improvements in social-emotional development, but does not influence cognitive development
   d. work is associated with higher levels of achievement and self-esteem

12. Levinson's theory of adult development focuses on
   a. the interaction of one's self with other people and society
   b. the role of stress in adult development
   c. how adult males differ from females in values and career choices
   d. how career choices are made

13. According to Levinson's theory of adult development, men
   a. typically settle into their final career choice in early adulthood
   b. follow career paths that are similar to women's paths
   c. question their career and family choices very little
   d. experience a midlife crisis and question their life structure

14. Role conflict refers to
   a. the belief that hard work pays off and relaxation promotes moral decay
   b. the feeling that one has too much to do and too little time to accomplish it
   c. the competing demands of various roles such as family and work
   d. the feelings that women experience when they are in careers traditionally held by men

15. The theory that successful aging requires a gradual withdrawal from society is
   a. Levinson's theory
   b. disengagement theory
   c. withdrawal theory
   d. activity adjustment theory

Answer the following set of questions for mastery orientation and learned helplessness. Use Table 15.2 in the text to check your answers.

QUESTIONS	MASTERY ORIENTATION	LEARNED HELPLESSNESS
What is the child's view of ability?		
What is the child's goal in the classroom?		
How does the child explain successes?		
How does the child explain failures?		
What is the child's reaction to failures?		

APPLICATION QUESTIONS

By answering the following questions, you will strengthen your understanding of the material in this chapter. These questions require higher level thinking skills such as integration and application of concepts. To get you started, there is a sample answer or outline provided for the first question. This illustrates one possibility, but there are other answers you could provide that might be just as good. For the other questions, you can check yourself by referring to the text (a hint is provided), or by asking a peer or your instructor to review your answer.

1. Based on research described in the text, what recommendations would you make regarding adolescents and work?
   [Sample answer provided]

2. What factors are likely to increase or decrease our achievement motivation as we move through childhood and adolescence?
   [Hint: Review the sections in the text on "Mastery-Oriented and Helpless Achievement Styles" and "Declining Achievement Motivation."]

3. What attributions do you typically use to explain your successes and failures? How would you modify these attributions to create healthier ones? (And what is a healthy attribution?)
   [Hint: Review the sections under "Achievement Motivation," as well as the section on "Mastery-Oriented and Helpless Achievement Styles."]

Chapter Summary and Guided Review (Fill-in the blanks)

1.	locus of control	26.	cooperative learning
2.	internal	27.	success
3.	external	28.	external
4.	stability	29.	cognitive
5.	effectance	30.	feedback
6.	responsive	31.	fantasy
7.	functional	32.	tentative
8.	symbolic capacity	33.	realistic
9.	internal	34.	career-related
10.	external	35.	life structure
11.	mastery orientation	36.	midlife crisis
12.	learned helplessness	37.	selective optimization with compensation
13.	incremental		
14.	learning goals	38.	discrimination
15.	entity	39.	role conflict
16.	performance	40.	role overload
17.	incremental	41.	spillover
18.	social	42.	substantive complexity
19.	cognitively	43.	preretirement
20.	informal curriculum	44.	honeymoon
21.	ability tracking	45.	disenchantment
22.	academics	46.	reorientation
23.	aptitude-treatment interaction	47.	activity
24.	desegregate	48.	disengagement
25.	inclusion		

Review of Key Terms

1.	need for achievement (n ach)	15.	entity view of ability
2.	spillover	16.	functional play
3.	ability tracking	17.	activity theory
4.	informal curriculum	18.	locus of control
5.	learning goal	19.	cooperative learning methods
6.	life structure	20.	role conflict
7.	attribution theory	21.	selective optimization with compensation
8.	substantive complexity		
9.	midlife crisis	22.	aptitude-treatment interaction (ATI)
10.	role overload	23.	incremental view of ability
11.	effectance motivation	24.	mastery orientation
12.	inclusion	25.	disengagement theory
13.	performance goal	26.	learned helplessness orientation
14.	mentor		

1.	C	6.	A	11.	B
2.	D	7.	C	12.	A
3.	A	8.	A	13.	D
4.	B	9.	D	14.	C
5.	C	10.	B	15.	B

Application Questions

1.   *Overall, I would have to recommend NOT working, or working a limited number of hours. Research shows that adolescents who work 20 or more hours a week while going to high school get lower grades than those who do not work at all or work less than 10 hours. The ones who work a lot also tend to be disengaged in school; they cut class and do not spend as much time on homework. Further, the more teenagers work, the less control their parents have in their lives, which may contribute to higher rates of delinquency and alcohol and drug use. Some of the problems with school and parents started before the teens started working, but increased once they started working.*

Not all work experiences for teenagers are negative. Work that teaches teenagers valuable skills and allows for some advancement can be valuable. Unfortunately, most teenagers get jobs that are menial and repetitive and provide little opportunity for decision making.

CHAPTER SIXTEEN

PSYCHOLOGICAL DISORDERS THROUGHOUT THE LIFE SPAN

OVERVIEW

This is a substantial chapter, covering a variety of psychological disorders. Some of these disorders are fairly unique to a particular age period, such as eating disorders during adolescence and dementia among older adults. Other disorders, though, are prevalent throughout the life span, most notably depression. Before getting into these specific disorders, the chapter discusses how experts distinguish abnormal from normal behavior, and which criteria are used to diagnose psychological disorders. Then, like other chapters, it covers the overall topic for each major period of the life span. For infancy, the focus is on autism. For childhood, attention-deficit hyperactivity disorder is highlighted. The section on adolescence covers eating disorders, drinking and drug use. Finally, the section on adults discusses stressful life experiences and dementia. Throughout all the sections, there is discussion of depression. For each disorder, characteristics, suspected causes, typical treatments and likely outcomes are presented. The chapter ends with a discussion of whether psychological disorders are adaptive, which is an intriguing application of evolutionary theory.

LEARNING OBJECTIVES

After reading and studying the material in this chapter, you should be able to answer the following questions.

1.   What criteria are used to define and diagnose psychological disorders?

2.   What is the perspective of the field of developmental psychopathology? What sorts of questions or issues are studied by developmental psychopathologists?

3.   What are the characteristics, suspected causes, treatment, and prognosis for individuals with infantile autism?

4.   In what ways to infants exhibit depression-like conditions? How is depression in infants similar to, or different from, depression in adults?

5.   What is the difference between undercontrolled and overcontrolled disorders?

6.   What are the symptoms, suspected causes, treatment, and long-term prognosis for children with attention-deficit hyperactivity disorder?

7.   How is depression during childhood similar to, or different from, depression during adulthood?

8.   How do interactions of nature and nurture contribute to psychological disorders? Do childhood problems persist into adolescence and adulthood? Explain.

9.   Are psychological problems more prevalent during adolescence than other periods of the life span? Explain.

10.   What are the characteristics, suspected causes, and treatment of eating disorders?

11.   What factors are associated with adolescent alcohol and drug use?

12.   What is the course of depression and suicidal behavior during adolescence?

13.   What sorts of stress confront adults? How do adults cope with stress? What factors influence stress and coping strategies?

14.   What factors influence depression during adulthood?

15.   What are the characteristics and causes of dementia?

16.   What are some of the treatments for psychological disorders across the life span?

The following summary provides an overview of the main points contained in this chapter of the text. Fill-in the blanks with terms that appropriately complete the sentence. Scattered throughout the summary are questions in parentheses. These are meant to encourage you to think actively as you are reading and connect this summary to the more detailed information provided in the text. You can answer these questions as you are filling in the blanks or you can complete all the blanks, then go back and reread the entire summary, addressing the questions in order to provide more depth of understanding.

WHAT MAKES DEVELOPMENT ABNORMAL?
Criteria for Diagnosing Psychological Disorders

There are three general ways to define abnormal behavior. The first criteria uses (1) _____, or whether a person's behavior falls outside the normal range of behavior. The second classification uses (2) _____, or the extent to which a behavior interferes with personal and social adaptation. The third classification is whether or not a behavior causes (3) _____. When applying any of these criteria, there are other factors to consider in defining abnormal behavior. The expectations about how to act in a particular context, or the (4) _____, must be considered, along with societal expectations about what behaviors are appropriate at various ages, or (5) _____.

More specific diagnostic criteria have been described by the American Psychiatric Association in the *Diagnostic and Statistical Manual of Mental Disorders (DSM-IV)*. This manual specifies symptoms and behaviors associated with all psychological disorders. For example, *DSM-IV* defines (6) _____ as at least one episode of feeling profoundly depressed, sad, and hopeless, and/or losing interest in and the ability to derive pleasure from almost all activities. This definition excludes depression that is "normal," such as depression following the loss of a loved one.

Developmental Psychopathology

Developmental psychopathology is the study of the origins and course of abnormal behavior across the life span. Some developmental psychopathologists believe that DSM is too focused on problems as diseases and that instead, psychopathology should be viewed as (7) _____. In addition, the psychologists in this field are interested in the same issues that concern developmental psychologists. (***Do you remember these issues from the beginning of the book?***)

THE INFANT
Infantile Autism

Autism is a disorder beginning in infancy that is characterized by deviant social development, deviant language and communication skills, and repetitive, stereotyped behavior. This is classified as a (8) _____ disorder in the *DSM*. The language of autistic children may include (9) _____, where a child repeats or echoes sounds or words produced by someone else. Contrary to stereotypes of autistic children as exceptionally bright, many (about 75%) are (10) _____. In particular, autistic individuals seem to have trouble understanding mental states and the role of mental states in behavior, showing a lack of a (11) _____. Some researchers believe these cognitive impairments underlie the social and emotional problems of autistic children, although there is some evidence that contradicts this. Others believe that autistic children have trouble with (12) _____ or representational thought. Another possibility is that autistic individuals cannot integrate pieces of information into meaningful wholes. Autism appears to have both genetic and environmental causes, although no specific causes have yet been pinpointed. Long-term prognosis for autistic children is generally (13) _____ and treatment usually focuses on intense (14) _____ training starting at an early age.

Depression

Infants can experience depression-like states although it is not yet clear whether they experience true depressive disorders. Infants are not capable of expressing the cognitive symptoms of depression, but can show behavioral symptoms and (15) _____ or bodily symptoms. Infants who have lost an attachment figure are the ones most likely to show depressive symptoms. A condition called (16) _____ occurs when infants who are raised in a stressful situation fail to grow normally and become underweight for their age. If removed from the stressful situation, infants recover their weight very quickly.

THE CHILD

Children who have undercontrolled disorders, or (17) _____ problems, engage in behaviors that disturb other people and conflict with societal expectations. Children with overcontrolled disorders, or (18) _____ problems, focus their problems inward. There is a gender difference in expression of problems. In general, (19) _____ are more likely to show externalizing problems and (20) _____ are more likely to show internalizing disorders.

Attention-Deficit Hyperactivity Disorder

According to DSM-IV criteria, children with attention-deficit hyperactivity disorder show inattentive, impulsive, and hyperactivity. Although all young children show these behaviors to some extent, children who are diagnosed with the disorder show them to a marked degree. Behaviors associated with hyperactivity vary with age. (*Can you describe behaviors that might indicate ADHD in infants and children?*) ADHD seems to be caused by a (21) _____ problem, but it is unclear precisely what this is. Many hyperactive children are treated with Ritalin, a (22) _____ drug that reduces symptoms of ADHD, and seems to improve academic performance. (*What are some concerns about using Ritalin to treat ADHD?*)

Depression

It is now recognized that children can become depressed. Initially, some researchers believed that children showed (23) _____ by expressing symptoms not generally associated with depression in adults. However, it is apparent that children can be diagnosed using the same criteria that are used with adults. This does not mean that children and adults display depression in exactly the same behaviors. Preschool children are more likely to display somatic and (24) _____ symptoms rather than (25) _____ symptoms that adults and older children display. Many clinically depressed children continue to experience some episodes of depression later in childhood, adolescence, or adulthood.

Nature, Nurture, and Childhood Disorders

Many people believe that the social (26) _____ has a powerful effect on development, including the development of abnormal behavior. There is a relationship between type of environment and whether a child has a disorder. However, this does not mean that the environment caused the disorder. It is possible that the disorder is (27) _____ based, or, because of the (28) _____ influence within families, the child's disorder may have helped create a disordered environment.

Do Childhood Problems Persist?

Early childhood problems are more likely to (29) _____ than persist into adulthood. However, not <u>all</u> disorders vanish--Many adults who have disorders had problems as children. (*What factors affect whether a problem persists beyond childhood?*)

THE ADOLESCENT
Is Adolescence Really a Period of Storm and Stress?
        Adolescence is not really a period of storm and stress as G. Stanley Hall suggested. However, adolescents do seem to be more vulnerable to some forms of psychological disorders.

Eating Disorders
        Eating disorders are more often associated with adolescence than with other periods, and are much more common among girls than boys. Refusal to maintain weight that is at least 85% of one's expected weight is termed (30) _____. Binging and purging is associated with (31) _____. Our society may increase the likelihood of eating disorders with its emphasis on thinness. In addition, some girls appear to have a genetic predisposition to develop an eating disorder, possibly because genes influence (32) _____. Further, girls who develop eating disorders typically experience disturbed (33) _____ relationships. (***What is the prognosis and treatment for adolescents with eating disorders?***)

Drinking and Drug Use
        Many adolescents have used, or currently use, drugs and alcohol. Three general factors have been found to distinguish problem drinkers from other adolescents. One factor is the individual's (34) _____, including lack of value placed on academic achievement and alienation from conventional values. Secondly, problem drinkers perceive their (35) _____ differently. (***How do their perceptions differ?***) Third, problem drinkers are more likely to have other problem behaviors, suggesting that their drinking is part of a larger syndrome of unconventional behaviors.

Depression and Suicidal Behavior
        Adolescents who are depressed display many of the same cognitive symptoms that depressed adults display, as well as other problem behaviors. The rate of (36) _____ has increased, making this the third leading cause of death among adolescents. Suicidal thoughts are common during adolescence. Adolescents are more likely than adults to attempt suicide, but are less likely to "succeed" at killing themselves. As with other behaviors, suicidal behavior results from an interaction of genetic and environmental factors. (***What are some of the factors that contribute to suicidal behavior?***)

THE ADULT
Stress and Coping
        Most adults must cope with some degree of stress in their lives. Stress depends on one's appraisal of a situation. What is stressful for one person, may not be stressful for another person. Most people expect to be stressed by major life event, but stress also results from (37) _____, or everyday annoyances. Young adults seem to experience the greatest number of life changes and associated stress, while middle-aged and older adults gradually experience fewer and fewer stressors. Ability to cope with stress does not change significantly across the life span, although styles of coping may differ. In one study, middle-aged adults used (38) _____ coping, where they tried to change the situation or eliminate the problem. Older adults used (39) _____ coping, where they tried to change their perception and emotional response to the problem. (***What are examples of each of these coping strategies?***)
        · When coping mechanisms fail, many adults develop some type of psychological disorder. A survey of prevalence of affective disorders and alcohol abuse showed that these were more common among young adults than middle-aged or older adults. In addition, women were more likely to report affective disorders, while men were more likely to report alcohol abuse.

Depression

Contrary to a popular belief, elderly adults are not more depressed than younger adults. This may be because depression is often undiagnosed in the elderly. (*Why might this be the case?*) Women are more likely than men to be diagnosed with depression. (*Why are women more likely than men to be diagnosed with depression?*)

The (40) _____ model suggests that psychopathology results from the interaction of a predisposition to a disorder and the experience of stressful events. Applying this to depression, a person might become depressed if they had a vulnerability for depression and if they experienced stress. Explaining depression also requires consideration of an individual's (41) _____, which include personality and coping strategies.

Aging and Dementia

Many people fear "losing their minds" as they get older. Dementia, sometimes called (42) _____, is not a normal part of aging. It refers to progressive deterioration of intellectual functioning and personality. One form of dementia is caused by (43) _____ disease, which is progressive and irreversible deterioration of neurons, resulting in increasingly impaired mental functioning. Some forms of this disease appear to have a (44) _____ basis. This is supported by the fact that this disorder often recurs in families, and by the finding that individuals with Down Syndrome, a chromosomal disorder, are very likely to develop Alzheimer's disease. (*What are some other explanations for Alzheimer's disease?*)

Another irreversible dementia is (45) _____ dementia, which results from cardiovascular problems such as strokes. Some forms of dementia are reversible. (*What factors might cause a reversible dementia?*) Some elderly adults may be experiencing (46) _____, which is mistaken for dementia because of the similar symptoms (*How can these two problems be distinguished from one another?*)

APPLICATIONS: TREATING PSYCHOLOGICAL DISORDERS
Treating Children and Adolescents

Treating children and adolescents for disorders is different from treating adults. Adults can initiate their treatment, while children rarely do. Treatment for children is also dependent on parental cooperation. Treatment is also going to differ since children and adults function at different cognitive and emotional levels. Treatment for children is as successful as treatment for adults, and (47) _____ therapies seem to work better for children than "nonbehavioral" therapies.

Treating Elderly Adults

Treating elderly adults is also challenging, in part because elderly adults are less likely than younger adults to seek treatment. When they do get treatment, elderly adults are responsive and can improve.

IS PSYCHOPATHOLOGY ADAPTIVE?

According to (48) _____ theory, some maladaptive behaviors may serve useful adaptive functions in coping with poor environments, if not in modern society, then perhaps in earlier times.

REVIEW OF KEY TERMS

Below is a list of terms and concepts from this chapter. Use these to complete the following sentence definitions. You might also want to try writing definitions in your own words and then checking your definitions with those in the text.

age norm
Alzheimer's disease
anorexia nervosa
attention-deficit hyperactivity disorder
bulimia nervosa
comorbidity
daily hassles
delirium
dementia
developmental psychopathology
diathesis/stress model
echolalia
emotion-focused coping

externalizing problems
failure to thrive
infantile autism
internalizing problems
major depressive disorder
masked depression
problem-focused coping
social norm
somatic symptoms
storm and stress
stress
vascular dementia

1. _____ is the existence of more than one disorder in an individual.

2. _____ are problems that are disruptive to the individual and include conditions such as anxiety disorders, phobias, and severe shyness.

3. The state that occurs when we perceive events to tax our coping capacities and threaten our well-being is called _____.

4. _____ refers to the notion that adolescence is a time of problems and emotional ups and downs.

5. The field of _____ concerns the study of the origins and course of maladaptive behavior.

6. _____ is a coping strategy that focuses on changing the situation.

7. A group of disorders characterized by progressive deterioration of intellectual functioning and personality is collectively called _____.

8. The term _____ is used to describe infants who are neglected, abused, or otherwise stressed fail to grow normally, becoming underweight for their age.

9. The _____ proposes that psychopathology results from the interaction of a predisposition to a disorder and the experience of stressful events.

10. A(n) _____ is a societal expectation about what behavior is appropriate or normal at various ages.

11. A disorder called _____ involves progressive and irreversible deterioration of neurons resulting in increasingly impaired mental functioning.

12. Chronic strains or everyday annoyances of varying magnitude are _____.

13.	Mental deterioration that results from cardiovascular problems such as strokes is diagnosed as

_____.

14.	_____ occur when individuals act in ways that disturb other people and conflict with societal expectations.

15.	An expectation about how to behave that prevails in a culture or subculture is called a

_____.

16.	Refusal to maintain a weight that is at least 85% of the expected weight for one's height and age is diagnosed as _____.

17.	Autistic children often exhibit _____, a form of language where a child echoes or repeats sounds or words made by someone else.

18.	Children may exhibit _____ when they indirectly show symptoms of depression.

19.	A diagnosis of _____ is made when individuals feel profoundly depressed, sad, or hopeless, and/or lose interest in activities, and are not able to derive pleasure from activities.

20.	_____ is diagnosed when there are significant problems with attention, impulsivity, and hyperactivity.

21.	A(n) _____ is a reversible condition characterized by periods of disorientation and confusion alternating with periods of coherence.

22.	Repeated episodes of binging and purging are diagnosed as _____.

23.	Bodily symptoms such as loss of appetite or changes in normal sleep patterns are called

_____.

24.	The disorder _____ begins in infancy or early childhood and is characterized by deviant social and language development, and repetitive, stereotyped behavior.

25.	_____ focuses on changing the appraisal of, and emotional response to, a problem.

MULTIPLE CHOICE SELF TEST

For each multiple choice question, read all alternatives and then select the best answer.

1.	Age norms are defined as
	a.	the ages when it is appropriate to act in a deviant manner
	b.	societal expectations about what behavior is appropriate at different ages
	c.	societal expectations about how to behave in different contexts
	d.	the average ages when people are most susceptible to various disorders

2.   Which of the following persons is most likely to be diagnosed as having a psychological disorder?
     a.   a child who cannot fall asleep at night because he is worried about goblins under the bed
     b.   a woman who can no longer to work because she is so upset about her appearance
     c.   a man who quits his job because it is no longer challenging
     d.   a woman who is sobbing because her husband has recently died

3.   According to developmental psychopathologists, psychopathology is a
     a.   pattern of behavior that develops over time
     b.   medical condition that you either have or do not have
     c.   disease that can be treated with medicine
     d.   developmental disorder that lies solely within the person

4.   A disorder that begins in infancy and is characterized by deviant social development and communication skills is
     a.   an externalizing disorder   c.   infantile autism
     b.   infantile dementia   d.   attention-deficit disorder

5.   Which of the following is an example of echolalia?
     a.   using "you" to refer to one's self
     b.   hearing the echo of a phrase after someone has said something
     c.   substituting one phrase for another
     d.   repeating something that has just been said

6.   Autistic children
     a.   typically outgrow the disorder as they get older
     b.   have a number of physical problems in addition to their deficits in social and communication skills
     c.   are often mentally retarded
     d.   show marked improvement after they enter elementary school

7.   Which of the following seems to be a promising explanation of the cause of autism?
     a.   Autistic children have cold, distant parents.
     b.   Autistic children have inherited a recessive set of genes for the disorder.
     c.   Autistic children are unable to verbalize their thoughts.
     d.   Autistic children lack symbolic thought and/or the ability to organize information into meaningful chunks.

8.   Children who act in ways that conflict with rules and other people are said to have
     a.   an internalizing problem   c.   masked depression
     b.   an externalizing problem   d.   autism

9.   Attention-deficit hyperactivity disorder
     a.   is a disorder that is diagnosed on the basis of too much motor activity
     b.   is primarily an attention deficit
     c.   is an overcontrolled disorder
     d.   is associated with mental retardation

10. Depression
    a. is displayed in similar ways across the life span
    b. is not present until children are old enough to verbally express their feelings
    c. is an undercontrolled disorder
    d. can be present throughout the life span but is expressed in different behaviors

11. Problems that exist in early childhood
    a. disappear when children enter elementary school
    b. are nonexistent by the time children leave school
    c. are more likely to disappear than persist, although some do persist
    d. typically are still present later in life

12. Eating disorders such as anorexia and bulimia
    a. are caused by the body's inability to properly metabolize food
    b. develop, in part, as a result of a genetic predisposition interacting with stress and social pressure
    c. are easily controlled with a properly managed diet
    d. are present during adolescence and then disappear

13. Adolescent problem drinkers
    a. are indistinguishable from other adolescents
    b. place less value on academic achievement and more value on independence than other adolescents
    c. typically have just this one area where they have a problem
    d. are generally intolerant of deviant behavior in others

14. With respect to suicide,
    a. adolescents are more likely to attempt suicide than adults but less likely to succeed
    b. adolescents successfully commit suicide at a higher rate than any other age group
    c. males and females are equally likely to end up killing themselves
    d. elderly adults commit suicide at a rate somewhat higher than adolescents and younger adults

15. One difference between Alzheimer's disease and delirium is that
    a. Alzheimer's disease affects mental functioning and delirium does not.
    b. Patients with Alzheimer's disease have periods of lucidity, while those with delirium do not.
    c. Alzheimer's disease occurs only in old age, while delirium occurs only at younger ages.
    d. Alzheimer's disease is irreversible, while delirium is reversible.

APPLICATION QUESTIONS

By answering the following questions, you will strengthen your understanding of the material in this chapter. These questions require higher level thinking skills such as integration and application of concepts. To get you started, there is a sample answer or outline provided for the first question. This illustrates one possibility, but there are other answers you could provide that might be just as good. For the other questions, you can check yourself by referring to the text (a hint is provided), or by asking a peer or your instructor to review your answer.

1. What gender differences are found across the life span in the diagnosis or course of mental disorders? What factors might account for these differences?
   [Sample answer provided.]

2. How would you explain the development of psychological disorders from the perspective of each of the major developmental theories (Freud and Erikson's psychoanalytic theories, Piaget's cognitive-developmental theory, Skinner and Bandura's learning theories, and Bronfenbrenner's ecological theory)?
   [Hint: Go back and consult earlier chapters, particularly chapter two, to gather information about the theorists that will help you explain or interpret psychological disorders. You might want to pick a specific disorder and systematically apply each theory to this disorder.]

ANSWERS

Chapter Summary and Guided Review (Fill-in the blank)

1.	statistical deviance	25.	cognitive
2.	maladaptiveness	26.	environment
3.	personal distress	27.	genetically
4.	social norms	28.	reciprocal
5.	age norms	29.	disappear
6.	major depressive disorder	30.	anorexia nervosa
7.	development	31.	bulimia nervosa
8.	pervasive developmental	32.	personality
9.	echolalia	33.	family
10.	mentally retarded	34.	personal qualities
11.	theory of mind	35.	social environment
12.	symbolic	36.	suicide
13.	poor	37.	daily hassles
14.	behavioral	38.	problem-focused
15.	somatic	39.	emotion-focused
16.	failure to thrive	40.	diathesis/stress
17.	externalizing	41.	personal resources
18.	internalizing	42.	senility
19.	boys	43.	Alzheimer's
20.	girls	44.	genetic
21.	neurological	45.	vascular
22.	stimulant	46.	delirium
23.	masked depression	47.	behavioral
24.	behavioral	48.	evolutionary

Review of Key Terms

1.	comorbidity	5.	developmental psychopathology
2.	internalizing problems	6.	problem-focused coping
3.	stress	7.	dementia
4.	storm and stress	8.	failure to thrive

9.	diathesis/stress model	18.	masked depression
10.	age norm	19.	major depressive disorder
11.	Alzheimer's disease	20.	attention-deficit hyperactivity disorder
12.	daily hassles	21.	delirium
13.	vascular dementia	22.	bulimia nervosa
14.	externalizing problems	23.	somatic symptoms
15.	social norm	24.	infantile autism
16.	anorexia nervosa	25.	emotion-focused coping
17.	echolalia		

Multiple Choice Self Test

1.	B	6.	C	11.	C
2.	B	7.	D	12.	B
3.	A	8.	A	13.	B
4.	C	9.	B	14.	A
5.	D	10.	D	15.	D

Application Questions

1.   *Overall, males and females are equally likely to have psychological disorders, although there are some differences in the types of disorders that affect males and females. In general, boys are more likely to show externalizing problems that put them in conflict with others, such as conduct disorders or hyperactivity. Girls are more likely to have internalizing problems that cause inner conflict, such as depression or eating disorders.*

There may be genetic or biological reasons for these differences. For example, hormone levels differ for men and women and could contribute to different rates of depression. Think about the dramatic hormone changes following the birth of a baby that can lead to postpartum depression in women. Hormones cannot account for all the differences, though, between men and women. Socialization may also explain differences in depression. Women are socialized to internalize their problems and it is socially acceptable for women to seek help for their problems. Men are socialized to externalize their problems and are not encouraged to seek help. Men and women may also learn to cope with their problems differently. Some evidence suggests that women ruminate about their problems more than men, which tends to prolong the problem, while men distract themselves from their problems, which tends to curtail the problem.

CHAPTER SEVENTEEN

THE FINAL CHALLENGE: DEATH AND DYING

OVERVIEW

This chapter covers some of the physical realities of death, such as biological definitions, factors that affect life expectancy, and leading causes of death at different ages. but the focus of the chapter is on psychological interpretations and reactions to death. How do people of different ages understand death? How do they grieve and cope with death? Two theories that are prominent in this chapter are Kübler-Ross's theory and the Parkes-Bowlby theory of attachment. Kübler-Ross proposed that our reaction to death goes through a series of five stages. Although flawed, the theory has been instrumental in highlighting different emotional responses to death. Parkes and Bowlby proposed four overlapping responses to grief that are similar to the separation anxiety experienced by infants. The chapter closes by looking at factors related to coping and ways to lessen the grief associated with death.

LEARNING OBJECTIVES

After reading and studying the material in this chapter, you should be able to answer the following questions.

1.   How is death defined? Why is the definition of death controversial? How does the social meaning of death vary across groups?

2.   What factors influence life expectancy?

3.   What is the difference between programmed theories of aging and damage theories of aging? What are specific examples of each type of theory?

4.   What are Kübler-Ross's stages of dying? How valid and useful is this theory?

5.   What is the Parkes-Bowlby attachment explanation of grief?

6.   What is the infant's understanding of separation and death?

7.   How do children's conceptions of death compare to a "mature" understanding of death? What factors might influence a child's understanding of death?

8.   What is a dying child's understanding of death? How do dying children cope with the prospect of their own death?

9.   How do children grieve?

10.   What is the adolescent's understanding of death?

11.   How do family members react and cope with the loss of a spouse, a child, and a parent?

12.   What factors contribute to effective and ineffective coping with grief?

13.   What can be done for those who are dying and for those who are bereaved to better understand and face the reality of death?

CHAPTER SUMMARY AND GUIDED REVIEW

The following summary provides an overview of the main points contained in this chapter of the text. Fill-in the blanks with terms that appropriately complete the sentence. Scattered throughout the summary are questions in parentheses. These are meant to encourage you to think actively as you are reading and connect this summary to the more detailed information provided in the text. You can answer these questions as you are filling in the blanks or you can complete all the blanks, then go back and reread the entire summary, addressing the questions in order to provide more depth of understanding.

LIFE AND DEATH ISSUES
What is death?
        Biological death is currently viewed as a (1) _____ rather than a single event. The Harvard definition of biological death is that of (2) _____ death. This means an irreversible loss of functioning in the entire brain. To be judged dead by this definition, a person must be totally

unresponsive to (3) _____; fail to move for one hour and fail to breathe for three minutes after disconnection from life support systems; show no (4) _____; and show no electrical activity in the (5) _____ of the brain. (***Why is there debate over when someone is actually dead?***)

Hastening someone's death when that person is terminally ill is referred to as (6) _____. Providing the means for another person to kill him or herself is called (7) _____. Some people state their desire to not have any extraordinary medical procedures applied in the event that they are hopelessly ill in a document called a (8) _____.

The meaning of death, and reactions to death, vary greatly across cultures and subcultures. (***What are some examples of cultural differences in the social meaning of death?***)

<u>What Kills Us and When?</u>

The average number of years that a person is expected to live, or one's (9) _____, is about 75 years in the United States. This represents a substantial increase over expectancies in earlier centuries. Life expectancies have increased because fewer people are dying young and adults are living longer as a result of better health and medical technology. The leading causes of death in the United States change across the life span. Infants typically die of complications surrounding birth or from congenital abnormalities. Children typically die from (10) _____. Adolescents and young adults are generally healthy, but susceptible to accidents and violent deaths (homicides and suicides). Middle-aged adults are more likely to die from (11) _____ diseases, such as cancer and heart disease.

<u>Theories of Aging: But Why Do We Age and Die?</u>

Theories of aging fall into two main categories. (12) _____ theories of aging focus on the genetic control of aging while (13) _____ theories of aging focus on the cumulative effects of damage to cells and organs over time.

An assumption of the programmed theories is that all species have a (14) _____ life span, or ceiling on the number of years that any member of that species can live. This figure varies across species, suggesting that (15) _____ genes may control how long we live. Research with twins shows that genes account for one-third of the variation in longevity, while nonshared environmental influences account for the remainder. Genetics influence aging, possibly because of the (16) _____, which refers to the fact that human cells can only divide a certain number of times. Cell division may be restricted because the stretch of DNA at the end of chromosomes, called the (17) _____ does not replicate itself like the rest of the chromosome does.

The (18) _____ theory, a damage theory of aging, proposes that DNA is damaged over the years and the body's capacity to repair this damage slows down. Another damage theory of aging is the (19) _____ theory, which suggests that DNA is damaged over time as cells are exposed to environmental toxins. Another possibility relates to (20) _____, which are molecules that are chemically unstable and react with other molecules to produce substances that damage normal cells.

Many factors, both genetic and environmental, interact to produce aging and bring about death. One technique that may extend life is (21) _____, or substantially limiting caloric intake.

THE EXPERIENCE OF DYING
<u>Kübler-Ross's Stages of Dying</u>

Kübler-Ross proposed that people who are dying progress through a common sequence of five stages. In the first stage, (22) _____ and isolation, a person responds to the news that he or she is dying by refusing to believe that it is true, a common defense mechanism to keep anxiety-provoking thoughts out of conscious awareness. In the second stage, the dying person responds with

(23) _____ or feelings of rage. In the third stage, the person tries to (24) _____ to gain more time and be given a second chance. When it becomes apparent that death is really going to occur, the dying person experiences (25) _____ and, if the person can work through the earlier responses to death, he or she may come to the final stage, which is (26) _____ of their death. Throughout all the stages, Kübler-Ross believed that people retained a sense of (27) _____ regarding their death.

Criticisms and Alternative Views

A major problem with Kübler-Ross's characterization of death is that dying people really do not experience these reactions in a stage-like fashion. For example, some experts believe that dying patients alternate between denial and (28) _____, rather than moving systematically from one reaction to another. Another problem with Kübler-Ross's theory is that it does not account for how the course of an illness affects one's perceptions. A third problem with Kübler-Ross's theory is that it ignores how a person's (29) _____ affects their response to dying. (*Can you explain how this factor can impact one's experience of dying?*)

THE EXPERIENCE OF BEREAVEMENT: AN ATTACHMENT MODEL

The term (30) _____ is used to refer to a state of loss, while (31) _____ refers to the emotional response to loss. Culturally defined ways of displaying reactions to loss is referred to as (32) _____. Many people experience (33) _____ prior to the actual death of a loved one, unless the death is quite sudden. Parkes and Bowlby characterize grieving as a reaction to (34) _____ from a loved one that progresses through several overlapping phases. The first reaction is (35) _____, which occurs in the first hours and days following a death. The second phase is (36) _____, which is most intense about 5 to 14 days after the death, and is accompanied by restlessness and preoccupation with thoughts of the loved one. Anger and guilt are also common reactions during this phase. The third phase is (37) _____ and (38) _____ when the person realizes that the loved one is gone for always. Finally, in the fourth phase of (39) _____, a person begins to move on with life by forming new relationships and getting involved in new activities.

THE INFANT

Infants experience death of a loved one as that person's (40) _____ from their life, but do not understand death as the ending of life. Infants separated from their attachment figures show reactions that are similar to the reactions of bereaved adults, including protest and despair.

THE CHILD
Grasping the Concept of Death

Young children are curious about death and begin to show some understanding of death, but have not reached a "mature" understanding. A mature conception of death requires understanding that death is:

- (41) _____;
- (42) _____, or cannot be undone;
- happens to everyone, or is (43) _____; and
- caused by internal or biological factors.

Preschool-aged children tend to think dead people retain some of their living capabilities and that death is reversible. Between the ages of 5 and 7, children begin to realize that death involves cessation of life, it is irreversible, and it is universal. It takes children a few more years, however, to fully understand that death is caused by biological factors. Children's understanding of death is affected by their level of (44) _____ development and by their life experiences. (*What life experiences affect*

The Dying Child

Terminally ill children are typically aware that they are dying and experience a variety of emotions such as anger and depression. (***How do terminally ill children of different ages respond to their situation?***)

The Bereaved Child

Children who lose a loved one grieve, but express their grief differently than adults do. They may display a variety of problems, including problems with sleeping, eating, and other daily routines. Because children are very dependent on their parents and do not have adult-level coping strategies, they are particularly vulnerable to long-term problems following the loss of a parent.

THE ADOLESCENT

Adolescents have developed a mature understanding of death and may spend time contemplating death and its meaning. Adolescents grieve similarly to adults, but are influenced by general themes or concerns of the adolescent period.

THE ADULT
Death Anxiety

Adults fully understand death, but may experience death anxiety, or concern about death and dying. (***What factors influence the degree of death anxiety that a person experiences?***)

Death and the Family Life Cycle

Adults who lose a spouse often experience other changes as well and are at greater risk for illness and physical symptoms. (***What effect do age and gender have on how someone fares following the death of a spouse?***) The loss of a child seems particularly difficult to cope with, in part because we do not expect children to die before their parents. The (45) _____ of the child does not really affect the intensity of a parent's grief. For an adult, the death of a parent may not be as disruptive as the loss of a spouse or child, because in some ways, it is expected.

Who Copes and Who Succumbs?

Some people cope more effectively with the loss of a loved one than others. There are three forms of "complicated" or (46) _____ grief. In one, people who experience (47) _____ grief spend longer grieving the loss than is typical. People who show (48) _____ grief exaggerate some reactions to loss and hardly show other reactions. The third form of pathological grief is showing an absence or delay of grief.

Several factors affect how capable a person is of coping with loss. Bowlby argues that early (49) _____ relationships impact on our later ability to cope with grief. (***Can you describe the relationship between early experience and later coping ability?***) An individual's (50) _____ and coping style also influence how well they cope with death, as does the closeness of the relationship between the bereaved person and the deceased. Reactions to death are also affected by the suddenness or unexpectedness of the death. Finally, the (51) _____ of death also influences how a person responds to the loss. Grief at any age can be positively affected by the presence of (52) _____, and negatively affected by the presence of additional (53) _____.

Below is a list of terms and concepts from this chapter. Use these to complete the following sentence definitions. You might also want to try writing definitions in your own words and then checking your definitions with those in the text.

anticipatory grief
assisted suicide
bereavement
damage theories of aging
death anxiety
denial
dietary restriction
error accumulation theory
euthanasia
free radicals

grief
Hayflick limit
hospice
life expectancy
Living Will
maximum life span
mourning
programmed theories of aging
telomere
total brain death

1. The _____ suggests that there is a limited number of times that a human cell can divide.

2. _____ is a defense mechanism where anxiety-producing thoughts are kept out of conscious awareness.

3. The technique of _____, eating a highly nutritious but very restricted diet, may increase life span.

4. _____ is the act of killing or allowing a person who is terminally ill to die.

5. _____ is the emotional response to loss.

6. A _____ program supports dying persons and their families through a caring philosophy.

7. _____ explain aging through systematic genetic mechanisms.

8. According to _____, DNA is damaged over the years through exposure to environmental agents and the body cannot keep up with the necessary repair.

9. _____ refers to an irreversible loss of functioning in the entire brain.

10. Concern about death and dying is called _____.

11. A _____ is a tiny piece of DNA on the end of chromosomes.

12. _____ is the ceiling on the number of years that anyone lives.

13. Culturally prescribed ways of displaying one's reaction to death are known as _____.

Chapter Seventeen

14. _____ are molecules with an extra electron that react with other molecules to produce substances that damage normal cells.

15. According to _____, damage to cells and organs accumulates over time and eventually causes a person's death.

16. Our _____ is the average length of time we can expect to live.

17. A _____ is a document used to indicate whether someone wants extraordinary medical procedures used to extend life when he or she is hopelessly ill.

18. Grieving that begins before a death occurs in anticipation of what will happen is called _____.

19. _____ refers to a state of loss.

20. Helping someone else bring about their own death is _____.

MULTIPLE CHOICE SELF TEST

For each multiple choice question, read all alternatives and then select the best answer.

1. The Harvard definition of biological death is
    a.   the point at which the heart stops beating
    b.   irreversible loss of functioning in the cerebral cortex
    c.   irreversible loss of functioning in the entire brain
    d.   failure to breathe without life support systems

2. Cross-cultural research on death and dying indicates that
    a.   cultures have evolved different social meanings of death
    b.   all cultures have similar ways of coping with death
    c.   people of some cultures do not experience grief
    d.   there is universal agreement on the definition of death

3. The average length of time that a person can expect to live is termed
    a.   life span
    b.   life expectancy
    c.   age norm
    d.   maximum life span

4. The leading cause of death in childhood is _____ and in middle age, the leading cause of death is _____.
    a.   congenital abnormalities; chronic diseases
    b.   accidents; suicides
    c.   hereditary defects; violent acts such as homicides
    d.   accidents; chronic diseases

5.	The Hayflick limit is
	a.	the number of times that a gene can "turn on" or "turn off" to bring about maturational changes
	b.	the ceiling on the number of years that anyone lives
	c.	the speed with which the body can repair damaged cells
	d.	the limited number times that a human cell can divide

6.	Theories that focus on the genetic control of aging are called _____ theories and those that focus on gradual deterioration of cells are called _____ theories
	a.	genetic; environmental
	b.	programmed; damage
	c.	damage; programmed
	d.	biological; psychological

7.	According to Kübler-Ross's stages of dying, a person who expresses resentment and criticizes everyone is in the stage of
	a.	denial and isolation				c.	bargaining
	b.	anger						d.	depression

8.	According to Kübler-Ross's stages of dying, a dying person who agrees to stop smoking and drinking in return for a little more time is in the stage of
	a.	denial and isolation				c.	bargaining
	b.	anger						d.	depression

9.	One of the biggest problems with Kübler-Ross's stages of dying is that
	a.	dying is not really stage-like
	b.	patients go through the stages in order but at different rates
	c.	they are focused on a person's cognitive understanding of death rather than the person's affective response
	d.	they describe a person's response to death of a spouse or parent but not the response to one's own impending death

10.	The emotional response to death is referred to as
	a.	bereavement					c.	mourning
	b.	grief						d.	depression

11.	In the first few days following the death of a loved one, the bereaved person
	a.	is usually unable to function
	b.	experiences anticipatory grief
	c.	experiences the worst despair of the mourning process
	d.	is typically in a state of shock and numbness

12.	Preschool-aged children are likely to believe that
	a.	death is inevitable and will happen to everyone eventually
	b.	dead people still experience sensations and perceptions, just not as intensely as live people
	c.	people die because of changes in internal bodily functioning
	d.	death is irreversible

13. Terminally ill children typically
    a.   accept their impending death with equanimity
    b.   have no idea that they are dying or what it means to die
    c.   go through Kübler-Ross's stages of dying in sequential order
    d.   experience a range of negative emotions and express a number of negative behaviors

14. Grief over the loss of a child
    a.   is greatest if the child is young
    b.   does not differ in intensity as a function of the age of the child
    c.   is less intense if the child dies from an accident beyond the parent's control
    d.   is more intense for fathers than mothers since mothers in our culture are encouraged to express grief more openly than fathers

15. Children's grief
    a.   can be reduced by not talking about death and the deceased
    b.   can be reduced if they have a number of other stressors to deal with at the same time
    c.   can be reduced if appropriate social support systems are in place
    d.   is always expressed openly through behavior such as crying

APPLICATION QUESTIONS

By answering the following questions, you will strengthen your understanding of the material in this chapter. These questions require higher level thinking skills such as integration and application of concepts. To get you started, there is a sample answer or outline provided for the first question. This illustrates one possibility, but there are other answers you could provide that might be just as good. For the other questions, you can check yourself by referring to the text (a hint is provided), or by asking a peer or your instructor to review your answer.

1.   In general, what factors contribute to the process of aging and death?
      [Sample answer provided.]

2.   Integrate the understanding of death with Piaget's stages of cognitive development and apply this to the practical situation of coping with the death of a pet or the death of a parent. For example, how would you help a child in the preoperational stage understand and cope with death of a parent? How would you explain that the pet dog has died? How would your conversations with children in the concrete operational stage and adolescents or adults in the formal operational stage differ from the conversation that you have with the preoperational child?
      [Hint: Review Piaget's stages of cognitive development from Chapter Seven and review the changes in conceptions of death that are described in this chapter.]

Chapter Summary and Guided Review (Fill-in the blank)

1.	process	28.	acceptance
2.	total brain	29.	personality
3.	stimuli	30.	bereavement
4.	reflexes	31.	grief
5.	cortex	32.	mourning
6.	euthanasia	33.	anticipatory grief
7.	assisted suicide	34.	separation
8.	Living Will	35.	numbness
9.	life expectancy	36.	yearning
10.	accidents	37.	disorganization
11.	chronic	38.	despair
12.	programmed	39.	reorganization
13.	damage	40.	disappearance
14.	maximum	41.	final
15.	species-specific	42.	irreversible
16.	Hayflick limit	43.	universal
17.	telomere	44.	cognitive
18.	wear and tear	45.	age
19.	error accumulation	46.	pathological
20.	free radicals	47.	chronic
21.	dietary restriction	48.	distorted
22.	denial	49.	attachment
23.	anger	50.	personality
24.	bargain	51.	cause
25.	depression	52.	social support
26.	acceptance	53.	stressors
27.	hope		

Review of Key Terms

1.	Hayflick limit	11.	telomere
2.	denial	12.	maximum life span
3.	dietary restriction	13.	mourning
4.	euthanasia	14.	free radicals
5.	grief	15.	damage theories of aging
6.	hospice	16.	life expectancy
7.	programmed theories of aging	17.	Living Will
8.	error accumulation theory	18.	anticipatory grief
9.	total brain death	19.	bereavement
10.	death anxiety	20.	assisted suicide

1.	C	6.	B	11.	D
2.	A	7.	B	12.	B
3.	B	8.	C	13.	D
4.	D	9.	A	14.	B
5.	D	10.	B	15.	C

Application Questions

1.   *Aging and death result from a combination of genetic and environmental factors. Research with twins shows that genes contribute to life expectancy--identical twins show similar patterns of aging. Laboratory research indicates that human cells are limited in the number of times that they can replicate, suggesting that there might be a genetically programmed clock for aging and death. Other research suggests that damage to the cells from environmental toxins and free radicals produced by normal metabolic provesses accumulates over time and eventually kills us. Unfortunately, we do not have much control over genetic factors and we all breathe and matabolize food and live in environments with some degree of pollution, pesticides, etc. At this point, the only method that has been shown to extend the life span (of animals in the laboratory) is dietary restriction: eating a highly nutritious, but very limited diet. It has yet to be demonstrated that this method works with humans.*

EPILOGUE

FITTING THE PIECES TOGETHER

OVERVIEW

There are two major objectives of this chapter. One is to summarize developments of each major age or stage of the life span by chronologically organizing the topical information presented in the earlier chapters of the text. You should be able to describe the physical, cognitive, personal, and social developments of infants, preschool children, school-aged children, adolescents, young adults, middle-aged adults, and older adults. A second objective is to pull out and summarize the major developmental themes running throughout the text. These themes help one understand the developmental changes occurring throughout the life span. You should be able to describe the major themes and apply or give examples of each one.

LEARNING OBJECTIVES

1.   What are the significant trends (physical, cognitive, personal, and social) of each major age or stage of the life span (infants, preschool children, school-aged children, adolescents, young adults, middle-aged adults, and older adults)?

2.   What are the major developmental themes running throughout the text?

CHAPTER SUMMARY AND GUIDED REVIEW

The following summary provides an overview of the main points contained in this chapter of the text. Fill-in the blanks with terms that appropriately complete the sentence. Scattered throughout the summary are questions in parentheses. These are meant to encourage you to think actively as you are reading and connect this summary to the more detailed information provided in the text. You can answer these questions as you are filling in the blanks or you can complete all the blanks, then go back and reread the entire summary, addressing the questions in order to provide more depth of understanding.

MAJOR TRENDS IN HUMAN DEVELOPMENT
Infants (Birth to Age 2)

        Infant development is remarkably (1) _____, changing relatively helpless newborns into fairly sophisticated toddlers. Newborns come equipped with (2) _____ and (3) _____ capabilities that allow them to respond to their environment. Many (4) _____ reflexes disappear as infants mature during the first year and are replaced by voluntary motor behaviors. According to Piaget, infants are in the (5) _____ period of cognitive development. During this period, they acquire (6) _____, or the understanding that objects exist even when they are not being perceived. They also acquire the (7) _____, which allows them to mentally represent ideas. Along with cognitive developments, infants are developing a sense of self and showing signs of distinct temperaments. According to Erikson, infants face the first (8) _____ conflict of trust vs. mistrust and must somehow resolve this conflict. Infants are also forming (9) _____ with caregivers that can influence their later relationships.

Preschool children (Ages 2 through 5)

Preschool children acquire gross motor control and fine motor skills necessary for many important tasks. According to Piaget, they are in the (10) _____ stage of cognitive development, where they often use perceptually salient features to solve a problem rather than the (11) _____ used by older children. Through application of the (12) _____ acquired at the end of the sensorimotor period, they master the basics of language. Preschool children have short attention spans and they typically lack (13) _____ skills that would help them learn and remember more effectively. Preschool children are often characterized as (14) _____, since they have difficulty understanding another person's perspective. This might cause them to have trouble communicating since they assume that their listeners know what they know. According to Erikson, preschool children wrestle with two conflicts. In the stage of (15) _____ versus shame and doubt, they must learn to assert themselves and in the stage of (16) _____ versus guilt, they try to implement bold plans. Although still very close to parents, preschool children begin to spend more time with peers. When describing people, they emphasize (17) _____ characteristics and activities rather than internal factors.

School-Age children (Ages 6 through 11)

School-age children are typically more self-controlled, serious, and (18) _____ than younger children. They also have developed better (19) _____ skills, allowing them to participate in a wider range of sports and activities. They are in Piaget's (20) _____ stage, which means they can reason logically about concrete problems. They master the finer points of language and communication, and can take the perspective of their listener. School-aged children show a greater understanding of self and others. They are faced with Erikson's conflict of (21) _____ versus inferiority, as they struggle to master scholastic and personal tasks. We also see the formation of a more stable (22) _____ during this period, parts of which are evident in adulthood. Some school-aged children move from Kohlberg's (23) _____ level of moral reasoning to (24) _____ moral reasoning as they realize that rules are agreements among people. The social world expands and (25) _____ of children is increasingly affected by agents outside the home.

Adolescents (Ages 12 through 19)

Adolescents undergo dramatic physical changes as they go through (26) _____ and experience their growth spurt. As a result, many adolescents are preoccupied with appearance. There are also significant cognitive changes. Adolescents can think more systematically and (27) _____ about hypothetical situations or problems as they progress in Piaget's (28) _____ stage. They are able to think about self and others in more sophisticated ways. According to Erikson, a major developmental task of this period is developing a sense of (29) _____. Adolescents are more serious about preparing for adult roles than younger children and they increasingly participate in making decisions about their lives. They are more involved with their (30) _____ group, which can influence them in both positive and negative ways.

Young adults (Ages 20 through 39)

Young adults are at peak physical capacity and peak (31) _____. Some will move from Kohlberg's level of (32) _____ moral reasoning to (33) _____ reasoning. They face Erikson's conflict of (34) _____ versus isolation, and experiment with romantic relationships and marriage. Many become parents and most face a number of family and career responsibilities.

<u>Middle-aged adults (Ages 40 through 64)</u>

Middle-aged adults show gradual physical declines, and are more susceptible to heart disease and other chronic illnesses. Women experience (35) _____ around age 50. Intellectual capabilities during this period are relatively stable. Expertise on the job and at home allows adults to effectively solve everyday problems. Creative achievement is often at its peak during this period. Middle-aged adults struggle with Erikson's conflict of (36) _____ versus stagnation as they raise their families and make contributions to society. As children leave home, middle-aged adults often pursue other interests and find satisfaction in watching their children live adult lives.

<u>Older adults (Age 65 and Up)</u>

Older adults experience some losses and declines in functioning. They take more time to learn things and may experience some (37) _____ lapses. They have difficulty solving (38) _____ problems, but experience no big change in cognitive and linguistic skills that are used everyday. Older adults face Erikson's conflict of (39) _____ versus despair as they review their lives and try to find meaning from their accomplishments. It is difficult to describe a single pattern of development, since there is immense (40) _____ among capabilities of older adults

MAJOR THEMES IN HUMAN DEVELOPMENT

1. <u>We are whole persons throughout the life span</u>. Physical, cognitive, personal, and social developments are intertwined during each period of the life span.

2. <u>Development proceeds in multiple directions</u>. Development becomes increasingly differentiated and integrated. It involves gains, losses, and changes that are simply different but not gains or losses.

3. <u>There is both continuity and discontinuity in development</u>. This issue raises questions about whether change is stagelike (qualitative changes) or not (quantitative changes), and whether or not early experiences predict later traits (or carry over to adulthood).

4. <u>There is much plasticity in human development</u>. Human beings have the capacity to change in response to their experiences.

5. <u>Nature and nurture truly interact in development</u>. Biological and environmental factors together explain both universal trends in development and individual differences in development. The best developmental outcomes arise from the <u>goodness of fit</u> between a person and the person's unique environment.

6. <u>We are individuals, becoming even more diverse with age</u>. There is an incredible amount of diversity among humans, which makes it difficult to form generalizations about them. And as we age, human development becomes less and less predictable.

7. <u>We develop in a cultural and historical context</u>. Development is affected by broad cultural and historical contexts, as well as the individual's immediate environment.

8. <u>We are active in our own development</u>. We actively explore the world and create our own understandings of the world rather than being passively molded by the world around us. The person and environment reciprocally interact and influence one another.

9. <u>Development is best viewed as a lifelong process</u>. Development in any one phase of life is best understood by viewing it as part of a lifelong process.

10. <u>Development is best viewed from multiple perspectives</u>. Development may be best understood by integrating multiple theories and adopting a contextual perspective that emphasizes variations in development.

MULTIPLE CHOICE SELF TEST

For each multiple choice question, read all alternatives and then select the best answer.

1. Which advance in cognition is instrumental in helping the child to move from trial-and-error problem-solving to a point where s/he can mentally devise a solution to a problem and then try it out?
   a. transformational logic
   b. acquisition of symbolic capacity
   c. movement from concrete-operational to formal-operational thought
   d. the ability to conserve

2. Preschoolers are MOST likely to be in which of the following stages?
   a. autonomy vs. shame and doubt; latency
   b. initiative vs. guilt; conventional morality
   c. autonomy vs. shame and doubt; preconventional morality
   d. industry vs. inferiority; preconventional morality

3. A marked weakness of the preoperational stage is the inability to:
   a. think logically
   b. use language effectively
   c. allow one thing to represent something else
   d. socially interact with their peers

4. One drawback of concrete operational thinking is difficulty with:
   a. any sort of problem solving task
   b. tasks that require mental consideration of tangible objects
   c. abstract or hypothetical tasks
   d. tasks that require understanding the perspective of another person

5. Erikson believed that young adults were struggling with the issue of:
   a. industry versus inferiority
   b. identity versus role confusion
   c. intimacy versus isolation
   d. generativity versus stagnation

6. Older adults (age 65 and over) are typically:
   a.   lower in self-esteem and life satisfaction than younger adults
   b.   in Erikson's stage of generativity vs. stagnation
   c.   superior to younger adults with regard to fluid intelligence, though their crystallized intelligence has deteriorated significantly
   d.   suffering from some sort of physical limitations

7. With the evidence in, it is MOST accurate to say that cognitive development is:
   a.   discontinuous and stage-like, as Piaget asserted
   b.   continuous, reflected in measures of quantitative change such as accumulation and loss of knowledge over time
   c.   largely maturational and independent of environmental influence
   d.   both stage-like and gradual, depending on the aspect being studied

8. To say that there is discontinuity in development means that:
   a.   changes smoothly and gradually occur across the life span
   b.   changes occur in distinct steps
   c.   early traits carry over and form the basis of later traits
   d.   change is a matter of quantitatively adding to what is already present

9. We are MOST LIKELY to be similar to someone else our same age during:
   a.   infancy
   b.   childhood
   c.   adolescence
   d.   old age

10. Which is TRUE with regard to the course of development across the life span?
   a.   In general, there is growth throughout childhood and young adulthood, stability during middle-age, and a decline in functioning during old age.
   b.   In general, there is growth throughout childhood and young adulthood, followed by steady declines in functioning beginning with middle-age.
   c.   In general, growth proceeds in an incremental fashion throughout childhood and adolescence, levels off during young adulthood, and begins to decline by age 40.
   d.   There is evidence of growth, loss, and change at every stage of the life span.

APPLICATION QUESTIONS

By answering the following questions, you will strengthen your understanding of the material in this chapter. These questions require higher level thinking skills such as integration and application of concepts. To get you started, there is a sample answer or outline provided for the first question. This illustrates one possibility, but there are other answers you could provide that might be just as good. For the other questions, you can check yourself by referring to the text (a hint is provided), or by asking a peer or your instructor to review your answer.

1. One theme that runs throughout the text is "There is both continuity and discontinuity in development." Explain what this means and give a concrete example from any area of developmental psychology.
   [Sample answer is provided.]

2. Another theme that runs throughout the text is "Nature and nurture both contribute to development." Explain what this means and indicate how research is typically conducted to study the effects of nature and nurture.

ANSWERS

Chapter Summary and Guided Review (Fill-in the blank)

1.	rapid	21.	industry
2.	reflexes	22.	personality
3.	sensory	23.	preconventional
4.	automatic	24.	conventional
5.	sensorimotor	25.	socialization
6.	object permanence	26.	puberty
7.	symbolic capacity	27.	abstractly
8.	psychosocial	28.	formal operations
9.	attachments	29.	identity
10.	preoperational	30.	peer
11.	logical reasoning	31.	cognitive functioning
12.	symbolic capacity	32.	conventional
13.	information processing	33.	postconventional
14.	egocentric	34.	intimacy
15.	autonomy	35.	menopause
16.	initiative	36.	generativity
17.	physical	37.	memory
18.	logical	38.	novel
19.	motor	39.	integrity
20.	concrete operations	40.	diversity

Multiple Choice Self-Test

1.	B	6.	D
2.	C	7.	D
3.	A	8.	B
4.	C	9.	A
5.	C	10.	D

Application Questions

1. *Continuity refers to growth that is gradual and incremental over time, while discontinuity refers to more abrupt, stage-like changes. Continuous growth is quantitatively adding more to something you already have (e.g., height), while discontinuous growth is qualitatively changing something (e.g., adding a new way to solve problems rather than just getting faster at using an old problem solving method).*

The research presented throughout the text makes it clear that there are some aspects of development that are continuous and others that are discontinuous. As one example of continuous and discontinuous development consider a language accomplishment noted in Chapter 7. At around 18 months of age, there is vocabulary spurt when acquisition of words increases dramatically. This occurs because toddlers come to realize that everything has a name and then want to learn all the names they can. The realization is a discontinuous change because it reflects a new understanding; the subsequent increase in vocabulary is continuous because children are adding more and more to what they already have.